István Szabó

PHILOSOPHICAL FILMMAKERS

Series editor: Costica Bradatan is a Professor of Humanities at Texas Tech University, USA, and an Honorary Research Professor of Philosophy at the University of Queensland, Australia. He is the author of *Dying for Ideas: The Dangerous Lives of the Philosophers* (Bloomsbury, 2015), among other books.

Films can ask big questions about human existence: what it means to be alive, to be afraid, to be moral, to be loved. The *Philosophical Filmmakers* series examines the work of influential directors, through the writing of thinkers wanting to grapple with the rocky territory where film and philosophy touch borders.

Each book involves a philosopher engaging with an individual filmmaker's work, revealing how it has inspired the author's own philosophical perspectives and how critical engagement with those films can expand our intellectual horizons.

Other titles in the series:

Eric Rohmer, Vittorio Hösle
Werner Herzog, Richard Eldridge
Terrence Malick, Robert Sinnerbrink
Kenneth Lonergan, Todd May
Shyam Benegal, Samir Chopra
Douglas Sirk, Robert B. Pippin
Lucasfilm, Cyrus R. K. Patell
Christopher Nolan, Robbie B. H. Goh
Alfred Hitchcock, Mark William Roche
Luchino Visconti, Joan Ramon Resina
Theo Angelopoulos, Vrasidas Karalis
Alejandro Jodorowsky, William Egginton

Other titles forthcoming:

Leni Riefenstahl, Jakob Lothe
Jane Campion, Bernadette Wegenstein

István Szabó

Filmmaker of Existential Choices

Susan Rubin Suleiman

BLOOMSBURY ACADEMIC
LONDON • NEW YORK • OXFORD • NEW DELHI • SYDNEY

BLOOMSBURY ACADEMIC
Bloomsbury Publishing Plc
50 Bedford Square, London, WC1B 3DP, UK
1385 Broadway, New York, NY 10018, USA
29 Earlsfort Terrace, Dublin 2, Ireland

BLOOMSBURY, BLOOMSBURY ACADEMIC and the Diana logo are trademarks of
Bloomsbury Publishing Plc

First published in Great Britain 2024

Cover image: Mephisto (1981) directed by István Szabó, shown: Klaus Maria Brandauer
(© Analysis Film Releasing Corporation / Photofest)

A catalogue record for this book is available from the British Library.

A catalog record for this book is available from the Library of Congress.

ISBN: HB: 978-1-3501-8183-0
PB: 978-1-3501-8182-3
ePDF: 978-1-3501-8184-7
eBook: 978-1-3501-8185-4

Series: Philosophical Filmmakers

Typeset by Deanta Global Publishing Services, Chennai, India
Printed and bound in Great Britain

The modern person must choose the framework, the telos, of his or her life— that is, choose him or herself. One can say with Kierkegaard that if you do not choose yourself, others will choose for you.

ÁGNES HELLER, *A Philosophy of Morals*

I made films because I wanted to tell stories that had to be told and that would help people to live. To realize that they are not alone in struggling with problems.

ISTVÁN SZABÓ, Interviewed in 2021

Contents

Acknowledgments

The bulk of the research for this book was done during the semester I spent as a senior fellow at the Institute for Advanced Study of the Central European University in Budapest, in the fall of 2017. I am grateful to the director, Nadia Al-Bagdadi, the administrator Eva Gönczi, and all the staff of the Institute for facilitating my work with cheerfulness and efficiency, and to the other fellows for providing intellectual stimulation as well as feedback on some of István Szabó's films that we watched together. I want specially to thank the director of the Hungarian National Film Archive, György Ráduly, and the librarian Evin Hussein (no relation to the filmmaker), without whose help I could not have gotten far. András Szekfü, an eminent specialist of Hungarian cinema, spent many hours talking (and sometimes arguing!) with me about Szabó's films and those of other important Hungarian directors; once the book was done, he read the whole manuscript and corrected some errors. For that, I am extremely grateful to him. And of course I am grateful to István Szabó, who gave generously of his time over several years in discussing aspects of his films with me and kindly invited me to a day of shooting on *Final Report* in Budapest in November 2018. My thanks to the producer of *Final Report*, Sándor Pál, and to the head of production at Filmkontroll Kft., Csaba Pék, for sending me the film still from that film and allowing me to reproduce it. My research assistant, Emile Levesque-Jalbert, saved me many hours of work by creating and formatting the list of References, and he is also responsible for the Index.

As always, my friends and family have been crucial in maintaining my sanity and providing encouragement. Csaba Horváth, Magdolna Jákfalvi and Judit Karafiáth in Budapest, Kristian Feigelson in France, and Catherine Portuges in the United States have all contributed to my thinking about Szabó's films.

My sons Daniel and Michael Suleiman; my sister Judy Sprotzer; my daughter-in-law Veronica Suleiman; my partner Laurence Barrett; and last but not least my grandchildren Emma, Pablo, Alexander, and Nessa have added the element of love to my life, without which intellectual work would lose its flavor and meaning.

Chevy Chase, Maryland, June 7, 2023

An earlier, shorter version of the Introduction was published as "Private Lives, Public History: Encountering the Filmmaker István Szabó" in *Encounters in the Arts, Literature, and Philosophy*, ed. Jéróme Brillaud and Virginie Greene. London: Bloomsbury, 2021.

The epigraphs drawn from István Szabó's films and interviews are quoted here with permission of István Szabó. The epigraph from Ágnes Heller's *A Philosophy of Morals* is quoted with permission of Wiley Publishing Company (successor to Basil Blackwell).

Introduction

Encountering István Szabó

István Szabó is one of the few Hungarian filmmakers to have earned a major international reputation over the past half-century. His 1981 film, *Mephisto*, was the first by a Hungarian director to be awarded the Academy Award for best foreign film, and he has received many other prizes and awards over his long career. Most of his films are in Hungarian, but *Mephisto* and several others are in German and he has also made films in English. All of his films have been shot principally in Budapest, the city he has called home since his early childhood.

Born on February 18, 1938, in Budapest, Szabó spent his first six years in the small city of Tatabánya, where his grandfather, a doctor, had been the founder of the city hospital and where his father, also a doctor, worked. In October 1944, following the German occupation of March 1944 and the deportation of close to half a million Jews from the provinces over the following months, Hungary fell into the hands of the infamous Arrow Cross Party, a Hungarian version of Nazism. Szabó's parents, both of them from Jewish families, had converted to Catholicism before he was born, but he remembers his mother's parents still observing Jewish rituals.[1] Conversion was no protection at the time however; the family therefore fled Tatabánya and sought refuge at a Catholic hospital in Budapest, where Szabó's father became one of only two surgeons who took care of a growing population of patients and fellow refugees. Six-year-old István was hidden separately in a Budapest orphanage for some time, but he doesn't like to talk about that. In April 1945, not long after Hungary was liberated by Soviet troops, his father contracted diphtheria from one of his patients and died. Decades later, Szabó still often spoke about his lifelong sense of loss, and what it meant to be left without a father.[2]

Szabó belongs to what I have called the "1.5 generation" of Holocaust survivors, who were children in Europe during the Second World War.[3] This terminology alludes to the common usage of the term "second generation" to designate children of adult Holocaust survivors, born after the war. The "1.5 generation" refers to Jewish child survivors (born before 1945) and to their memory of persecution and trauma, but it can apply to anyone who experienced the Second World War as a child in countries where the war was fought, not only to Jews. The major fact about experiencing trauma as a child is that one is not able to fully understand what is happening. Of course most adults don't "fully understand" either, but at least they have a vocabulary and certain concepts that allow them to try and make sense of their experience; young children don't only lack these tools for understanding the events around them, they often don't even remember those events later on, except in the most fragmentary and incomplete way. Yet, despite—or perhaps because of—the absence of understanding and of coherent memories, children who experience trauma are affected by it very deeply. Childhood trauma has crucial consequences for an individual's personality precisely because the child has no way of explaining the experience to him or herself, and children have even less control over what happens to them than the most helpless adult. Jewish children in Europe during the war often survived in hiding with false names, separated from their parents, having to pretend to be someone else at a time when they barely knew who they were to begin with. Non-Jewish children also suffered; many experienced bombardment, displacement, and separation from parents, especially from their fathers who were in the Army.

Szabó himself is very conscious of the importance that his experience during the war had for him and for all those of his generation. In one of the first interviews he gave, when he was twenty-five years old, right after the success of his first short films that had been presented at an international film festival, he told his interviewer how he came to make his ten-minute long film "Variations on a theme," which is about the war: "It was born of the understanding that my generation too, even though we were barely eight years old when the war ended, is a generation wounded by war. Half of my friends lost their fathers in the war. I did too. No more war!"[4] More than fifty years later, in a conversation I had with him in Budapest in October 2017, he mentioned that he had recently been invited to a film festival in France whose theme was "Film and War," and added with a laugh: "It looks like just about all of my films fit the rubric!" That's because of his childhood during the Second World War, he said. "That marks you, you don't just move on from it."[5]

Before I ever met István Szabó in person, I had encountered some of his films. I must have seen *Mephisto* in the 1980s, though I have no memory of doing so then. I vividly recall seeing his next film, however: *Colonel Redl*, released in 1985. Starring the marvelous Austrian actor Klaus Maria Brandauer, who had also been the star of *Mephisto*, *Colonel Redl* takes place in the waning years of the Habsburg Empire; it ends with archival footage of the assassination of Crown Prince Franz Ferdinand and of early battles of the First World War. The story focuses on the life of an Army officer, Alfred Redl, who rises from an impoverished peasant childhood in the far eastern region of the Empire, Galizia, to the highest post in the Habsburg intelligence service, only to die an ignominious death by his own hand when it turns out that he has sold military secrets to the Habsburgs' historic enemy, the Russian Czar. Alfred Redl was a real person, an out-and-out traitor and double agent, who used his highly privileged position to collect large sums for the secrets he sold over a period of more than five years.[6] In Szabó's film, however, he appears as a complex character, a closeted homosexual and a parvenu never comfortable in his skin, who gives away secret information only once, in a fit of self-hatred. The figure that Szabó draws of him could have stepped out of the pages of Joseph Roth's celebrated novel *The Radetzky March* (1932) or of Sándor Márai's posthumous bestseller *Embers* (1942), which also explore the inner lives of Habsburg Army officers in the waning years of the Empire.

Colonel Redl made a profound impression on me. When I thought about it afterward, I realized it was not only because of the psychological complexity of the main character but also because I associated several scenes with Budapest, which was second only to Vienna as a capital of the Austro-Hungarian Monarchy (as the Habsburg Empire was known after the "compromise" of 1867, which accorded a degree of autonomy to Hungary). Budapest is my native city; I was born there just a year and a half after Szabó himself. Like him, I was a young Jewish child in hiding in 1944–5; unlike him, I left the country with my parents a few years after the war, and for more than three decades I never looked back. Once we arrived in the United States, I was bent on becoming an American girl, with no complications. Throughout middle school, high school, college, graduate school, then marriage, motherhood, and the first years of a teaching career, I almost never thought about Budapest and talked about it only rarely with my two sons, despite the fact that my mother—whom my sons knew and loved—never lost her thick Hungarian accent. But she too avoided reminiscing about Budapest. She was resolutely turned toward the present, and her memories of Hungary—the anti-Jewish laws of the 1930s, the war, then communism—were mostly not the kind to wax nostalgic about.

Then, things shifted. In 1984, after my mother had fallen ill (it was the beginning of her dying, which occurred four years later), I returned to Hungary for two weeks with my sons and became temporarily what I called a tour guide of my own life. That return trip jogged my earliest childhood memories: the war, but also the time after it, when life in Budapest seemed quite wonderful for a while. The outings to the Buda hills with my mother, the walks along leafy Andrássy Avenue right near our apartment building in Pest, the summers spent in a resort town nearby where I learned to dance and swim, all that came back to me with a power that surprised me. Compelled, I started to write about my childhood. My scholarly interests also took a sharp turn, as I embarked on writing about, and teaching new courses on, literature and films of the Holocaust and about memory of the Second World War and the Occupation in France. Until then, I had specialized in literary theory, avant-garde movements, and feminist criticism; those interests did not disappear, but they were upstaged by my new ones. It was as if the return to Budapest had opened a door I had kept resolutely shut for many years; once I opened it, I discovered a terrain that stretched from Budapest to Paris but that somehow also included New York, Chicago, and Cambridge, Massachusetts.

True, the "memory boom" in literary and cultural studies was also taking off around that time, so my personal turn corresponded to a wider intellectual turn in academic scholarship. Pierre Nora's immensely influential volumes *Les Lieux de mémoire* appeared between 1984 and 1992, and Claude Lanzmann's epochal film *Shoah*, which insisted not so much on the events of the Holocaust as on survivors' memories of them, appeared in 1985. But looking back on it, what strikes me as significant is the way the collective phenomenon intersected with my personal history. The by now almost hackneyed dictum that "all scholarship is autobiographical" found here a solid confirmation.

Still, my involvement with Hungary, and with the films of István Szabó, might not have continued without the intervention of History with a capital H. The fall of the Berlin Wall in 1989 opened up Hungary, like the rest of Eastern Europe, to the world. In 1991, I saw Szabó's first English-language film, *Meeting Venus*, featuring an international cast headed by Glenn Close and the French actor Niels Arestrup. The film recounts the rocky but ultimately successful road taken by a production of Wagner's *Tannhäuser* at the Paris Opera in 1990. The production was slated to celebrate post-Wall Europe, where international cooperation would be the norm. But the Hungarian maestro Zoltán Szántó (played by Arestrup) has to struggle against multiple obstacles in getting to opening night. These include in-fighting among the singers, due to national as well as personal rivalries—already, the demons of nationalism were rearing their heads, as Szabó realized. Frustrating demands from the French labor unions, Szántó's deteriorating marriage back in Budapest, and his stormy love affair with the diva Karin Anderson (played by Close) add further complications. At one point, Szántó returns to Budapest for a few days with Anderson, who is giving a recital there; this causes a major break in his marriage (the ending of the film leaves that question unresolved) and also gives Szabó a chance to take his hero back to his native city. Budapest plays a major role in many of Szabó's films—it's a city he clearly loves and has filmed beautifully. But in *Meeting Venus*, all the scenes in Budapest take place indoors—the concert hall, the conductor's apartment, and the hotel where the diva is staying.

It is all the more curious that the memory I carried with me for many years was of the conductor proudly showing off the city to his new love. Only upon seeing the film again in preparation for writing this book did I realize my error and begin to ponder its significance. In my memory, Szántó took Andersen up to the "Fisherman's Bastion," a neo-Gothic structure on Castle Hill from where one has a panoramic view of the city. Nowadays it's always full of tourists and is not a spot that Szabó particularly likes—he filmed it only once (in a scene in *Mephisto*), whereas the Danube and its bridges, and some streets near the river on the Pest side, with turn of the century apartment buildings, recur like a leitmotif in his works. Was my false memory linked to the fact that my mother had once written to me, around the time I was getting ready for my first return to Budapest in 1984, that the Fisherman's Bastion was among the few things she still remembered of the city of her youth? In a conversation I had with Szabó in Budapest in December 2017, I mentioned that I loved his films because they raised questions that made the audience think. But he pointed to his head and said, "Not here." Then he pointed to his heart: "Here." What he seeks in his films, he said, is first of all to touch a viewer's emotions, not her reason. My own experience of *Meeting Venus* seems to bear that out. Of course, he wants the viewer to think as well, and indeed my false memory spurred a lot of thinking—but feeling comes first.[7] The idea that he wants his films to affect viewers' emotions, and by extension to "help them live," is a long-standing one with Szabó and recurs in many of his published interviews, down to the present day. In November 2021, upon receiving the Lifetime Achievement Golden Olive Award from the Cineuropa Film Festival in Lecce, Italy, the 83-year-old filmmaker declared (in English): "The only reason to make a film is to help the audience to understand they are not alone dealing with their problems."[8]

Less than a year after seeing *Meeting Venus*, in the spring of 1992, I received a letter sent to my Harvard address: a new Institute for Advanced Study had just been founded in Budapest, and I was invited to join the first cohort of fellows, starting in September. The writer of the letter clearly had no knowledge of my Hungarian background; the invitation was addressed to the Harvard professor, not to the fledgling autobiographer seeking traces. Of course, I jumped at it. In the beginning of February 1993, I moved to Budapest for six months. The Collegium Budapest, located in a historic eighteenth-century building on Castle Hill, a stone's throw from the Fisherman's Bastion, provided a roomy office and a community of scholars, as well as a comfortable apartment in a nice part of town. The time I spent there was like a dream—a dream recorded, for every night I would sit at my laptop computer and write in detail about the day's activities: my meetings with Hungarian colleagues, lectures I heard (and also gave) at the Collegium and elsewhere, exhibits I attended, films I saw (only Hungarian ones—I wanted to educate myself), and perhaps most importantly, the walks I took around the city, often circling back to the neighborhood where I had grown up. And then there were the endless conversations with friends and strangers about the meaning and consequences of the "regime change" (*rendszerváltás*) as the transition from communism was called in Hungary. At the end of those six months, I had a huge manuscript that, with cutting and pruning, would eventually be published as a memoir, *Budapest Diary: In Search of the Motherbook*. My love affair with the city and the talks with Hungarians about how their lives had been transformed by the larger history after 1989 constituted, along with my almost obsessive search for traces of my childhood and family, the heart of the book.

Among the films I wrote about in detail in *Budapest Diary* was István Szabó's *Sweet Emma, Dear Böbe* (*Édes Emma, Drága Böbe*), which I saw in Budapest in July 1993, a few months after its release. Once again, I found that Szabó's preoccupations and my own had intersected. *Sweet Emma, Dear Böbe* is a film about the "regime change"—about what happens when two young women schoolteachers from the provinces, who had been trained to teach Russian in elementary school and who live in quasi-impoverished circumstances in a teachers' dormitory in Budapest, are suddenly told that they will have to teach English from then on and learn it fast. Russian would no longer be a required part of the curriculum. As I wrote in my diary that evening, "Szabó is merciless in showing the effects of 'the Change' even on the smallest institutions: petty bickering among the teachers, desperate attempts by former communists to divorce themselves from their Party past, and everywhere a generalized anxiety about the future."[9] The story of Emma and Böbe does not end well. Like many others, the two young women are caught by a huge historical wave that threatens to drown them. The "new Europe," Szabó seemed to be saying, brings with it new freedoms, but also new hardships and even death to people with minimal resources.

Although I met many intellectuals and even one or two filmmakers while I was in Budapest, it never occurred to me to try and meet István Szabó. I hadn't seen enough of his films and hadn't written about them, and he was famous. What reason could I possibly give for wanting to meet him? The fact that I admired his films and felt a kinship with his preoccupations was not enough.

Now fast forward to 2000. *Budapest Diary* had been published in 1996 and I was at work on a book that would take several more years to complete, focusing on public and private memories of the Second World War and the Holocaust. In my original plan, the "memory book," as I called it, would be focused exclusively on France, even though the broader issues it raised—about trauma, memory, national identity, and Jewishness—were relevant to other times and places.

But that summer, in Paris, I saw István Szabó's film *Sunshine* (1999) and realized that I must write about it for the memory book. It's hard to describe the deep emotion and intense personal involvement I felt while watching that film. It was in English (starring Ralph Fiennes, Jennifer Ehle, and Rosemary Harris, among other luminaries), but it was about Hungary—and not only Hungary but Jews in Hungary. Almost double the length of Szabó's other films (three hours long), *Sunshine* tells the story of a Jewish family in Hungary over four generations, from the "Golden Age" of Hungarian and Hungarian-Jewish history in the late nineteenth century to the end of communist rule. The three main protagonists, father, son, and grandson, are all played by Fiennes, in a tour de force performance that earned him many award nominations and the Best Actor award at the Europa (Berlin) film festival. The story is of Jewish assimilation (including a change in the family name from the Jewish-Germanic Sonnenschein to Sors), followed by the upheaval of the First World War, then a growing climate of antisemitism culminating in the anti-Jewish laws of the late 1930s, then war again, deaths in the Holocaust, a diminished life under communism, and finally a kind of liberation after 1989.

Dubbed into Hungarian, *Sunshine* (*A napfény ize*, "A Taste of Sunshine") received enormous attention in Hungary and stirred up some heated debates. While many viewers, especially among Jews, loved the film, others criticized it. It should not have been made in English, some said; it made Hungary look bad in the eyes of Western viewers, said others; still others said that Szabó's handling of the postwar period was not true to the way things really were. And what did Szabó think he was accomplishing by having the grandson take back the family's original name at the end? Was he suggesting that all those whose names had been "Magyarized" generations earlier should revert to their

Germanic (or Serbian or Czech or Romanian) names? Only antisemites made suggestions like that! And so on.[10] In the United States, passions were not aroused; the film received mixed reviews in the press. Some critics objected to having a single actor play all three major roles; others found the characters not complex enough, especially when compared to Szabó's earlier films with their rich attention to individual psychology. Jewish audiences by and large loved the film, however, and it also had many screenings among Hungarian-Americans. As for me, I wrote a long essay that was published in a journal in 2001 and eventually found its way into my memory book.[11] This time, I did seek out an opportunity to speak with István Szabó. Just around the time I was finishing my article, in the fall of 2000, Columbia University organized a symposium about the film, with Szabó in attendance. I flew down to New York from Boston for the event. After the screening, a historian and a literary scholar specializing in Hungary discussed the film with Szabó, and then the audience had a chance to ask questions. I raised my hand and asked a question, which I hoped would show that I had really studied the film. He answered appreciatively, and I felt authorized to go up to him afterward. I was too shy to speak Hungarian with him, especially since his English is excellent. But I was thrilled to have met the man, after having been acquainted with some of his films over many years.

Thus began a personal acquaintance that has meant a great deal to me. In 2006, while I was in Budapest to attend a conference, Szabó agreed to meet me for a formal interview to talk about his work. As part of my preparation, I watched his first three feature films, in Hungarian, which had established his international reputation as a young filmmaker in the 1960s: *The Age of Daydreaming* (*Álmodozások kora*, 1964), *Father* (*Apa*, 1966), and *LoveFilm* (*Szerelmesfilm*, 1970). All of these films featured young men and women of Szabó's generation, who came of age after the war, under communism. Since that was also my generation, these films gave me a glimpse of what I might have become, had my family not left Hungary in 1949. The question of emigration is raised in each film, and in *Lovefilm* it is central: the film tells the story of a young couple who have been in love since childhood, but who are separated in 1956 when she decides to leave the country after the October uprising and he decides to stay. Among Szabó's early films, it is the one that struck me most deeply—for obvious reasons, given my own displacements, but it is also formally among Szabó's most complex works, a memory film that skips around among different moments in the lives of its protagonists, from the time of the Nazi occupation in 1944 to the "Young Pioneer" years of the early 1950s, and then the 1956 uprising and the "softer" years of the late 1960s. Running through it like a guiding thread is an existential question that I found fascinating: How do individuals make choices at historically critical moments such as war and revolution, when public history interferes blatantly with private life? Szabó has asked this question, in one form or another, in just about all of his films. In *Lovefilm*, the lives of the two protagonists are permanently inflected by the divergent choices they make in 1956. My family left Hungary before then, but I imagine that my parents must also have struggled with the question—and their decision to leave obviously determined the rest of my own life.

On a sunny day in September 2006, I met Szabó in a café on Castle Hill, not far from the Collegium Budapest. He arrived punctually, and we got down to our interview with no preliminary chitchat. We spoke in English to make it easier to transcribe (I had brought along a voice recorder), and also I hoped that the distance provided by another language might allow him to talk more freely. (At the end of the formal interview we switched to Hungarian, and all of our subsequent conversations over the years took place in that language.) Our conversation lasted more than two hours; we talked about his childhood, the war, the question of emigration (why did he and his mother stay in Hungary after the war, when they could have emigrated to New York where an uncle lived?), and the complications of Jewish identity in Central Europe.[12] Although he was brought up as a Catholic, people still thought of him as Jewish, he said: "In this part of the world, that's how it goes." "The exclusion of those who don't belong?" I asked. "Yes, exclusion is the most important element of the tribe mentality. Those who aren't Hungarian . . ." Rereading the transcript of that interview today, when Hungary's prime minister Viktor Orbán rests his power and his popularity on the hatred he foments of "migrants," I realize how prescient Szabó was—more exactly, how correctly he diagnosed the "tribe mentality" that seems to be gaining ground all over Europe at present.

One thing that was very much on Szabó's mind during our conversation was the painful subject of a recent scandal around his name, which had occupied the Hungarian press for several months and had also been reported in the *New York Times* and other newspapers abroad. The previous January, a journalist had published a long article exposing his discovery that for several years when Szabó had been a student at the Film Academy, he had written reports for the Secret Service about his classmates and others linked to the institution.[13] Given Szabó's long-standing reputation in Hungary as a filmmaker of integrity, whose concerns encompassed ethical questions as well as the ways that individual lives are inflected by History, this revelation devastated many people. But didn't they realize, Szabó told me, that he had been an eighteen-year-old boy forced into cooperating with the Secret Service along with many others, including two of his classmates? And that the whole episode lasted only a few years, that it was over before he had even made his first film? He felt angry and frustrated, convinced that he had been targeted precisely because of his international reputation: "They needed someone they could attack, and since I'm the best known. . . ." He didn't explain who "they" were, but it hardly mattered: they were whoever stood to gain (or thought they did) from exposing compromising facts about the communist years. After the opening of Secret Service archives all over Eastern Europe in the 1990s, it appeared that in Hungary as in other communist countries, half the country had been writing reports about the other half. Actually, less than 1 percent of Hungarians and about 2 percent of Germans were enrolled as informants.[14] While some who did that undoubtedly acted out of ideological conviction, many others had been forcibly enrolled, by means of threats and blackmail, into acting as "agents" during the harsh years immediately following the 1956 uprising.

In January 2000, just after he had finished a long novel in which he expressed his lifelong admiration for his father, the celebrated writer Peter Esterházy discovered, to his horror, that the same father had written detailed reports for the Secret Service for more than two decades, from 1957 to 1979. Esterházy wrote a book about his discovery, and his description makes clear that the system itself—which went to absurd lengths to enroll and oversee its so-called agents—was the main culprit, not those it forced into its clutches.[15] Nevertheless, and even for people who were able to escape from those clutches relatively quickly, like Szabó and his classmates (that too was part of the system's absurdity: agents could be dismissed just as they had been enrolled,

for no obvious reason), the whole experience must have been fraught with
feelings of guilt and self-loathing as well as helplessness. They could, after all,
have refused to cooperate and faced the consequences. Easier said than done.

As I was getting ready to write this book, I struggled with the question of
how much importance to ascribe to that painful episode from Szabó's youth.
Clearly I could not ignore it, even if this book is not a biography but a study
of his films. But I couldn't make it a centerpiece either. Szabó himself has said
that everything one needs to know about this episode is in his films. Following
that lead, one could argue that his emphasis on existential and ethical choices

Figure 0 *István Szabó in Budapest, December 2017. Photo Susan Rubin Suleiman.*

in individual lives, as well as his often repeated statement that private lives can be destroyed by History, have their source in that youthful experience. Such an insight does not get us very far, however, in understanding his films; it reduces their general import, and the importance of Szabó's concerns, to mere personal history. A theme that underlies all of Szabó's oeuvre is precisely that personal history is indissociable from public history —History with a capital H—which is always ready to interfere with, and often to destroy, individual lives.

The challenge, here as in many other instances, is to acknowledge a traumatic personal past—whether your own or someone else's—without letting it overwhelm you. One thing one can learn from encountering István Szabó (the man and his films) is that complexity is all (Figure 0).

* * *

When I told Szabó that this book would appear in the "Philosophical Filmmakers" series, he protested: "I am not a philosopher!" It's all right, I told him, I'm not a philosopher either, if that means being the possessor of a degree in the academic discipline of philosophy. One does not need such a degree in order to be preoccupied with philosophical questions. Szabó's importance as a filmmaker lies not only in his attention to film's formal elements (which is abiding and real, though not the primary focus of his work) but in his deep and ongoing engagement with urgent existential questions of our time. How do individuals attempt, and often fail, to create a viable self and a life in extreme historical situations over which they have no control? This is the single most important, profoundly philosophical question that haunts Szabó's work, as indeed it does the work of many other Central European intellectuals and filmmakers of the twentieth century, from Czeslaw Milosz or Ágnes Heller to Andrzej Wajda, Márta Mészáros, or Jiri Menzel. Szabó himself put it this way (somewhat hyperbolically) in 1987, when communism was on its way to collapsing in Hungary and other parts of Eastern Europe: "Perhaps never, and nowhere, has history interfered as drastically, permanently, unavoidably in people's everyday life, their fate, their relationships, their character, as in this corner of the world."[16]

In the chapters that follow, I explore the ethical, political, and existential implications of entanglements between individual lives and public history as they are developed in Szabó's films, starting with his Hungarian works of the 1960s and 1970s, which earned him international recognition while still a young man, then in the so-called German trilogy of the 1980s, the films he made after the fall of the Berlin Wall in the 1990s and the early 2000s, and finally, the Hungarian works after 2005. Given Szabó's achievement as a filmmaker and his international renown, it is surprising that his oeuvre overall has received relatively little scholarly attention. Aside from John Cunningham's fine monograph from 2014, *The Cinema of István Szabó*, there exist no comprehensive studies of his work in English; and even in Hungarian, the only book devoted to him, József Marx's authoritative *István Szabó*, dates from more than twenty years ago. Szabó has received a great deal of attention from newspapers and magazines in Hungary, however, and has given important interviews to journalists over the years, many of them published in hard-to-find or long-gone papers. Luckily, most of these have been preserved in the library of the Hungarian National Film Archive, in voluminous dossiers devoted to Szabó. I am pleased that this book can provide a bridge between the Hungarian sources, which I have used in abundance, and the English-speaking world.

The title of each chapter is in the form of a question that points to an existential choice faced by individuals in a specific historical situation. Chapter 1 is about emigration. Whether to leave or to stay home was a choice faced by many ordinary Hungarians throughout the years of the communist regime (1949–89), but especially after the failed revolution of October 1956, when hundreds of thousands left the country. Chapter 2 asks: Why do men (but it could be women as well) of talent and ambition acquiesce to, and sometimes even love, figures of authority who restrict their freedom? And what are the consequences, for the individual and for the larger society, of such acquiescence? Chapter 3 deals with the fraught question of Jewish identity, which has been part of the Jewish experience in Europe ever since Jews were allowed to enter civil society after the French Revolution. I examine the "Jewish question" not as it has existed for antisemites, but as it was (and continues to be) a question faced by Jews themselves. The final chapter is about the idea, or more exactly the ideal, of community, both in its interpersonal and its larger societal aspects, after the historical upheaval which changed the face of Europe in 1989.

The question of community has preoccupied Szabó throughout his career, and it has become more and more pressing with the rise of right-wing nationalisms and the temptation of authoritarianism, not only in Hungary but the world over. For Szabó, love of one's home and country is a positive emotion, but it can be perverted into a "tribe" mentality based on the exclusion of those who don't belong. How to affirm community and cooperation without falling into tribalism? This is the question posed by Szabó's last film to date, *Final Report* (2020). It is one that we must all face in the decades to come, if this fragile planet of ours is to survive.

Notes

1 Szabó mentioned this in my 2006 interview with him: Suleiman, "On Exile, Jewish Identity, and Filmmaking in Hungary."

2 The biographical information here is based on the biography by Marx, *Szabó István*, 21–8; Marx does not mention Szabó having been hidden in 1944–5, but Szabó spoke about it very briefly in my 2006 interview with him: Suleiman, "On Exile, Jewish Identity, and Filmmaking in Hungary."

3 Suleiman, "The 1.5 Generation."

4 Lelkes, "Három kisfilm sikeréröl a rendezővel, Szabó Istvánnal" (About the Success of Three Short Films, with the director István Szabó). Clipping at Hungarian National Film Archive library in Szabó's Personal Folder, 1963–82. Unless otherwise indicated, all translations from Hungarian and French, here and throughout, are my own.

5 Personal conversation, Budapest, October 20, 2017.

6 Schindler, "Redl—Spy of the Century?."

7 Personal conversation, December 14, 2017.

8 See the video from the award ceremony in November 2021: https://cineuropa.org/en/video/413542/ For an earlier formulation of the same idea, see the long interview with Szegő from 1987, "Ingerelnek a felfuvalkodott, gőgös emberek" (I can't stand swellheaded, arrogant people), reprinted in Szabó, *Beszélgetések Szabó István Filmrendezővel* (Conversations with Filmmaker István Szabó).

9 Suleiman, *Budapest Diary*, 172.

10 I discuss the Hungarian debates in detail in my book *Crises of Memory and the Second World War*, 128–31.

11 Suleiman, "Jewish Assimilation in Hungary, the Holocaust, and Epic Film: Reflections
    on István Szabó's *Sunshine*." Revised version in *Crises of Memory and the Second World
    War*, chap. 5.

12 Suleiman, "On Exile, Jewish Identity, and Filmmaking in Hungary."

13 Gervai, "Egy ügynök azonosítása" (The identification of an agent). For coverage in
    the United States, see Dempsey, "The Past, the East Learns, Is Always Present," and
    especially Deák, "Scandal in Budapest."

14 Deák, "Scandal in Budapest."

15 Esterházy, *Javított Kiadás* [Revised Edition]. The book has been translated into
    many languages, but not into English. *Harmonia Caelestis* was the title of the novel
    Esterházy had just finished, a paean to his father, when he discovered the latter's
    hidden past. For a long and detailed discussion of the Szabó affair and its broad
    historical and philosophical implications, see Rév, "The Man in the White Raincoat."

16 Szegő, "Ingerelnek a felfuvalkodott, gőgös emberek" [I can't stand swellheaded,
    arrogant people], 14.

1

To Leave or to Stay?

Existential Choices under Communism

It is true, is it not, that you yourself would like to be young, would feel that there is something beautiful in being young but also something very serious, that it is by no means a matter of indifference how one employs one's youth, but that before one there lies a choice, a real either/or.

SØREN KIERKEGAARD, *Either/Or*

"It would be good to travel." "Where?"
"Anywhere"

JÁNOS AND EVA, IN *Age of Daydreaming*

About halfway through *The Age of Daydreaming* (*Álmodozások kora*), Szabó's first feature film, the protagonist, János, and his new girlfriend Eva are sitting in a movie theater that runs nothing but newsreels, including old ones. She has invited him to come with her because one old newsreel features her as a twelve-year-old conductor of the Young Pioneers' railway. Built in 1948 by the then-fledgling communist government as publicity for the hoped-for future, the railway connected two hills in Buda and was staffed entirely by schoolchildren. (It still exists, but today it's a tourist attraction called the Children's Railway.) When János hears about her role, he delightedly exclaims, "me too!" He does not appear in the newsreel, but he too had been a Young Pioneer conductor. This shared memory of childhood reinforces their budding romance, and once they settle into their seats they continue to talk in whispers while the images on the screen evoke the violent history of the preceding decades: Hitler's speeches and Nazi marches, the roundups of Jews, the end of the war, then the first communist years in Hungary (including the launching of the Young Pioneers' railway), and eventually the anti-Soviet uprising of October 1956 brought to a sudden end by Soviet tanks rolling down a snowy boulevard in Budapest (Figure 1).

Why did Karcsi, a Young Pioneer who she had told him was her first boyfriend, leave the country in 1956, János asks—and the verb he uses is "disszidálni," to leave in dissidence, commonly used about those who left the country under communism. She's not sure why Karcsi left, Eva replies—various reasons. And did she think about leaving too? János asks. Oh yes, she answers, she tormented herself about it for days and days: to leave or to stay? In the end, she was too afraid—what if she was shot at the border? Was that all? he asks. Her replies come tumbling out: "I ran all around the city, I didn't want to be left

Figure 1 The Age of Daydreaming *(Álmodozások kora)*, *1965, Eva and János in the newsreel movie theater. In courtesy of National Film Institute Hungary—Film Archive.*

out." "Out of what?" "Of . . . history," she says after a pause, with a quasi-self-deprecatory smile. Then: "I wanted to prove I was a good Hungarian." Prove to whom? he asks, but instead of answering she continues. "I didn't want to start over, finding new friends, new ways of thinking. I realized that a thousand things held me back. I was born here, formed here." Then, suddenly, he asks: "Are you a communist?" Yes, she replies, with another small smile. "And you?" "I'm an engineer," he says, poker-faced. She asks why he didn't leave. "I never thought of leaving," he replies. "My life is here. I don't like to roam."

In our first conversation, in 2006, István Szabó mentioned this scene as proof that the communist regime of the 1960s did not censor artistic expression the way some have claimed. The fact that János could reply, when asked whether he was a communist, that he was an engineer, was a sign of the regime's leniency. True, every script had to be approved by the authorities (the screenplay for *The Age of Daydreaming* went through six versions before it was authorized!), but "it was possible to negotiate."[1] In this instance, Szabó explained, the negotiated solution was to add "Grown-up adolescents" as the film's subtitle, presumably to suggest that his protagonists had not yet reached the age of responsible adulthood. But Szabó could have mentioned an earlier scene as well, when the talkative barber who gives János a haircut and who is definitely an adult, says to one of the clients in the shop: "I'm not a communist, I'm a realist. I don't believe in fairy tales. My wife is the one who goes to church," thus equating communism with religion and rejecting both. The barber is a minor character who appears only in one brief scene in the film; yet Szabó, who wrote the screenplay, gives him some of the most provocative lines in the film.

It's true that by 1964, when *The Age of Daydreaming* was first shown, the Kádár regime in Hungary had entered its "consolidation" phase after the harsh repression that followed the 1956 uprising, which had included the execution of the reformist communist leader Imre Nagy and several of his associates, as well as prison sentences for many of the participants. By the early 1960s, Hungary had moved toward what would later be called "goulash communism," which depended on an implicit contract with the population: a degree of personal freedom, including some private enterprise and artistic expression, would be tolerated, as long as politics were left to the government. In fact, the years between 1963 and 1969 have been called the "unrepeatable golden age" of Hungarian filmmaking, when the regime became more relaxed but still supported the nationalized film industry, and television had not yet replaced movie houses, which multiplied all over the country.[2] Szabó had the good fortune to start his career right at the beginning of that golden age, very soon after graduating from the Film Academy; the success of his first short films (including the prize-winning *Koncert*, which he had made while still a student[3]) no doubt contributed to this. While most other young filmmakers had to work as assistants on older directors' films for many years, he was given a chance to direct his first feature film at the age of twenty-six, after his work as "first assistant" on an important film directed by János Herskó, *Párbeszéd* (*Dialogue*, 1963). Herskó, a decade older than Szabó, was a professor at the Film and Theater Academy during Szabó's last years there and would subsequently become head of a studio at the state-run Mafilm Company, where he strongly supported Szabó's work. His sudden emigration in 1970 (he "disszidált," left on a trip to Sweden and never came back) came as a shock to many of his colleagues, including Szabó. Herskó became a professor of film studies in Stockholm and returned to Hungary in 1989, where he again taught courses (though not full time) at the Film and Theater Academy.

Herskó's *Dialogue* was certainly of interest to Szabó, for it told an individual story in the larger context of the history of postwar Hungary; and unlike many films of the 1950s, it managed largely to avoid a propagandistic effect—to put it more precisely, it did not shirk a critical view of the years between 1949 and 1953, when the regime under Mátyás Rákosi was at its most repressive. While not exactly subtle in psychological exploration, *Dialogue* traces the love story of a couple (a young Jewish woman who returns from Auschwitz in 1945 and a young working-class man, not Jewish, who was in the resistance during the war) from its idealistic beginnings (building a new society after the war) through the years of hard-line communism (when the man is imprisoned for not being sufficiently Stalinist), the reforms after 1953 and the upheaval of 1956, all the way to the more prosperous and relaxed years of the early 1960s. It was while working on *Dialogue* that Szabó made the acquaintance of the veteran actors Miklós Gábor and Imre Sinkovits, who play relatively minor roles in *The Age of Daydreaming*—but Gábor would perform superbly as the star of Szabó's next film, *Father* (*Apa*, 1966).

Getting around the Censor in the 1960s

In his first three feature films, released between 1965 and 1970, which all focus on young intellectuals in Budapest who were born just before the war and came of age in the 1950s and early 1960s, Szabó found a way to talk about potentially dangerous subjects, like emigration (which was strongly condemned by the regime and its spokesmen), or like ideological nonconformity (János works as a sound engineer in the state-run television station but is not a communist) without incurring the wrath of the authorities. How did he do it? One way was to put the most provocative lines, like those of the barber who "doesn't believe in fairy tales," into the mouths of minor characters who are expendable to the plot. It's as if Szabó were saying that these statements are "parenthetical" and only the most attentive viewers will notice them.

Along somewhat similar lines, one often finds a taboo subject mentioned in the middle of a longer monologue or exchange, which again functions like a parenthesis. János's question about why Eva didn't leave in 1956 is one such instance because in 1964 the subject of the uprising was still a very delicate one. In her survey of Hungarian films about 1956, Catherine Portuges notes that very few mentioned the subject in the decade following the event, and those that did had to tread carefully; historical research about the 1956 uprising was also taboo for many years.[4] *The Age of Daydreaming* was among the first films to mention emigration in 1956, and Szabó manages not to sound judgmental about those who left.

Another, even more delicate example occurs soon after Eva and János first meet, when they are shown walking through the city, then happily running as it starts to snow. She asks him, " Do you like snow?" Oh yes, he answers, he even ate it sometimes as a kid after building a snowman. That's interesting, she responds—her father, who had been in a concentration camp, told her they used to eat snow there. Yes, says János, his father said they did the same thing when he was at the river Don—a reference to the disastrous battle where the Second Hungarian Army was destroyed by Soviet troops in January 1943. Which camp was her father in, János asks. "Auschwitz," she replies. And then they talk about something else.

In this exchange, both Eva and János refer to painful subjects in Hungarian history, but almost casually, the way one talks about events one knows about but has not experienced personally. The two young people, like all their contemporaries, grew up with these facts, but only as hearsay from their fathers. Eva's reference to Auschwitz tells us that she is Jewish, a fact that illuminates her later statement, in the movie theater, that one reason she stayed in 1956 was to "prove she was a good Hungarian." The fraught relation between Hungarianness and Jewishness and the deportations in 1944 that landed more than 400,000 Hungarian Jews in Auschwitz were close to being taboo subjects in the early 1960s (though not entirely so, as I will discuss in Chapter 3), and Szabó evokes them in *The Age of Daydreaming* only in this brief and indirect way. He would do so more directly in *Father*, but a full treatment had to wait until his 1999 film, *Sunshine*. He does evoke at least fleetingly the persecution of Jews and the fraught issue of Jewish identity in these two early films, but the subject was so delicate at the time that the Hungarian critics who wrote about the films back then almost unanimously failed to mention it, according to Szabó's biographer József Marx.[5] Hungarian critics also largely ignored the allusions to emigration in *The Age of Daydreaming*, which occur at several moments in the film, not only in the scene at the cinema. (Two other moments when emigration in 1956 is alluded to, both times "parenthetically," occur in the sequence where János plays ping-pong with an old schoolmate who mentions that he had spent time in Canada, and one where János's earlier girlfriend, Habgab, mentions that her parents are divorced and that her father left the country in 1956, after which "he never even sent us anything.")

Indirection and parenthetical mentions that could be ignored (or "ignored") by the viewer were one way to insert difficult subjects into the film without calling down the censor on your head. Another way was to situate the action in an earlier time, but with parallels to the present that audiences would be quick to understand. Miklós Jancsó's first great success, *The Round-Up* (*Szegénylegények*), which came out around the same time as Szabó's first films, in 1966, is presumably about the brutal repression, by Austria, that followed the failed revolution of 1848 in the Hungarian countryside, but its viewers could draw their own parallels with more recent history. Jancsó is in many ways the opposite of Szabó in his aesthetic and thematic choices, preferring the *puszta* (Hungarian plain) as a setting instead of the city, using few words instead of the complex dialogues created by Szabó, and relying on very long takes instead of Szabó's more fragmented style.

Szabó's early films were innovative in more than just subject matter—notably, in the way they looked. While Szabó appreciated the training he had received from Hungarian directors like János Herskó or Félix Máriássy (who was the lead teacher of Szabó's class in the Film and Theater Academy and whose works Szabó greatly admired), their influence on him was more thematic than stylistic. Máriássy and Herskó, like some other Hungarian directors who had been young men during the war (Máriássy was born in 1916, Herskó in 1926), sought ways to represent Hungary's wartime and postwar history without overly simplifying it to fit into the ideological orthodoxy and without avoiding some painful subjects. Máriássy's 1955 film, *Spring in Budapest* (*Budpesti tavasz*), for example, was the first film to allude to the infamous shootings of Jews into the Danube by Hungarian Arrow Cross thugs in the winter of 1944–5, an event that Szabó would take up in his own way in *Lovefilm* a few years later. But stylistically, Máriássy's film was quite traditional, harkening back to the melodramas of the 1940s and earlier. Szabó's first films, by contrast, immediately signaled their indebtedness to the French New Wave and other Western cinemas of the period, as well as to the whole tradition of European avant-garde filmmaking. In his extended 1972 interview with the film historian András Szekfü, Szabó recalled the month he had spent on a student scholarship in Paris, where he practically lived at the Cinémathèque, watching every film he could get his hands on, including the early films of Dziga Vertov, Jean Vigo, and Luis Bunuel;[6] and of course, like many others his age, Szabó was a fervent admirer of Truffaut, Bergman, and Fellini (among others). In *The Age of Daydreaming*, snippets from Truffaut's *Jules et Jim* and Fellini's 8 ½ are heard on János's shortwave radio in his room, and later a huge advertising poster for Truffaut's *The 400 Blows* makes its way down the street on a cart near János and Eva as they walk toward the cinema.

It is in the two subsequent films of the trilogy, however, that Szabó demonstrates fully the formal mastery and the aesthetic taste he shares with the great European directors of the period. Like Truffaut, he directs child actors with stunning effectiveness: in both *Father* and *Lovefilm*, as much as half the running time is devoted to the childhood of the protagonist, with many scenes involving two or three children in conversation, and often a whole class. In one memorable scene in *Father*, the young Takó (Dániel Erdély) explains to two elementary school friends *c*. 1950 that Jesus and the communists have much in common, since both want to create equality and lift up the oppressed. And since one of the boys is from an aristocratic family, which makes him a "class enemy," Takó thoughtfully (and astonishingly) points out that these days it's the young Count who is among the oppressed—adding that the oppression in his case is no doubt a form of punishment for his class's misdeeds. The combination of childish naiveté and sly reasoning is beautifully reinforced by Szabó's camera, which zooms in on Takó's face as he elaborates his theory and then lingers on the faces of the other two boys.

Like Fellini, Szabó creates images of great formal beauty by means of costuming and movement—for example, in the fantasy sequence in *Father* where the boy's father, a doctor, is shown dressed in operating whites, moving in a kind of ballet with the nun nurses who wear white wimples, as in some of Fellini's sequences in *8 ½*).[7] And, again like Fellini in *8 ½* or like Bergman in *Smiles of a Summer Night*, Szabó can shift suddenly from reality to fantasy to memory or dream, yet keep the viewer's attention on the story that is unfolding (Figure 2).

Even in the lenient years of the early 1960s in Hungary, this kind of self-conscious formal experimentation ran the risk of being considered too "subjective," which was implied in the term "auteur film" (*szerzői film*) as used by Hungarian critics. It may have been a reason why Szabó sometimes reacted negatively when the term was applied to his work, even though he was literally the author of all his films of the 1960s and 1970s, responsible for the story and the screenplay as well as directing. Szabó's emphasis on his protagonists' individual psychology, including their tendency toward self-reflection and memory, could similarly be criticized as an unhealthy subjectivism, at odds with the Marxist emphasis on so-called objectivity. One influential critic, writing in the widely read weekly *Élet és Irodalom*, recognized *Father* as an important film and a "sincere and beautiful experiment" on Szabó's part, but regretted that both the protagonist and the filmmaker appeared to be "befuddled" (*tanácstalan*) in the face of life's problems.[8] He added that while this befuddlement was

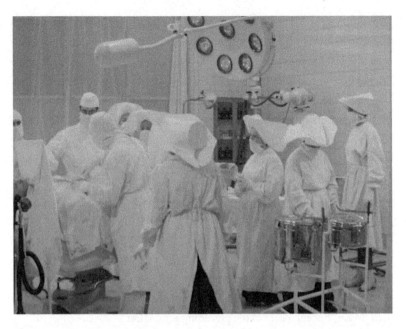

Figure 2 Father *(Apa), 1966, the doctor surrounded by nurses. In courtesy of National Film Institute Hungary—Film Archive.*

"sympathetic and poignant," still it was a befuddlement—not a positive term. A few years later, the same critic wrote about *Lovefilm* that Szabó should have focused less on memory and nostalgia for the past, "like an old, Americanized Hungarian" (a dig at all those who had left the country in 1956) and more on the present: "on the task at hand, the project to be accomplished."[9]

Such criticism was undoubtedly facilitated by the presence of a single actor, András Bálint, in all three of the films; while the three protagonists have different names, indicating that they are not the same person, the "type" or persona of the young man in all three films is very much the same. In his 1972 interview with András Szekfü, Szabó himself expressed some regret at having made the character so similar in the three films. He described the persona as "pensive, struggling, self-ironic, yet taking things very seriously; observing everything, hesitating rather than acting on the world."[10] The description fits, but it does not do full justice to the Bálint figure, nor to many of the other characters we meet in these films. Like most people, the films suggest, the young men and women whose stories are told do not think of themselves as historical actors but as individuals struggling with personal choices. They are not ideologues, even if ideas interest them; and although they have lived through some dramatic historical moments—most notably the failed revolution of 1956, when they were just reaching young adulthood—they nevertheless see their lives in individual, not collective, terms. Eva tells János that she didn't want to be left out of history in 1956, but ultimately her choice to remain in Hungary was based on her sense of who she was and what she could envisage herself doing, or not doing. At the same time, as educated young people, Eva and János and their friends harbor dreams and ambitions that transcend the purely personal. Eva, upon embarking on a career as a magistrate after graduating from the Law Faculty, declares to an interviewer that she wants to enact laws that will persuade people to live "authentically," not hypocritically, as they do now; János and the other young engineers seek to come up with innovations that will go beyond what they consider the outdated technologies espoused by their bosses, the engineers of the preceding generation.

In sum, these early films are about a cohort, even if a single (male) protagonist is at the center of the story. Szabó emphasizes this collective aspect in the famous scene in *Father* where Takó, now a young man, swims across the Danube to prove himself to himself, thinking that he is alone in the water—but when the camera pulls back, we see dozens of similar young men who are doing the same thing. This kind of reminder that more than one person is involved becomes a signature in Szabó's trilogy; in *The Age of Daydreaming*, the final sequence shows a row of telephone operators, each repeating the same message: "It's time to wake up." In *Lovefilm*, which I discuss in detail later, a similar sequence occurs toward the end, when the protagonist stands in a post office in Budapest, writing a letter to his lover who left Hungary in 1956; but next to him is a whole row of other people, men and women, young and old, tracked by the camera, who are doing the same thing. Such sequences emphasize that the individual story we have just followed is situated in a collective history, where people share similar experiences despite the specificities of their life stories.

Zoltán Fábri (1917–94), a filmmaker from the older generation whom Szabó greatly admired and one of the first Hungarians after the war to gain international recognition (his 1955 film *Körhinta* [Merry-go-round] was shown at Cannes), explained to an interviewer in 1994 that, starting in the 1960s, he had sought more and more consciously to choose themes that would allow him to "analyze the conflicts of a vulnerable person—an ordinary man who had trouble maintaining his place in the storms of history."[11] Fábri's "ordinary men" were a generation older than Szabó's protagonists, which means that they lived through the stormiest times of the country's history. Fábri's *Utószezon* (*Late Season*,1965), for example, focuses on the belated pangs of conscience of an elderly Hungarian who apparently denounced his Jewish employers to a policeman during the German occupation in 1944, leading to their deportation and death. This film, which also features the Eichmann trial in its plot, was among the first feature films in Hungary to show images (filmed by Fábri) of Jews wearing the yellow star, as well as archival images borrowed from Resnais's *Night and Fog*. Szabó may have intended to allude to it in the sequence in *Father* where Takó and his friends are enrolled as extras in a film showing Jews being herded by Arrow Cross thugs (Hungarian Nazis) on the Chain Bridge in Budapest. After that filming, Takó and his friends sit pensively on the Danube bank, and one remarks: "Aren't we glad we missed all that."

Indeed, for Szabó's cohort in these films (as for Szabó himself), the war is only a memory of early childhood. They may have all been "wounded by the war," as Szabó stated in an interview as early as 1963,[12] and the war may have engraved indelible images in their mind: bombed-out bridges over the Danube and dead horses in the street that people cut up for food are among the recurring images in Szabó's oeuvre. What's more, the war left many of them fatherless, a hugely significant factor in a young person's life. But the war was not a time that confronted them with difficult choices. They were too young to make them, too young to be responsible.

Szabó's first films spoke to his contemporaries in a personal way. The film historian András Szekfü, who was a student at the time (he is just a few years younger than Szabó), recalled a decade later how *The Age of Daydreaming* had affected him: "I still remember the film's wrenching effect on me, as I made my way from the darkness of the screening to the street. In the film's protagonists I saw myself, my own generation on the screen."[13] But Szabó spoke not only to Hungarians. The *Age of Daydreaming* won the Silver Sail for best first film at the Locarno film festival in 1965, and *Father* won the Grand Prix at the Moscow film festival in 1967 as well as several other prizes, and went on to important screenings in New York and Paris. With that, at the age of twenty-nine, Szabó was launched as a significant director in world cinema; he also gained a prestige at home that would be confirmed and amplified by his Oscar win a decade and a half later.

Leaving and Its Consequences in *Lovefilm*

Unlike its two predecessors, *Lovefilm* did not win any prizes or nominations, but it is my personal favorite in the 1960s trilogy, possibly because it deals most explicitly with the "to leave or to stay" question, which has special meaning for me. Hungary has the unenviable distinction of being a country where people have had to ask themselves that question quite a few times over the course of the twentieth century and right up to today. In Szabó's last film to date, *Final Report* (2020), when the nursing staff at a hospital the government has decided to close are forced to move to different jobs, some mutter that they prefer to leave the country. During the 1920s and 1930s, when state-sponsored antisemitism increasingly thrived (from the numerus clausus laws limiting Jewish university enrollments in the 1920s to the much more draconian exclusionary laws of the late 1930s), the question confronted mostly Jews and provoked the departure of some very great talents in the arts and the sciences.[14] In 1944–5, when the Red Army invaded the country, thousands of Hungarians chose to follow the German Army in its retreat, many of them eventually settling in the United States. In 1948 and 1949, when the communists rose to full power in the country, many Hungarians again preferred to leave, including my own family.

Among the postwar emigrés was the world-renowned writer Sándor Márai, who devotes some beautiful pages in his autobiography to reflections on why he or anyone else who is attached to a native land and its language may decide one day to leave and never return. As Márai describes it, his choice was between collaborating with the new regime, even if only passively— accepting to be "recruited" as a famous author and receiving material rewards in exchange—or maintaining his personal freedom.[15] The price he paid for his choice, besides the estrangement of permanent exile, was that his works became taboo in Hungary for close to four decades. He and his wife eventually settled in San Diego, California, where he continued to write and publish, always in Hungarian. In 1989, after his wife's death, Márai committed suicide at the age of eighty-eight, just months before the fall of the Berlin Wall. By then, his works had begun to appear again in his native land and he was even invited to return, but he never did.

It was in 1956, as a result of the failed revolution, that the greatest number of Hungarians had to face the "to leave or to stay" question, and some 200,000 of them chose to leave.[16] In a country whose total population was less than 10 million, that is a considerable number, more than 2 percent. József Marx remarks, with a bit of exaggeration, that "in the late fall of 1956, there was not a single family in which the 'to leave or to stay' question did not arise."[17] It was an existential question par excellence, for it implied not only a leave-taking from home but the choice of a whole new life and self. Existential choices are choices of oneself, of who one is, as Nietzsche put it in *Ecce Homo*, or of who one will be. They can also imply a farewell to who one *was*: Márai speaks about saying farewell to his "real 'I,'" the I he recognized only in his native land.[18] The philosopher Ágnes Heller, who wrote extensively about the concept of existential choice, put it this way: "Choice of yourself is a choice of destiny; more precisely, choosing yourself is tantamount to knowing yourself as a person of a particular destiny."[19]

Heller's view may appear too voluntaristic, allowing for no role of the unconscious in determining life choices; indeed, like Jean-Paul Sartre, Heller was quite wary of psychoanalysis, but she recognized that rationality does not suffice to account for an existential choice. She was careful to stipulate that her theory should not be confused with theories of rational choice. The notion of a "leap," which she inherited from Kierkegaard, takes account of the non-rational aspect of existential choices: "one takes the risk and dives in."[20] Heller herself left Hungary in 1977, after a number of run-ins with Communist Party orthodoxy, but like many political exiles, she returned both for visits and then permanently after 1989.

Of course, "diving in" can also consist in choosing *not* to move or leave. The Hungarian Jewish writer György Konrád, who survived the war in Budapest as a child (he was born in 1933), recounts in his autobiography that he decided more than once not to leave Hungary. He could have emigrated to Israel in 1949 with his family, but they decided to stay. He could also have left in 1956, when many of his friends did and "became professors in the United States." In Konrád's opinion, "Everyone who left was right, as was everyone who stayed."[21] He did not add the obvious corollary: although there was no "correct" choice, once the choice was made, it had consequences. Among the consequences, for those who left during the communist years, was the possibility of reprisals against their family members who stayed behind; to "leave in dissidence," as one Hungarian friend reminded me, was not merely to emigrate but possibly to deprive your family members of certain privileges for some years. Not to mention the fact that leaving itself was not simply a matter of getting on a train or plane, since it was illegal. Yet, many thousands did choose to leave and managed to do so, one way or the other.

István Szabó has stated more than once in interviews that it is not enough to know the techniques of filmmaking; one also has to "have something to say."[22] One thing he has to say in *Lovefilm* is precisely about the consequences of leaving, and it can be summed up like this: an existential choice is free (to the extent that any choice can be called free within certain determinisms of place and time), for it affirms the agency of the individual making it. But once the choice has been made, the one who made it must live with what follows from it.

Lovefilm explores in beautiful cinematic detail the story of two young people who have loved each other since childhood, but one leaves the country in the fall of 1956, while the other stays. Jancsi (diminutive of János) and Kata grow up together in the same Budapest apartment building, almost like brother and sister, and their story is told against the background of Hungary's wartime and postwar history. Like the other protagonists of Szabó's trilogy, these two young people were born a year before the outbreak of the Second World War. Their earliest memories date to the Nazi occupation of 1944 (when Jancsi was hidden, briefly, because of his Jewish origins, a fact Szabó presents but does not dwell on) and the arrival of Soviet troops in the winter of 1944–5. Their first school years are spent during the Rákosi regime, and both become (obligatorily) members of the Young Pioneers; as adolescents, they take part in May Day parades, carrying flags and placards with the leader's photograph. Separated for a while, they meet again as young adults and fall in love: it's 1956, the year of choices. Jancsi and Kata are not active in the uprising of October, but they are caught in the street fighting while standing in line to buy bread, along with other ordinary people, most of whom are terrified by the shooting. Very soon after that, Kata suddenly announces to Jancsi on the telephone that she is leaving and pleads with him to go with her; but Jancsi stays.

Szabó emphasizes the momentousness of Kata's choice by the way he films her in close-up, her face anxious, as she speaks into the telephone. (Kata is played by Judit Halász, who also appears in *The Age of Daydreaming* and *Father*, as well as in Szabó's important 1980 film, *Confidence*.) For still more emphasis, Szabó shows the close-up twice. It first appears early in the film, where it functions as a flash-forward. Although the film's temporal structure is not linear, there is a roughly chronological progression in the memory sequences about the couple's childhood and adolescence, but images from 1944 and 1956, which are clearly the most important in the protagonists' lives, often disrupt this chronology, as in the instance of Kata's phone call, which is first shown between two memories dating to around 1945. The second shot of Kata on the telephone occurs much later, in more or less the right place chronologically, right after the sequence where Kata and Jancsi are caught in the crossfire on the street in October 1956. Significantly, Szabó makes no attempt to motivate Kata's choice to leave, emphasizing its suddenness. In the original scenario, he included a scene between the street sequence and the phone call, where Kata and Jancsi are sitting at her kitchen table and she is arguing for them to leave together. By omitting this scene in the final version, Szabó reinforces the dramatic impact of the phone call, as well as its quality as an existential "leap." In my meeting with him in November 2019, Szabó told me a lovely anecdote that may be relevant here. After *Lovefilm* was finished and already about to play in theaters in Budapest, he realized that he had to cut ten minutes—so, armed with scissors, he went to every single movie theater in the city where the film was scheduled to be screened and made the cut manually![23] It's possible that the scene around the kitchen table disappeared on that occasion. Kata's choice, which will determine the rest of her life, remains unexplained (Figure 3).

Figure 3 Lovefilm (Szerelmesfilm*), 1970*: *Kata tells Jancsi she is leaving. In courtesy of National Film Institute Hungary—Film Archive.*

The film's present action begins ten years later, when Jancsi says goodbye to his current girlfriend at the train station in Budapest. He is on his way to visit Kata in France, where she has attended university and started a modest career as a fashion designer. By 1966, Hungarians could travel to the West if they obtained permission, although we are not told what Jancsi's declared reason for travel is—in fact, we know very little about his present life, other than that he is an educated young man living in Budapest, evidently with a job (which is not specified) and with the wherewithal to afford a trip abroad. This, as well as the fact that the characters are played by the same actor and have the same first name, János or Jancsi, has led some commentators to speculate that the protagonist of *Lovefilm* is the same person as the protagonist of *The Age of Daydreaming*, so that the latter functions as a prequel to the former.[24] There is not much point to such speculations, however, just as it makes no sense to ask how many children Lady Macbeth had. Szabó himself discourages attempts to "fill in" details about characters that are not given in the films themselves. In *Lovefilm*, for example, the character of Bözsi, a young woman who lived in the same apartment house as Kata and Jancsi and who was murdered during the war, appears in several flashbacks, including one where she gave them swimming lessons that they both remember vividly. But as to exactly who Bözsi was in relation to their families, we don't know and it doesn't matter, Szabó told an interviewer.[25]

Although we know little about Jancsi's present circumstances, we are given a great deal of information about his childhood and adolescence, in memory sequences triggered as Jancsi sits on the train. *Lovefilm* is in many ways a study in and about memory—its importance in individual lives as well as its imbrications with collective history, a subject Szabó would explore in even greater detail a few years later in *25 Firemen's Street* (which I discuss later in this chapter).

Memory is already foregrounded in *Lovefilm*'s opening shot, in which the camera lingers over a pile of family photographs. Some clearly date to before the First World War, when women wore long, corseted dresses, others to the 1920s (short hair, chemise dress), and still others to later. We see couples, a father with his young child, parents with children, and an older woman who must be a grandmother—but soon the camera zooms in on photos of a little boy and then of a boy and girl in various poses, before resting on a photo of four toddlers lined up in a playground, all of them wearing snowsuits and white shoes. This photo will be seen later in Kata's apartment in France, one of the few items she took with her when she left—it is clearly a marker of the long personal history between the two protagonists. The relation between family photographs and individual and collective memory has been explored in great detail by contemporary theorists.[26] Photographs constitute an archive that not only acts as a mnemonic device and as a means of transmission between generations but can also evoke a collective history, as in the evolution of women's fashions that we see here.

Right after the opening montage of photos we see a close-up of Jancsi today, speaking directly into the camera: "I have been dreaming a lot about Kata." This sentence echoes the opening of the poet Miklós Radnóti's prose text *Ikrek Hava* (*Under Gemini*), which recounts the narrator's memories of his younger sister and which Szabó has said was an inspiration for his film.[27] (Jancsi takes a copy of Radnóti's book to France as a gift to Kata.) Jancsi's first-person narration recurs at several moments in the film, emphasizing both its subjective quality and its memorial aspects. Even when the action moves forward, after the couple's reunion during the few days they spend together, it is constantly doubled by reminiscences, not only by Jancsi but also in the dialogues between him and Kata: "Do you remember . . .?" At one point, they disagree about a detail as they recall the lessons Kata's mother improvised for them and a few other children during the war: Did she use a small blackboard to write on, or was it a piece of dark paper? This kind of attention to detail can appear superfluous, but it is precisely through visual details (which may or not be accurate) that memory functions, as Szabó suggests.

Visual detail is also what characterizes film as an art form, of course. In one of the great set pieces in *Lovefilm*, a dinner party of Hungarian exiles in France, one of the guests, a Jewish woman named Klári (Rita Békés), recounts to Kata and Jancsi her harrowing escape from being shot into the Danube by Arrow Cross thugs in 1944; she mentions that her last memory of Budapest is the iron railing she saw before jumping into the freezing water and swimming for her life (Figure 4). The camera focuses mainly on her face as she tells her story, so we do not see a railing. But a bit later, Jancsi comments in voiceover that just as Klári's outstanding memory is of the railing, his own war memory is above all

Figure 4 Lovefilm *(Szerelmesfilm), 1970: Klári tells her story to Jancsi and Kata. In courtesy of National Film Institute Hungary—Film Archive.*

of the knapsacks he and Kata wore as they hurried to the air raid shelter during a bombing raid. By then, we have already seen several shots of the two children descending into the shelter, with identical knapsacks on their backs, but in this instance what we see while Jancsi mentions knapsacks is an iron railing in the city, evoking a memory not of the war but of a moment years later, when Kata runs away from him after he tries to kiss her. The complex interactions between narration and visual representation (in this instance, what we see does not correspond to what we hear), and between various moments in time and the images associated with them, make *Lovefilm* structurally one of the most intricate in Szabó's oeuvre. The only other work that is even more complicated structurally is *25 Firemen's Street*, which adds the major element of dream to the mix of memory and history. But dream also figures, albeit less prominently, in *Lovefilm*: at one point toward the end, Jancsi realizes that a scene he had thought of as a memory (and which had been shown visually as such), of him and Kata kissing on a streetcar, was actually a dream.

The imbrication of personal memory and collective history is brought to the fore in two complementary ways. First, there are what might be called "faux newsreel" sequences, which refer to events or images that many viewers will recognize as historical, but that are filmed here as if they were Jancsi's memories. For example, quite early in the film, we see several men dragging a dead horse on the street and then cutting into its flank for meat. This was not an uncommon occurrence in Budapest in the winter and spring of 1945, and it was recorded in black and white newsreels at the time; in fact, Szabó started *Father* by showing just such archival footage in order to situate that film's action historically. He has explained in interviews that he spent many hours as a young filmmaker watching historical newsreels, and he often used them in his early films, as in the opening of *Father* or in the sequence of János and Eva at the cinema in *The Age of Daydreaming*. In *Lovefilm*, however, he does not use the archival footage of men dragging the horse, but rather reconstitutes the scene in color, so that it appears just like all the other, purely personal memory sequences. Similarly, the May Day parade that Jancsi and Kata participate in is staged and filmed in color, like Jancsi's other memories, in contrast to *Father*, where Szabó included archival footage of actual May Day parades during the protagonist's childhood; and the image of Russian tanks barreling down the street in 1956, which he showed as a piece of archival footage in both *Father* and *The Age of Daydreaming*, is here filmed directly, as a reconstruction. *Lovefilm* was Szabó's first color film, and it is possible that he excluded the use of black and white footage in order to maintain tonal consistency, but what also happens as a result is that well-known images from Hungary's recent history become transformed into instances of personal memory.

The other way Szabó introduces the collective element into this very subjective film is by including other people's stories to provide a context—and an occasional contrast—to the story of Kata and Jancsi. The most elaborate version of this is the dinner party in France where Klári recounts her escape from the Arrow Cross. Jancsi and Kata are among the guests, along with a middle-aged man and two women, including Klári. The hosts are a young Hungarian couple, whose little boy joins them for a few minutes after he wakes up from his nap—just long enough for the adults to sing him some childhood songs they all know, and to have his father point to the television set when the weather report comes on with a map of Europe: "Look, look, there is Hungary!" The fact that all these guests know some of the same songs, despite their differences in age and life experiences, is highly significant, as is the father's excitement when he points out Hungary to his child. These Hungarians are all exiles of a kind, and while some want nothing more to do with Hungary ("Go to America," the older man advises Jancsi, while Klári declares that she never wants to see Budapest again after what happened to her), they all share some common memories tied to that country and find pleasure in that fact: even Klári sings along with the others. She does not know songs from the communist era, however, as she left the country before then. Musical memories, Szabó suggests, can signal differences as well as commonalities, especially between generations. The other middle-aged woman at the party, an attractive blonde who knows all the songs that Jancsi and Kata learned as schoolchildren under the Rákosi regime, explains to Jancsi that she was a choir director in 1950, when "you were still drinking hot cocoa and working on the Young Pioneer Railway."

It is clear, incidentally, that not all these emigrés are Jewish; exile and emigration from Hungary, especially in 1956, were not specific to Jews but affected the whole country. One of Szabó's great achievements in *Lovefilm* is that he depicts the emigrants from 1956 without judging them. The only other Hungarian film that struggled with the question of "to leave or to stay," György Révész's much earlier *At Midnight* (*Éjfélkor*, 1957), also focused on a couple who made opposite choices in 1956, but the film clearly comes down on the side of the man who stays, not the woman who leaves—hardly surprising for a film released only a year after the event, when the Kádár regime was still punishing "counterrevolutionaries."

Those Hungarians who chose to leave, whether in 1956 or earlier, share a trait that Szabó emphasizes in *Lovefilm*: they are all foreigners in their adopted country. The former choir director is now married to a Frenchman and has started to dream in French, she tells the others at the party. But we can be sure that she speaks French with an accent, since she left Hungary as an adult; the same must be true of the middle-aged man, who nevertheless insists on leading the others in singing *La Marseillaise* instead of the Hungarian national anthem. Later in the film, a childhood friend of Kata's and Jancsi's who left in 1956 and ended up in the United States, Karcsi, suddenly shows up in his American Army officer's uniform: he is currently stationed in Germany. During their brief but joyous reunion (Karcsi was one of the toddlers in the photo that sits on Kata's bookshelf), Karcsi explains that he is afraid of being sent to Vietnam, but he can't really protest the way some young Americans are doing, by burning their draft cards, for example. "I'm a dirty foreigner [in America], just glad to be alive," he says ruefully before taking his leave.

The condition of the displaced "foreigner"—or of the exile, the refugee, the emigrant, the expatriate, each of those terms with its own particular resonance and connotation—always implies separation from the place of origin, and most often from the native tongue. Many emigrants derive a certain pride from "acting as if one were at home wherever one happens to be," as Edward Said put it (this being the obverse of not feeling truly at home anywhere); others feel a permanent sense of nostalgia and loss, acutely prone to "the melancholy tension of separation from one's origins," in Victor Burgin's elegant phrasing.[28] But whether they are happy or melancholy, all emigrants experience, if not permanently then at least from time to time, the feeling of *being between*: between homes, between cultures, between landscapes, and between languages. Interestingly, Szabó explores this theme in *Lovefilm* through the only character who is not an emigrant but merely a traveler, Jancsi. Jancsi's displacement from home is temporary, since he will return to Budapest at the end of his brief visit to France. But he experiences the bitterness of feeling like an exile as he wanders through the streets of the French town while Kata is at work, repeatedly asking in an interior monologue: "Bonjour Monsieur, Bonjour, Madame, Bonjour Mademoiselle, savez-vous où est la Hongrie?" ("Do you know where Hungary is located?") He never asks the question out loud, but the implication is clear: none of these French men and women know, or care, where Hungary is. The earlier scene where the father excitedly points to Hungary on a map for his little boy acquires a particular meaning in retrospect: only to emigrants living outside the country is the question of its location—or more exactly, the question of what other people know about its location—compelling.

The status of *being between* is explored at greater length, visually, in an earlier sequence, again from Jancsi's perspective. Since he has never seen the sea (Hungary's landlocked status after its loss of territories in 1919 is a topos of much Hungarian literature), he and Kata take a brief holiday on the coast. The mood of this sequence is generally one of playfulness and pleasure in the present moment, as the two young people frolic in the waves, but at one point, while they're lying on the beach, Jancsi's mind suddenly turns to the house he lives in, in Budapest, on Firemen's Street. We then get a number of quick alternating shots, as the facade of the building and a wider view of the street alternate with close-ups of Kata's body lying on the sand, Jancsi's face as he looks at her, and the waves lapping on the shore behind her. Accompanying this series of images and the sound of the waves is Jancsi's internal monologue: "If I open my eyes, I see Kata and the sea; if I close my eyes, I see the house on Firemen's Street." But someone who is actually there, on that street in Budapest, can touch the building's stones, he muses, whereas what he touches is Kata's hand. Once he is back home, the situation will be reversed: he will see Kata if he closes his eyes, but will not be able to touch her.

What this sequence drives home is the fact that there is no way to unite those two spaces, those two worlds, in reality; they can only be united, fragmentarily, in Jancsi's mind. The separation between worlds is what makes the love in *Lovefilm* impossible or at best bittersweet. The love between Kata and Jancsi has no future because neither of them is willing to change course: Jancsi will not move to France, as Kata begs him to, and she will not return to marry him in Budapest. As Kata herself puts it, love requires a shared project, an envisaged future. All they have, by contrast, are their shared memories. The reviewer who remarked, critically, that Szabó's hero (and Szabó himself, in this film) focused on memories rather than the future was right, but he missed the point: rather than being a flaw in the film, the absence of a future for this particular couple is its very subject. It would require a new existential choice on the part of one of them to bring about a traditional happy ending—but can existential choices, once made and lived with, be reversed? The passage of time, Szabó suggests, makes some choices irreversible. Jancsi's future, like Kata's, will unfold independently of the other's.

On his way home, after he arrives at the Gare de l'Est in Paris and deposits his suitcase in the train compartment, Jancsi runs outside to look at the city he has not had time to visit. Among the succession of quick shots that capture a typical day in the capital (people on a café terrace, cars on a busy street, advertisements on storefronts, and travelers arriving or leaving the station), we see a street sign: *rue du 8 mai 1945*. The streets and boulevards of Paris are full of allusions to historical events, and this sign evoking the day the Second World War ended in Europe seems particularly apt. Not only do Jancsi's and Kata's first memories date to around that time, but the Iron Curtain, which made 1956 into a moment of choice for Hungarians, was a consequence of the end of the war. While it would be simpleminded to suggest that History alone is responsible for how individual lives evolve, the street sign points to Szabó's long-standing preoccupation with the way collective events influence the fate of individuals.

Those Who Stay: Visions of Home in the 1970s

When Jancsi arrives back home, in *Lovefilm*, the first thing we see is the gallery above the inner courtyard of the apartment building where he lives. One standard feature of Budapest apartment buildings that date from the early part of the twentieth century is the inner, rectangular courtyard that you enter from the vestibule; the stairway leading up to the various floors is tucked into one corner. Framing the courtyard are the narrow galleries that run around each floor, generally with wrought-iron railings. The doors to individual apartments open onto the gallery. If you are on a high floor, you can look down before entering the apartment and see the whole courtyard with its crown of railings below you; looking up from a low floor or from the courtyard itself, you see the sky and the crown of galleries rising above you. Szabó often shows these courtyards and railings and galleries in his films—they are immediate identifiers of Budapest. Jancsi walks along the gallery to his apartment, and we notice the worn-out condition of the walls, with peeling paint everywhere: this building could use some refurbishing. When he enters the apartment and puts down his bag in the living room, we note the furnishings, dating probably from many years before the war: a white tile stove in a corner, dark walls, a painting of a landscape in an ornate gold frame, a brown velvet armchair, and an oval table covered in gray felt. Like the gallery outside, the interior is shabby. The viewer who recalls the bright blue walls and light curtains of Kata's French apartment is sure to remark on the difference. Since *Lovefilm* was Szabó's first color film, he was very meticulous about getting all the colors right—this has remained a preoccupation of his ever since.[29]

Right after this interior view, we get a quick shot of the building's facade and recognize it as the same facade that Jancsi saw in his mind's eye while lying on the French beach next to Kata. Now he is back in Budapest. Home.

"Somehow everything was connected to the city": That is how the writer Iván Mándy put it in recalling the time, around 1970, when he and Szabó were thinking of collaborating on a film. The subject would be not only about dreams but also about Budapest, a city both men loved and featured in their works. They spent many hours together, Mándy recalled, watching newsreels about the city and comparing their dreams about "the streets, the parks, the old cafés, the soccer fields, the galleries [in apartment buildings], the wrought-iron railings, the stairwells, the dark and shadowy backstairs. And the people who lived in that house, who rejoiced and struggled, and whose figures are lost in shadow like the back staircase."[30]

The project with Mándy never materialized, but his reminiscences about it are a precious source for understanding Szabó's work in the years immediately following *Lovefilm*. In 1971, a year after *Lovefilm* premiered, he made a series of shorts about the city that he put together under the title *Budapest, Why I Love It* (*Budapest, amiért szeretem*). It was as if he were seeking to answer the questions raised in *Lovefilm*: Why does Jancsi refuse to follow Kata into emigration? Why does he choose to return to his shabby apartment in the once sparkling but now dusky Eastern European capital he calls home? And what does home mean, exactly, for a young man like Jancsi—or for Szabó?

One thing it means is a shared history, with its accompanying Muses, memory and dream. What defines a nation, Ernest Renan wrote, is that the people in it "have many things in common," including a "rich heritage of memories."[31] The same can be said about a family, or (stretching things a bit) about the inhabitants of a house who know each other and have lived in proximity for a long time. The first of the shorts that make up *Budapest, Why I Love It* is a thirteen-minute film titled *Dream about the House* (*Álom a házrol*). Like the others in the series, it consists entirely of visuals and music, with no dialogue. It begins with a tracking shot across the Elisabeth Bridge over the Danube, from Buda to Pest, approaching a main thoroughfare known to all inhabitants of the city; after reaching the Pest side, the camera travels along almost empty streets in the early morning, past parked cars, churches with their tall steeples, storefronts, and the occasional pedestrian crossing the street or waiting for a streetcar. Finally, it comes to rest in front of a house, the by now familiar apartment building of *Lovefilm*. It is in the area known as Ferencváros, Budapest's 9th district, an inner city neighborhood where proud buildings from the late nineteenth and early twentieth century mingle with more modest working-class lodgings. This particular building has an ornate facade that bespeaks a prosperous past, but it has a thick coating of grime and we may assume that it is quite run-down inside.

All of the action that follows takes place on the sidewalk outside the front door of the house: in true dreamlike fashion, the interior of the building has been transplanted into the street. There are tables and chairs, a sewing machine, and even a bed; an old grandfather clock hangs on the outside wall, and various people come up to it at intervals to adjust the time. Many images are repeated, as they are in dreams. A small Christmas tree rests on a side table, while a family near it consumes a holiday meal featuring a large fish (often found on Catholic tables at Christmas time), carefully carved and distributed by the old woman who presides at the table; earlier, we saw the same fish still alive, displayed on a porcelain platter; later, we will see the old woman packing away the Christmas decorations. Two other old women sit next to the sewing machine, and the one who is operating it suddenly slumps over; by the time the doctor hurries up with his bag, all he can do for her is to close her eyes (Figure 5).

Meanwhile, people enter and exit through the main door: a young couple kisses each other goodbye, and soon the young woman emerges (several times), wearing her wedding dress; later, they separate. Two men wearing blue uniforms drag a man from the building—who are they, and when? In 1919, blue-uniformed Romanian troops invaded Budapest to root out "Reds" after the fall of the Commune led by Béla Kun, but the dream gives us only the image, not its precise meaning. Soldiers wearing Hungarian khaki uniforms come back from the war (is it the Second World War?). An old man with a backpack shows up and is greeted joyously by two women. Is he a Jew returning from forced labor service? Again, we can only guess, while the music plays. Boys run on the sidewalk or else lean against the wall—among them, we recognize the child actor (András Szamosfalvi) who played Jancsi as a boy in *Lovefilm*. A sexy young woman, her open blouse partially exposing

Figure 5 Dream about the House (*Álom a házrol*), *1971. Mafilm 8. Copyright National Film Institute Hungary—Film Archive.*

one breast, also leans against the wall; later she will show up with her blouse primly buttoned. Meanwhile, crossing our field of vision several times, looking right at the camera, is a baker in his white smock and cap, carrying a platter of dinner rolls.

Whose dream is this? It could be anybody's who has lived in that house for many years. Szabó manages, in the space of thirteen minutes, to evoke a whole collective history as it may have been experienced and then remembered, in dream fragments, by an inhabitant of the building. By bringing the intimacy of the interior into the street, Szabó makes the dream about the house both anonymous and unanimous, individual yet inseparable from what is lived in common. The film ends with a group portrait, as all the figures we have seen pose together in front of the door.

The other shorts in *Budapest, Why I Love It*, are less focused on a single place, but they too have an oneiric quality. Fish swim in a telephone booth, pigeons ride the streetcar, and beautiful young women wave from the roofs of apartment houses. The second in the series, "The mirror," features a mirror in a shop window that registers all the people who stop to look at themselves, and even those who stopped to do so decades ago: women carrying parasols from around 1900, girls primping then and later, and men young and old examining themselves. It's as if Szabó wanted to record every possible kind of face one might see in the Hungarian capital, a project that also underlies the segment titled "The Square." We see children playing (among whom we once again recognize the boy from *Lovefilm*), well-dressed women chatting on a bench, men playing cards on another bench, and lovers embracing on a third. A boy hangs by his legs from a tree while girls play hopscotch.

In all these films, the Danube is a presence in the background, its image recurring obsessively beneath the pulsating rhythm of the Bach musical score. Along with the streets and houses of the capital, Szabó's traveling camera never tires of filming the river and its bridges: at dawn, at dusk, flown over by pigeons, crossed by that other icon of the city, the yellow streetcar. Houses provide stability, while the river and the streetcar move; together, they add up to a vision of home.

In his book *The Poetics of Space*, the philosopher Gaston Bachelard noted that "every space that is truly inhabited carries with it the essential notion of the house or home" (*maison*, in French, means both).[32] In his films of the 1970s about Budapest, Szabó seems to be running with that idea. For those who remain there, he suggests, Budapest becomes (or maybe it has always been, and that is why they choose to stay) the inhabited space that defines home.

Dream about the House, presented on its own, was awarded the top prize for a short film at the Oberhausen film festival in 1972. But Szabó was not finished with that house yet, or with dreams about (or within) home. In 1973 he released *25 Firemen's Street* (*Tűzoltó utca 25*), a full-length feature film that brought the dreamers indoors: the film's subtitle, in Hungarian, is *Dreams from the House*.[33] *25 Firemen's Street* went on to win the Golden Leopard for best film at the Locarno film festival, beating out Jacques Rivette's *Céline and Julie Go Boating*, among other major competitors.

The first thing we see is an apartment building exploding, producing billowing smoke: a piece of city planning in Ferencváros *c.* 1970. The building falls three times while the opening credits roll. After that, a written text informs us:

> Our house is a piece of the past—its inhabitants live in the web of their memories. The most important choices in their lives confronted them during the years of war, and that is also when they faced the crucial tests of their humanity. Perhaps during this night they will finally say goodbye to the house, and to that past.

We soon learn that the destroyed house is not the house with the dreamers but one near it. The wrecking ball will soon transform the neighborhood, and no doubt this house will fall as well, but for now it still stands, its facade familiar. The camera goes inside and starts looking in through the windows at the lives of the inhabitants. We don't know who these people are yet, but we have seen some of their faces before, notably in *Lovefilm*. András Bálint, our hero Jancsi, is here cast in a relatively minor role as the son of Rita Békés, who played the Holocaust survivor Klári in the earlier film and is a major character (not Jewish) in this one; Ervin Csomák, who played a minor role as Kata's father in *Lovefilm*, here appears in a larger role as Békés's husband, a baker, while the Polish actress Lucina Wynnicka, who played the blond chorus director in *Lovefilm*, has a principal role as the brunette Mária, whose family story is the most developed one in the film. (Szabó often uses an international cast in his films, doing postproduction synchronization of their dialogue into Hungarian, or in some cases German or English.) The effect on the viewer who recognizes these actors is akin to how one feels upon recognizing an acquaintance from home in a foreign country: "I know you!" Szabó has often spoken, including in my conversations with him, about the community that is established on the set of a film, not only among the actors but the cinematographer and the rest of the crew, many of whom have accompanied Szabó over decades. The viewer who recognizes familiar faces among the actors from film to film becomes part of that community for the duration of the viewing.

25 Firemen's Street is very much a film about community, both its protectiveness and its fragility. Intergenerational families inhabit almost every apartment, or inhabited it in the past before the older members died. As Mária's grandmother says around the time of the First World War, when Mária was a beautiful young woman being courted by two different men, "The family matters above all." But neighbors also matter, and in many of the sequences we are not sure whose dream we are in: the young man played by Bálint will end up marrying a girl who lives in the house, but he also dreams about two other women neighbors. Szabó explained in some interviews that during this one night, "everyone in the house dreams the same dream"—but in most of the sequences, we are aware of a particular dreamer, or at least a particular family, whose story we are in, even if neighbors are also involved. When Mária and her family—who we come to realize are assimilated Jews with a proud tradition of Hungarian patriotism, a Jewish "type" Szabó would study in detail in his 1999 film *Sunshine*—are forced to move out of the house in 1944, they leave their valuables with several neighbors, who restore them to Mária after the war. A decree by the Hungarian government after the Nazis invaded Hungary in the spring of 1944 forced Jews to move into specially designated "yellow-star houses" in the capital—Szabó does not spell this out, but trusts his audience to recall it; evidently Mária's family is forced to move into one of those houses. A few years later, when one of Mária's non-Jewish neighbors, an aristocrat, is in turn forced to leave the house (again, no explanation is offered: around 1951, the hard-line Rákosi regime forced "class enemies" to move to small villages far from the capital, an exile that could last several years), he leaves his valuables with Mária.

The fact that Szabó leaves all historical explanations aside may appear puzzling, given that this film was shown in many international venues. Evidently, he assumed (not necessarily correctly) that his Hungarian viewers were familiar with the history and that others would get the point even without knowing the details. When Szabó returned to some of this history in his English-language film *Sunshine* many years later, he was careful to fill in the blanks—and was blamed for it by some Hungarian critics, who accused him of having made a film for Americans![34]

It speaks to the powerful effect of Szabó's film that even without explanations, the viewer understands the import of the historical events that haunt the dreamers of the house. It almost doesn't matter which war we are in, or what the exact circumstances are: what matters is that at crucial moments of collective experience, some people are hunted while others must decide whether to help them or not. An officer in a blue uniform stands in the middle of the courtyard looking up at Mária's grandmother, who stands by the railing of the gallery, and asks her in French: "Have you seen any Reds, Madame?" "Non, mon colonel," she answers, "we haven't seen any Reds." But in fact, her family is sheltering at least one "Red," despite the danger to themselves. That is the point the viewer needs to understand, not the fact that this is 1919 and that the officer is part of the Romanian Army (although, of course, knowing that fact adds substance to one's viewing experience). Twenty-five years later, during the Nazi occupation, the baker's wife hides people in the attic, presumably Jews, and she too is in danger for it, but she saves their lives. The building's concierge behaves less honorably, but when she becomes the one who feels hunted (as a collaborator, after the war) and asks for help, the baker's wife protects her as well, signing an affidavit that the concierge knew what was going on but didn't betray her. The fact that the concierge is an unsympathetic figure adds an element of coercion to her plea for help: the baker's wife seems to feel obliged to sign the affidavit, even though she could refuse with impunity. Is this Szabó's version of humanism, a refusal to judge even unsympathetic characters as long as they are not outright evil? In this house on Firemen's Street, a microcosm of Hungarian urban society, there are no real villains.

The main point is that History (with a capital H) has been a major element in individuals' lives in Hungary throughout the twentieth century, and, more sharply, that in extreme historical circumstances people are confronted with choices that impinge on the rest of their days—and nights. "[H]istoric and political events of 30 or 40 years earlier and personal traumas have an impact, and even today penetrate [their] dreams"—that is how Szabó put it to an interviewer in commenting on the film.[35] The introductory text stated, "Perhaps during this night they will finally say goodbye to the house, and to that past." In the morning, as the inhabitants emerge from their night full of historic dreams, the baker's son (played by Bálint) repeats that thought: "Dear mother, we must say goodbye to this house." But is a traumatic past—or what Joyce's Stephen Dedalus calls the nightmare of history—so easily liquidated? Szabó himself shows otherwise. People say goodbye and go on with their lives, but they carry their past, and even that of their neighbors, with them.

Would an actual departure, emigration, make a difference? At several points in the film, characters leave: for Australia, for Brazil, for America. "You must go. Here it's all finished," one man tells Mária before the war. As we know from *Lovefilm*, even those who leave carry their dreams with them; yet the changes in their physical world, starting with the places they inhabit, will ineluctably transform their notion of home. In *25 Firemen's Street*, Szabó experiments with the idea that a single shared space (albeit one with many doors) can constitute a collective home. Significantly, not a single sequence of the film occurs outside, on the streets of Budapest. After the first shot of the house nearby being blown up, every sequence takes place in the confines of the apartment building, except for the brief ones that show Mária and her children in the room with other Jews who have been forced out of their homes—yet another interior. After she is released, Mária is right back in the house on Firemen's Street, with no transition outside. Yet, even though we don't see the city, we are aware that this apartment building, like the stories of its inhabitants, exists only in Budapest in the twentieth century.

The last of what I call Szabó's "why I stayed in Budapest" films, *Budapest Tales* (Budapesti Mesék, 1977), presents yet another vision of home, but in this instance the home is not a house; it's a yellow streetcar, an emblem of Budapest in Szabó's films. Abandoned and lying on its side near a body of water, the streetcar is righted and set back on its rails by a group of people (among whom we again recognize András Bálint as well as several others who appeared in *25 Firemen's Street*) who come together after what appears to have been a collective catastrophe. Szabó had already inserted a somewhat extraneous sequence about a streetcar into *Father*, where the heroic father fantasized by Takó as a boy gets an abandoned streetcar moving again with the help of other people. In *Budapest Tales*, the streetcar itself becomes home: its inhabitants sleep, cook, make love, give birth, recite poetry, sing songs, and plan for the future within its walls. Once the first group gets the car moving (the rails must lead to "the city" and the "depot," they reason), more people join them. Fights break out with marauding soldiers; a doctor who strays into the woods is murdered by other soldiers; and a woman gives birth to a pair of twins who grow into young boys, marking the passage of years. Snowy landscapes are followed by summers; the streetcar traverses a forest fire, emerging from it blackened but intact (it gets repainted). It even survives possible extinction, when the rails suddenly end at a body of water. "There is no redemption," one character declares. But eventually the inhabitants find a solution: they dismantle the streetcar piece by piece, carry all the pieces across the water, and rebuild it on the other side.

Clearly, this is an allegory, a "tale" in the sense of fairy tale or folktale. (The film's title in Hungarian, *Budapesti Mesék*, makes this explicit: "mese" is the word for fairy tale or folktale.) "I wanted to make a film so simple that anybody could understand," Szabó explained to an interviewer. "So I told a fable so simple and clear about human beings whose only need was to stay alive and together."[36] When the streetcar finally rolls into the city center, it encounters other streetcars just like it, recalling the collective endings of Szabó's earlier films. The last word belongs to the character played by András Bálint (in one of his last roles in a film by Szabó): "We're alive!" he proclaims triumphantly.[37]

Aside from its familiar actors, *Budapest Tales* includes a number of familiar objects from Szabó's iconography: the grandfather clock from *Dream about the House* and *25 Firemen's Street*, family photos (as in *Lovefilm* and *Father*), a woman trying on different pairs of glasses (as in *The Age of Daydreaming*), and even a large fish swimming in somebody's dream. There are some lovely moments in it, as when the streetcar is shown in a panoramic view from above, traveling along woods covered in snow, or when its inhabitants start dancing during a stop. But the film is too schematic, or to use Szabó's words, too "simple and clear" to touch a viewer emotionally. The characters have no names, just descriptors in allegorical fashion: Widow, Soldier, Barber, Girl Who Knows Colors. The one exception is the young man played by Bálint, who has a name, but it too is allegorical: Fényes, which means bright or shining. The story as a whole comes across as an allegory, even if we cannot be sure what its intended meaning is: People have a need to rebuild after a catastrophe. Humans seek shelter and can make a home almost anywhere. With sufficient goodwill, a community can overcome even seemingly impossible obstacles and work toward a common goal. These are all worthy sentiments, and some critics have found the film powerful precisely because of its generality. David Paul calls it "a philosophical poem about community building, trust and security," whose power comes from the fact that the characters "represent general qualities."[38]

An alternative allegorical reading would look for specific equivalences between episodes in the film and postwar Hungarian history, but that strikes me as a futile exercise, as well as quite alien to Szabó's way of working. Graham Petrie, in his discussion of the film (written shortly after its release), mentions some of the possible historical parallels: postwar conflicts within Hungary and the 1956 uprising, for example. Petrie puts its well, however, when he states that the film is "both too overtly and too obscurely allegorical" to be effective.[39] At various unexpected moments, characters embark on detailed monologues about their personal obsessions, often in the form of advice (how to stanch a wound, how to write a good petition letter to a government office) that produces an almost comic effect by appearing totally out of context. The clichés offered up by the after-dinner speaker at the Christmas dinner toward the end also come across as ironic: Undertake only work that you can do. Think about the future. Etcetera.

The "simple and clear" meaning of the film itself, however (no matter how one interprets it), is not meant to be seen ironically, and that is precisely the problem: the combination of earnestness and abstraction with quasi-realism (the births, the deaths, the conflicts, and the city at the end) does not work. By contrast, abstraction and outright satire, with no attempt at realism, can be highly effective, as demonstrated in Gyula Gazdag's *Bástasétány 74*. Made in 1974 but censored for a decade thereafter, the film is a quite hilarious spoof on social issues, notably the housing shortage, in the form of an operetta with cloying waltzes, frilly costumes, and characters breaking into song at incongruous moments. But biting satire is not a mode that Szabó favors.

Budapest Tales demonstrates, *a contrario*, that Szabó's greatest talent lies in what is missing in this film: the psychologically complex exploration of individual characters' choices and emotions, situated in the concrete social and historical world of Central Europe. He would demonstrate this talent brilliantly in his films of the 1980s and beyond, starting with his 1980 film *Confidence*—which also inaugurated his collaboration with the cinematographer Lajos Koltai, who has shot all but one of Szabó's films to this day (the cinematographer of *The Door* was Elemér Ragályi). *Confidence* (*Bizalom*, 1980), whose more accurate English title would be *Trust*, is a two-person drama set in the last months of the Second World War in Budapest: a man and a woman, both of them connected to the anti-Nazi resistance—he by long-standing engagement and she by virtue of being married to a member of the resistance—are thrown together in hiding under false identities, having to pretend that they are man and wife. The question of how much they can trust each other is the driving force of the film, confirming Szabó's ongoing preoccupation with the possibilities of community and interpersonal trust (a subject I will turn to in the last chapter). But unlike *Budapest Tales*, *Confidence* is firmly set in the historical world of 1944–5 in Budapest, with the grittiness of its streets and houses and the claustrophobic furnishings of the room in an outlying district of the capital where the protagonists spend almost all of their time. This concreteness makes all the difference.

Confidence was awarded the Silver Bear at the Berlin Film Festival and was nominated for an Academy Award, a herald of Szabó's coming successes.

Notes

1   Suleiman, "On Exile, Jewish Identity, and Filmmaking in Hungary." Szabó mentioned the six rewrites of the film to me in a personal conversation, December 21, 2017; they were also mentioned in Marx, *Szabó István*, 209–10.

2   Zombory, Lénárt, and Szász, "Elfeledett Szembenézés" [Evaded Self-Scrutiny], 246.

3   *Koncert* (1962), which I discuss in Chapter 4, won a prize at the Oberhausen film festival and was nominated for an Oscar in 1964. *Variations on a Theme* (1962), an innovative antiwar film, provoked newspaper articles in Hungary and caused some controversy when it was refused to be shown at Oberhausen. See Marx, *Szabó István*, 94 and 100.

4   Portuges, "The Political Camera," 151–71.

5   Marx, *Szabó István*, 122.

6   Szekfü, *Igy filmeztünk 2* [How we filmed 2], 243.

7   In a personal conversation in 2018, Szabó mentioned the operating room scene in *Father* (1966) as an "hommage to Fellini" because "the camera turns from above, just like in *8 1/2* with the nuns" (Budapest, July 2, 2018).

8   Nagy, "Kűzdelem az árvasággal" [Struggle with Orphanhood], 9.

9   Nagy, "Nosztalgia és Küldetés" [Nostalgia and the Task at Hand], 13.

10 Quoted in Marx, *Szabó István*, 167. The full interview was published recently in Szekfü, *Igy filmeztünk 2*, 237–71.

11 Quoted in Zombory, Lénárt, and Szász, "Elfeledett Szembenézés," 247.

12 Lelkes, "Három kisfilm sikeréröl a rendezővel Szabó Istvánnal." [On the success of three short films, with filmmaker István Szabó].

13 Szekfü, "Az álmodozásoktól a mesékig" [From Daydreaming to Tales], 79.

14 See Marton, *The Great Escape: Nine Jews Who Fled Hitler and Changed the World*.

15 Márai, *Memoir of Hungary, 1944-1948*, 349–79.

16 The figure of 200,000 emigrants in 1956 is mentioned by (among others) Lénárt, "Emigration from Hungary in 1956 and the Emigrants as Tourists to Hungary," 368.

17 Marx, *Szabó István*, 122.

18 Márai, *Memoir of Hungary*, 367.

19 Heller, *A Philosophy of Morals*, 10.

20 Ibid., 25. Her refusal of rational choice theory is on p. 10.

21 Konrád, *A Guest in My Own Country*, 228.

22 See, for example, the interview with Papp, "Mondani kell valamit" [One has to say something], 34–5, and the one with Szépesi, in *Könyvjelző*, March 2012. Both are at the Hungarian National Film Archive Library, in Szabó's personal folder.

23 Personal conversation, Budapest, November 13, 2019.

24 Dragon, *The Spectral Body*, 37, 45, and *passim*. Dragon, in pursuing a psychoanalytic interpretation focused on the "secret" of Jewishness in Szabó's early films, "fills in" a great many elements that Szabó leaves unexplained or ambiguous.

25 Szekfü, *Igy filmeztünk 2*, 253. Dragon (*The Spectral Body*.) assumes that Bözsi is Jancsi's aunt, that she is Jewish and married to a Jewish man, and that she is murdered because she is Jewish. This is not at all clear in the film, however—she and her husband are shot execution style, standing against a wall, and could be members of the resistance.

26 See, in particular, Hirsch, *Family Frames* and Bán and Turai, eds., *Exposed Memories*.

27 Szabó, interview with Pongrácz.

28 Said, "Reflections on Exile," 148; Burgin, "Paranoiac Space," 29.

29 In an interview with Karen Jaehne published in 1978, he asked: "Do you know how long a filmmaker spends on details of that nature? Color, shadow, decor? So, of course I'm pleased when somebody does actually talk about the pictures and the colors" (Jaehne, "István Szabó: Dreams of Memories," 34).

30 Quoted in Marx, *Szabó István*, 178.

31 Renan, *Qu'est-ce qu'une nation?*, 15 and 31.

32 Bachelard, *La Poétique de l'espace*, 24.

33 Firemen's Street, Tűzoltó utca, is an actual street in Budapest's 9th district, but number 25 is not the house we see in Szabó's films.

34 I discuss the Hungarian reception of *Sunshine* and the debates it provoked among Hungarian critics in Chapter 3, as well as in my book *Crises of Memory and the Second World War*, chapter 5.

35 Jaehne, "István Szabó: Dreams of Memories," 36.

36 Ibid., 40.

37 After *Budapest Tales* (1977), Bálint appeared in a secondary role as the Army doctor Sonnenschein in *Colonel Redl* (1985) and in a cameo as a doctor in *Final Report* (2020). Apart from his work with Szabó, he has had a long and distinguished career as an actor, appearing in more than a hundred films (including TV films) as well on the stage; he was Artistic Director of the highly regarded Radnóti Theater in Budapest from 1985 to 2016.

38 Paul, "Szabó," 178.

39 Petrie, *History Must Answer to Man*, 225.

2

What Price Glory?

The Talented Individual and State Power

Don't blink, Hendrik. Look History in the eye.

THE GENERAL, In *Mephisto*

Always be grateful to the Emperor.

REDL'S MOTHER, In *Colonel Redl*

In 2004, Szabó released his English-language film *Being Julia*, a theatrical comedy starring Annette Bening and Jeremy Irons that is undoubtedly the most lighthearted of all his works; in a BBC interview, Szabó compared it to a "soufflé." The film's producer, the Canadian-Hungarian Robert Lantos, called it a "romp."[1] Based on a novel and then a play by Somerset Maugham, with the screenplay by the British playwright Ronald Harwood, *Being Julia* is one of the rare works by Szabó that features a woman in the role of chief protagonist (the others are *Sweet Emma*, *Dear Böbe* and *The Door*). It is the story of a famous actress on the London stage, the Julia of the title (Annette Bening), who undergoes a mid-life crisis when she feels herself aging (she is forty-five) but emerges triumphant after she succeeds in completely upstaging a younger woman, who is also her romantic rival, on the opening night of a play. All ends well, however: the play is a huge hit, and even the younger actor can look forward to a long run where she "will learn much" by working with Julia, as the latter's husband and the theater's director (Jeremy Irons) tells her.

Being Julia takes place in 1938, we are informed by a title early in the film, but the only reference to the History that interferes with people's lives occurs toward the end, when theatergoers lining up on opening night are treated to a street performance by an actor satirizing Neville Chamberlain in the wake of the Munich accords of September. "If [the accords] fail, the King and Queen and I will all go to Canada," he intones. "You will stay here." Such a warning about Hitler's doings on the Continent had little resonance in the cosseted world of the London theater and its audiences *c.* 1938, the film suggests. Nor was it likely to be of much interest to moviegoers who saw it in 2004, since this was not billed as a "historical film." I was all the more intrigued, therefore, by a remark that Szabó made during one of our conversations in the fall of 2017:

> Actually, if you think about it, *Being Julia* is very similar to *Mephisto*. They take place around the same time, the 1930s, and both films are about characters who want to be in the limelight, who will do anything to get ahead, to be the best, to be the star. They are the same character, in fact: The only difference is that one lives under a fascist dictatorship, while the other lives under good King George V!

He leaned toward me, hammering the words:

> Everything depends on who the boss is. They live in two totally different worlds. But if you transplanted them, Höfgen would soon be competing with Laurence Olivier, want to outdo Olivier, while Julia would compete with Leni Riefenstahl. Would she say "No thanks, I don't want to make films here"? Not on your life! She would accommodate to the regime, you can bet on that.[2]

I am still pondering that remark. Did Szabó mean that character or individual psychology—"personality," in the sense used by the authors of *The Authoritarian Personality*—alone determines one's actions, independently of circumstances? Or, on the contrary, that History plays the major role in designating who is a hero or a villain, a victim or an executioner? Szabó's film *Mephisto* (1981), along with the other two films that belong to his so-called German trilogy of the 1980s, *Colonel Redl* (1984) and *Hanussen* (1988), suggests yet another possibility: that certain historical situations confront talented individuals— mainly, though not exclusively, artists and intellectuals—with existential and ethical choices that they are, by virtue of their character, unable to resolve in a satisfactory way. The three films add up (albeit not in chronological sequence) to a sweeping view of Central European history, from the waning years of the Habsburg Empire to the consolidation of Nazi power in the mid-1930s. *Mephisto* takes place from around 1930 to 1936 in Germany, *Colonel Redl* from around 1880 to 1914 in Austria-Hungary, and *Hanussen* from 1919 to 1933 in Hungary, Austria, Czechoslovakia, and Germany.

Each film features a male protagonist (though Szabó's remark about Julia opens the way to at least the theoretical possibility that a woman might occupy the role) whose talent and ambition propel him to great heights, but who is eventually destroyed—if not physically, then morally—by a brutal power whose nature he misjudges or whose force he underestimates. All three protagonists are based on historical figures of some significance, who have been the subject of various artistic and historical portrayals. *Mephisto* gives screen credit to Klaus Mann's novel by the same title, and *Colonel Redl* to John Osborne's play *A Patriot for Me*, but the protagonists of all three films bear Szabó's authorial imprint; he cowrote the screenplay for each with the Hungarian writer Peter Dobai. *Mephisto* was the first film Szabó made with financing from abroad (the producer, Manfred Durniok, was from West Germany), but he also obtained backing from the Hungarian studio Objektiv Films, and the filming was done mainly in Hungary.[3] As with almost all of his other films, Szabó used both Hungarian and non-Hungarian actors who spoke their lines in their native language, with dubbing afterward. It is difficult to determine an "original" version in Szabó's films as far as language is concerned—even his early Hungarian films used a few non-Hungarian actors who had to be dubbed, and his films in German or English all exist in Hungarian versions and have screenplays in Hungarian as well as German or English.

An allegorical reading of these films would note the parallels between the autocratic or totalitarian systems portrayed in them—in particular in *Mephisto*—and the communist regimes in Eastern Europe after the Second World War. Such a reading would claim that by displacing the history to a slightly different place and an earlier period, Szabó was in fact exploring the situation of talented men like himself in relation to the admittedly "softer" totalitarianism of the Kádár regime. According to one specialist of Eastern European cinema, Aniko Imre, *Mephisto* is understood by Eastern European viewers to be "about the compromised, yet tragic situation of the resistant intellectual [in relation to communism]," whereas in the West "the local allegorical reading can easily be ignored in favor of 'global' [universalist] theories."[4] It's not clear what these "global" theories might be, other than an exclusively psychological interpretation of the protagonists that would ignore their historical situation altogether— something I find difficult to imagine. Apart from this, Imre presents the provocative argument that Szabó's depictions of Eastern European intellectuals' relation to the West, in *Mephisto* and in his 1990 film *Meeting Venus*, are analogous to Frantz Fanon's self-portrait in *Black Skin White Mask* as a colonized Black intellectual in relation to the colonizers.

A Hungarian journalist has recently been even more specific in drawing parallels, seeing not only in *Mephisto* but in the whole German trilogy and in other of Szabó's films an allegory of the filmmaker's own youthful entanglement with the Kádár regime's Secret Service. The article adopts a neutral tone, but it demonstrates the shortcomings of an allegorical reading that seeks simple equivalences between an artist's life and his work. The author is right to note that "betrayal, self-deception, collaboration, and the conflict between the individual and state power" are ongoing preoccupations in Szabó's work, but to reduce these to mere reflections of a major event in Szabó's life is inadequate— or worse still, irrelevant.[5]

My own approach will avoid such allegorical readings as too obvious to be of much interest, even while also avoiding a "universalist" bent that would ignore the specificities—historical, cultural, and geographical—that these films take pains to represent. A universalizing interpretation does not necessarily overlook historical specificity. It is not a contradiction to say that *Mephisto* tells the story of an actor in 1930s Germany who must choose whether or not to collaborate with the Nazi regime and that, at the same time, it presents a universal problem. Szabó himself put it well, in a 1982 interview published soon after the film won the Academy Award for best foreign film: after summarizing the specific story of his central character ("an actor is seduced by and gets very near to a nerve center of the vast web of Nazi power"), he noted that the story "delineates a universal problem concerning twentieth-century intellectuals: the relationship between history and the individual."[6]

Step by Step: The Road to Degradation in *Mephisto*

Klaus Mann's novel *Mephisto*, first published in 1936, opens with a Prologue titled "1936." It describes in great detail the glittering birthday party that the "air force general/prime minister" (read Hermann Göring) is throwing for himself in the grand lobby of the Berlin State Opera. Like a camera panning over a landscape, Mann's omniscient narrator scans the crowd of dignitaries and ordinary social climbers (over 2,000 invitations had been sent out, he tells us) and reports bits of their conversations. "They say decorating the Opera House for tonight cost sixty thousand marks," one foreign diplomat remarks to another. "Nice little birthday party," the other replies.[7] Certain guests stand out in the crowd, some by their absence: the Führer, for example, has excused himself, but the minister of propaganda, "overlord of the spiritual life of millions," is present, as is the director of the State Theater, Hendrik Höfgen, "privy councillor and senator" (11). It's a grand party, notes the narrator: "Such glitter, such noise. It was difficult to tell which shone the brighter, the jewels or the medals." A page later, he comes back to the charge: "Yes, it was certainly a magnificent party. All the guests appeared to be enjoying themselves to the fullest [. . .]. They danced, gossiped, flirted. They admired themselves. They admired one another. Most of all, they admired power, the power which could give such a party" (8, 9).

As his comments make clear, the narrator's attitude is not neutral in this novel; his voice often drips with sarcasm. He tells us, for example, that the general/prime minister, in giving himself this party for his forty-third birthday, fancies himself as a "fairy-tale prince," and that on his wedding day, he "had had two proletarians executed" (9). But no one elicits more of the narrator's acid comments than his main character, Hendrik Höfgen. Already in these first pages, during which we learn that Höfgen, now at the height of his prestige, hails from a modest family in Cologne that was quite unknown in that city before his phenomenal rise (p. 6), we are also given entry into Höfgen's devious mind. After Höfgen makes a snide remark about the Führer's absence to the propaganda minister, who everyone knows is a sworn enemy of their host the general/prime minister, the narrator comments: "With these observations, delivered in the gentlest manner, Höfgen betrayed his friend the prime minister, the protector to whom he owed all his prominence, to the jealous minister of propaganda, whom he held in reserve in case of emergency" (13). The narrator obviously wants us to know that Höfgen is a smooth operator and a despicable human being, always ready to betray those who trust him if he thinks it's in his interest.

After the Prologue, which has already pinned Höfgen to the wall (now it's just a matter of showing how this scheming opportunist made it to the top), Klaus Mann's novel leaps back to Hendrik Höfgen's early days as a left-wing actor in Hamburg, around 1930. From there on the plot is linear, describing Höfgen's rise to stardom from betrayal to betrayal, together with the rise of the Nazis to the most brutal kind of state power. Mann, son of the world-renowned novelist Thomas Mann, wrote *Mephisto* in exile in Amsterdam, after he and his whole family had been forced to leave Germany. His novel is a cri de coeur, a bitterly satirical indictment of Nazism and of those artists and intellectuals who made their peace with it—or to use a metaphor more pertinent to the subject at hand, who sold their souls to it. One of these was Mann's own one-time brother-in-law, the acclaimed actor Gustaf Gründgrens, who was famous (among other roles) for his portrayal of Mephisto in Goethe's *Faust*. Gründgrens was married to Mann's sister Erika from 1926 to 1929.[8]

Gustaf Gründgrens, like his fictional double, started out as a communist but switched sides when Hitler came to power and enjoyed a brilliant theatrical career under Nazism as well as after the war. He was gay, as was Klaus Mann (the two were apparently lovers while Gründgrens was married to Erika[9]), but Höfgens is portrayed as heterosexual in the novel as well as in Szabó's film. Making Höfgen gay would have introduced a distracting diversion from the main theme, Szabó explained in an interview.[10] What is at stake in both works is not sexuality but the overweening ambition that drives a talented artist to collaborate with a ruthless dictatorship. As we know, the Nazis persecuted homosexuals, but they willingly turned a blind eye when it suited them.

There are a number of important differences between Mann's novel and Szabó's film, but none more striking than their opening scenes. Mann's Prologue, quite apart from the narrator's acid commentaries, which condemn Höfgen the minute we see him, establishes a temporal structure—starting the story at the end—that eliminates any ambiguity about Höfgen's evolution toward becoming a collaborator with Nazism. The narrative logic of terminus ad quem makes that evolution appear inevitable. Thus, in the novel, it is not only Höfgen's "character" that explains his embrace of collaboration, even if the narrator takes pains to drive home that Höfgen is cowardly as well as calculating. The teleological drive of the narrative accomplishes much of that work.

Szabó too is interested in showing Höfgen's evolution—but by starting the story in the beginning, he allows Höfgen a certain freedom. To put it in philosophical terms, Szabó recognizes the contingent nature of human choices in the course of a life; those choices are not predetermined, even if they gather momentum as they progress and even if one can retroactively ascribe them to an individual's "character." Apart from its philosophical import, contingency also makes for a better story: instead of knowing in advance how all (or almost all) of the protagonist's choices will turn out, the viewer is free to anticipate various possibilities and to feel both suspense and surprise, prime ingredients of a good plot.

The first time we see Höfgen in the film, he is having a tantrum in his dressing room—at this point he is a provincial actor in Hamburg, and he listens to the wild applause for a visiting star from Berlin who is adulated by the public. He almost literally tears his hair out, screaming "No! No!," trying to wrap his head in a cloth as if to shut out the sound of another's success; finally, he stands in front of his mirror, grimacing. But despite this early indication of Höfgen's unstable, narcissistic character, or simply his unquenchable thirst for recognition, we do not know from the start where he will end up. Only gradually, step by step, as the result of a number of choices which *could have turned out otherwise*, does he become an active collaborator of the Nazi regime, gaining fame and fortune in the process but losing his soul.

The idea of a narrative that progresses "step by step," with no prior knowledge of where it is heading, is the basis for one of the great works of modern Hungarian literature, Imre Kertész's autobiographical novel *Fatelessness* (*Sorstalanság*), published in 1975. Kertész, who was deported to Auschwitz and other camps as a teenager and who in 2003 became the first Hungarian writer to be awarded the Nobel Prize in Literature, explained more than once that this linear temporality was the only way he could truthfully render his protagonist's experience of deportation and survival. At every step of the way, the adolescent boy encounters a reality he is not able to anticipate. While this is especially true of the reality of the death camps (how could one anticipate the unthinkable?), in philosophical terms all life can be said to unfold step by step, offering existential choices along the way. There is, of course, a radical difference between Kertész's protagonist, who has almost no opportunity to make choices (though he does have a few—for example, he realizes upon his arrival in Auschwitz that he must lie about his age, for those under fourteen are sent to the "wrong" side) and a relatively free agent like Höfgen. But Kertész's notion of the "step by step"—which is another word for contingency—is very much relevant to Höfgen's story as well. Indeed, in his Nobel Prize acceptance speech, Kertész explained that his writing of the book was itself a step-by-step process: "So I proceeded, step by step, on the linear path of discovery."[10]

The Austrian stage actor Klaus Maria Brandauer, in one of his first film roles, gives a career-making performance that brings out the attractiveness as well as the more deplorable traits of Szabó's central character. Down to the very end, by which time the viewer has plenty of reasons to condemn him, Höfgen retains a degree of our sympathy, or at least of our understanding. This is in keeping with Szabó's often-stated desire to lead viewers to identify sufficiently with his main character so that they can imagine themselves in the latter's situation and wonder how they themselves would—or should—have acted in his place. In one of our conversations, Szabó even had recourse to a rather baroque analogy, comparing some of his films to "vaccines" that inoculate the viewer against the mistakes portrayed on the screen. Medical analogies occur quite often in interviews with Szabó, possibly because his father, whom he revered and who died when Szabó was seven years old, was a doctor. He has also mentioned that after finishing the *gymnazium*, he applied both to medical school and film school but was accepted only in the latter.[11]

Mephisto opens with theatrical performances both on and off stage. On stage, Dora Martin, the star from Berlin, performs the lead role in an operetta as the bewigged Madame du Barry, while offstage Höfgen performs his hysterical envy in private; shortly thereafter, having collected himself and gotten dressed properly, he joins the other actors in the troupe in the canteen where they gather after the show and gives yet another performance, congratulating the visiting star on her outstanding job. She is not taken in, however: "You fraud," she laughs goodnaturedly, "you didn't even see the show! But you're very talented, I hear." "Say it louder," he begs her, and she obliges so that the others can hear her. Clearly, he craves recognition, but that craving goes hand in hand with his drive to excel. Höfgen is an actor who works hard at his craft.

His sense of himself as an actor is again emphasized in the following scene, a tour de force of directing and cinematography as well as performance. The scene takes place in the studio of Höfgen's lover and dance teacher Juliette, a beautiful mixed-race woman played by the German actor Karen Boyd. "You're late," she announces to him in a disapproving voice as she lies on her bed, before telling him to get undressed for his lesson. She then teases him about his manhood: "You don't drink beer like a real man—I can't even imagine you saying these words: 'Get me a beer'!" Höfgen, now in his underclothes, responds mildly that he doesn't drink (she is sipping wine from a glass) and waits for her to join him as the music starts (Figure 6). While they dance in front of the barre on the mirrored wall, with Höfgen imitating Juliette's graceful movements, she clearly comes across as the dominant figure, teacher to pupil. This continues even as she retreats to her bed, instructing him to dance alone ("Faster! Faster!") and then teases him: "If you liked music, you wouldn't feel tired, Heinz"—she insists on calling him by his given name, which he dislikes. The power dynamic starts to change, however, when Höfgen stops dancing, strips off his undershirt, leaps onto her bed, and starts to embrace her while she screams with delight. All the while, they are talking: "Why do you always laugh at me, Juliette?" "Would you love me if I didn't?" "I love you anyway." "Heinz, you love only yourself. Your only concern is pretending, you always wear a mask." At that point, Höfgen jumps off the bed and runs to the mirror, facing her and yelling: "My eyes are not my eyes, my face is not my face, my name is not my name—because I'm an actor! Do you know what an actor is?

Figure 6 Mephisto, *1981. Objektiv Stúdió, Manfred Durniok Produktion für Film und Fernsehen. Copyright National Film Institute Hungary—Film Archive.*

A mask." He says this jubilantly, fully assuming (in the existential sense) his chameleonic status as an actor.

In fact, many theorists of theater from Diderot on have described the actor as a "man without qualities," able to adapt to any role. Things become more problematic if an actor continues performing even when he is not on stage, or when he can no longer tell the difference between theater and reality; but at this moment in the film, those issues are not present. Höfgen returns to the bed (Juliette invites him: "Come!") and they wrestle, laughing, while he strips her naked, drags her by her arms and legs to the mirror, and collapses onto the floor with her head between his legs. Both of them quiet now, he pulls a paisley shawl off the barre and drapes it over her.

It's a stunning scene, dramatically and cinematically. Unusually for a Szabó film, it contains two long takes that last a minute or more: Höfgen and Juliette wrestling on the bed: Höfgen dragging her to the mirror and settling on the floor with her. Höfgen and Juliette are clearly playing an erotic game together, one they may have played before, where they take turns as the dominant or submissive partner. The contrast with Klaus Mann's version of the scene is enormous. In Mann's version, Juliette remains the dominant partner throughout; she plays the role of a textbook dominatrix, sporting a pair of long green patent leather boots and a red leather whip that Höfgen gave her, and that she uses on him. He himself is the textbook masochist, cowering before her like a little boy, submitting to the whip and then begging her to "come to him" in bed. There is no triumphant assertion of himelf as an actor ("When the public likes me a little—when I have a success—I owe it all to you," he tells her), let alone an alternation of roles between him and Juliette. He remains a needy, unattractive figure from the beginning of the scene to the end.[12]

Unlike Szabó's Juliette, about whom we know almost nothing other than what her lithe body and fine-looking face suggest, Mann's Juliette is introduced in some detail in this scene: the daughter of an African mother and a German father who spent time in Africa before abandoning the mother and daughter, Juliette has had a hard life. By the time she arrived in Germany as a young woman, by herself, her father was dead; she earned her living as a tap dancer, but her excessive drinking drove her further and further down the social ladder into prostitution and dancing in sailors' dives under the billing of "Princess Tebab" or "the black Venus." It was in such a dive that Höfgen had discovered her. Physically, Mann's narrator describes her as a "half-caste" who looks like a "pure-blooded black," with "thick pouting lips" against "blazing white teeth, which she bared in laughter and in rage," and a flat nose "that seemed as good as nonexistent: it was a hollow, rather than an eminence, in the middle of this evilly attractive face." The narrator concludes, "The proper background for Juliette's barbaric head was primeval jungle" (48–9).

One might expect that contemporary feminist and postcolonial critics would reproach Mann for his racial stereotyping, or at least seek to excuse him on the grounds that it was considered acceptable to describe a Black woman in this way in 1936. But surprisingly, two analyses of the film, by highly intelligent critics writing around the turn of the twenty-first century, reproach Szabó instead, accusing him of edulcorating Mann's "radical" description of Höfgen's black lover. Dagmar Lorenz, in an otherwise far-ranging analysis of *Mephisto* and *Colonel Redl*, notes that Szabó "transformed Mann's ugly stripper into a goodlooking black woman whose sense and honesty leave no room for the shock effect intended by Mann."[13] Lorna Fitzsimmons, writing several years after Lorenz, mounts a more sustained attack: Szabó's film, according to her, "suppresses" the "transgressiveness" of Mann's "radical satire." Fitzsimmons believes that "Mann satirizes German colonialism and contemporaneous denigration of Africans," but nothing in the novel suggests such a reading. In the dance lesson scene in particular, she argues, "Szabó recuperat[es] the working-class tap-dancer/prostitute from the subversiveness of her Sadeian namesake and contain[s] her within the heterosexual passivity of Shakespeare's heroine."[14] No viewer who looks at this scene in the film without preconceptions would consider Juliette passive! But around the year 2000, Szabó's brand of humanism, in which "sense and honesty" are positive values, along with the cinematic depiction of a Black woman as beautiful and playful, evidently looked passé compared to "Sadeian subversiveness." Two decades later, after we have witnessed countless senseless acts of public and private violence and dishonesty the world over, Sadeian excesses have lost some of their avant-garde glamour.

Szabó explained in his interview with John Hughes exactly why he had dropped the sadomasochistic aspect of Mann's central character. It was because of his theory of identification, which is also why he (like Mann) made Höfgen heterosexual:

> I didn't want to give people the chance to say, "This man is collaborating with the Nazis because he is a pervert and a fetishist; and since I am not a pervert and fetishist, I could not collaborate with the Nazis. . . ." The evil of Nazism does not result from perversion and homosexuality. Fascism and anti-Semitism are ultimately a special kind of perversion: the perversion of the soul. One must show this essential horror of the distortion of the human spirit. So you must get the "normal" audience, so vulnerable to this soul-perversion, to identify with the character.[15]

As the foregoing quote makes clear, Szabó does not view Höfgen as an admirable character; but by presenting his choices step by step, he engages the viewer in a way that Mann's sardonic commentaries do not. In the novel, the narrator's constant interpretations of Höfgen's actions, always seen as either cowardly or coldly calculating, may actually end up irritating the reader, who feels coerced in his or her responses. Szabó invites his viewers to project themselves into Höfgen's place and draw their own conclusions.

Some of the most powerful scenes in the film are those where we see Höfgen confronting a personal or professional choice that has ethical or political implications and either talking himself into a compromised position or simply leaping into one. On the morning after Hitler is declared Chancellor, in January 1933, Höfgen's wife Barbara—the daughter of a respected and wealthy liberal intellectual, whom Höfgen married partly because of her high social standing but from whom he is now estranged—arrives in his apartment in Berlin with the newspaper while he is still in bed. Hitler is Chancellor! They must leave the country, she tells him. Leave the country? Whatever for? Hitler is just a clown, Höfgen says, putting on his dressing gown; anyway, there are political parties opposing him. Besides, he himself is "just an actor," not involved in politics, so he has nothing to fear. By now, Höfgen is a well-known star of the stage in Berlin, including his outstanding performance as Mephisto in Goethe's *Faust*, and he has also starred in films. "But don't you realize what's happening here? They'll force you to take a stand," his wife cries. "I'm an actor, I need the German language and *Heimat* [home]," he responds. Barbara leaves for Paris; he stays in Berlin.

Here is an instance where the question of "to leave or to stay" in a repressive political regime, which in Szabó's early films appeared as an existential question faced by ordinary people, takes on a strong ethical dimension. It's one thing for a young person who grows up under communism to leave the country when the occasion presents itself, or to stay because that country is, despite everything, home; it's quite another thing for a public figure—and by 1933 Höfgen is undoubtedly a public figure—to face the choice of collaborating or not with a brutal regime that threatens to undo every democratic norm. The economist and philosopher Albert Hirschman, in his influential book *Exit, Voice, and Loyalty*, described three different responses—choices, really—that individuals adopt in the face of what he called "decline in firms, organizations, and states." Hirschman started from a simple economic model, where decline referred to a lessening of the quality of certain products and what consumers could do about it. They could stop buying the product and switch to another one—that's what Hirschman called "exit." Or they could complain to the company and demand improvements—that's what he called "voice." Finally, they could keep on buying the same product in the hope that it would improve—that's what he called "loyalty." Things get more complicated when we move from laundry soap to governments, but Hirschman shows that his model can be useful in thinking about how individual citizens respond to a repressive political regime.[16] The word "decline" may not be the right one when it comes to totalitarianism, but we may consider a totalitarian regime as a decline from democracy. Loyalists are those who, whether for opportunistic reasons or out of ideological conviction, espouse the regime and seek to join those in power. Those who stay and express criticism or disagreement, in one way or another, are manifesting voice (often with dire consequences). Those who exit, especially if they are public figures, can also be considered as manifesting voice, but it's a voice of condemnation which declares that no improvement is possible within the existing regime, at least for the near future.

In the case of Nazi Germany, exit was clearly the most honorable response on the part of public figures or intellectuals who were horrified by Hitler's seizure of power. Under Nazism, attempts at voice would most often end in death, as shown in the fates of two of Höfgen's actor colleagues in *Mephisto*: Hans Miklas (György Cserhalmi), a convinced Nazi from the early days, becomes disillusioned with the regime's brutality and drafts a letter of protest for which he seeks signatories; Otto Ulrich (Peter Andorai), a communist, tries to organize resistance. They are both murdered in short order. (Höfgen plays a role in both of their stories, and I'll come back to it.)

Höfgen's wife Barbara, along with many other liberal or anti-fascist intellectuals at the time, chooses to exit the moment Hitler comes to power. Still, it could be argued that in January 1933, the Nazis had not yet shown their true colors, at least not to people who were not intensely involved in politics. At this point, while we may wonder whether anything will occur to shake Höfgen out of his comfortable view of himself as "only an actor" who can keep aloof from those in power, we can understand why he chooses to stay. But as events unfold and as new choices present themselves, Höfgen becomes more and more compromised and in need of self-deception in order to justify his actions.

This is already evident in a sequence that occurs some weeks later. Höfgen is on a film shoot in Budapest, where we see him on horseback in what appears to be a lighthearted comedy set during the period of the Habsburg

Monarchy. But the filming is disrupted when the news arrives that, in Berlin, the Reichstag has burned. As we know, the Reichstag fire of February 27, 1933, was the excuse Hitler needed to assume emergency powers as Chancellor, and it signaled the end of democracy in Germany. Höfgen appears to understand this, and after the filming is over he tells the director—who has confided to him that he plans not to return to Berlin and advises him to do the same—that he will go to Vienna. But when he receives a letter in Vienna from another actor, a young woman who assures him that the new government will welcome him because it "needs men of talent," and not cause him any trouble on account of his left-wing past, he immediately gets on the next train to Berlin. The effect is highly dramatic, without any words of self-justification on Höfgen's part. It's clear that by getting on that train he has made a sudden existential choice (the Kierkegaardian "leap"), seduced by his colleague's flattery. Once he arrives in Berlin, he cannot help but notice all the new uniforms and swastikas that greet him, but he does not appear to regret his decision. On the contrary, he flatters the actress who will star with him at the State Theater, for she is the fiancée of the newly powerful air force general and prime minister (a stand-in for Göring).

From here on, Höfgen's collaboration with the regime is foreseeable, but Szabó still maintains the step-by-step approach as we follow Höfgen's professional rise, accompanied by his gradual moral degradation. One key moment on the road to success is his renewed performance as Mephisto at the State Theater, not long after his return. Szabó takes great pleasure in presenting stage performances in his films, and *Mephisto* is full of them. At one point we see a montage of ten shots taking up less than one minute, indicating the diverse roles that Höfgen plays during his first years in Berlin, from bewigged eighteenth-century costume dramas to modern drawing-room comedies. But Goethe's *Faust* (Part I) gets special treatment: no fewer than three substantive excerpts are performed from the play, two of them on stage and one in a rehearsal.[17] The second stage performance is crucial, for it occurs in 1933, after Höfgen's return to Berlin. Wearing a black and red satin cape, his face completely covered by thick white makeup and his head as smooth as a billiard ball, Höfgen cuts a striking figure as he prances around Faust. The excerpt Szabó chose contains some of the most famous verses of Goethe's dramatic poem. At their first meeting, when Faust asks Mephisto who he is, the latter replies:

> I am the spirit that ever denies!
> And rightly so: since everything created,
> In turn deserves to be annihilated:
> Better if nothing came to be.
> So all that you call Sin, you see,
> Destruction, in short, what you've meant
> By Evil is my true element.[18]

Mephisto the nihilist speaks the truth about himself, in terms that have also been used to describe the Nazi regime: destruction for its own sake, or what humans call radical evil, is his true element. The General/Prime Minister, outfitted in his dress uniform with a row of medals, is so impressed by Höfgen's performance that he invites the star to his box during intermission (Figure 7). When the spectators return to their seats, they can see the actor and the General, each in his own costume, engaged in lively conversation. Szabó emphasizes the significance of this scene by a shot of the whole audience in

Figure 7 Mephisto, *1981. Objektiv Stúdió, Manfred Durniok Produktion für Film und Fernsehen. Copyright National Film Institute Hungary—Film Archive.*

the orchestra with heads turned toward the box, as if it were the stage. It is in fact a performance worth watching, for it acts out in real life the kind of pact that Faust and Mephisto enact on stage. But the roles are reversed, for in this real-life scene Höfgen is the Faust figure. Although the General from then on playfully calls Höfgen "Mephisto" or "my Mephisto," in their interactions it is he who plays the role of the Devil. In a later scene, the General (brilliantly acted by the German actor Rolf Hoppe) tells Höfgen that he has "learned a lot" from watching him on stage.

After this first meeting, Höfgen becomes more and more ensnared in the General's web, accepting invitations to "intimate" gatherings at the General's house as well as to public events where he is called on to speak about art in the new Germany. Good actor that he is, he learns very quickly what words to use to describe the ideal characteristics of Nazi-sponsored art: *strong, courageous, victorious*, the opposite of the "degenerate" art that preceded it. But the more he is compromised, the more he is forced to find new excuses and justifications for his actions. In fact, he engages in a common form of self-deception, what Jean-Paul Sartre called bad faith (mauvaise foi). When his Black lover Juliette (now living in Berlin, called there by Höfgen, who seems genuinely devoted to her) challenges him by asking why he accepted to attend an art opening where he praised the "strong, courageous" sculptures (enormous neoclassical nudes in the manner of Hitler's favorite sculptor Arno Breker) by a sculptress the General admires, he tells her that he had no choice. They asked him to go, and he "couldn't refuse. Anyone who says the contrary is lying." Besides, he adds, the General is a "nice guy" and knows a lot about theater. Since we have just witnessed, in the preceding scene, how well Höfgen can play the role of spokesman for Nazi art, his declaration of helplessness appears like a perfect example of bad faith; as for his calling the General a nice guy, it shows a certain lack of attention to reality. Juliette, for her part, is not taken in: "You're a well-behaved boy, who always wants to behave well," she tells him with some irony. A very different figure, a paternalistic Army officer, will use almost exactly the same words to praise the young cadet Alfred Redl in Szabó's next film, *Colonel Redl*.

As if to prove that Höfgen does in fact have a choice, soon after this the General informs him that he has "plans" for him. "You can say No, but then you won't be doing as much for our cause as you could," he tells him. The General's plan is that, since he is such an eloquent speaker ("You're more than an actor," he says), Höfgen should become Director of the Berlin State Theater, a position that will bring him closer to the inner circles of Nazi power. But of course he must first divorce his wife, who is in Amsterdam, actively opposing the Fatherland, and he must put a stop to his "shameful" relation with the "Negro" woman, Juliette Martens. The General obviously has a file on Höfgen (he is leafing through it as he speaks to him), and he is displaying his knowledge of the actor's private life in order to intimidate him. Höfgen caves in immediately, asking only that they "shouldn't hurt" Juliette but allow her to leave the country.

The next scene starts with a headshot of Höfgen: "What shall I do? Should I say Yes? Or maybe I should emigrate to America! Do I want this? They need me, just imagine!" He seems to be asking these questions of himself, but the next shot shows that he is talking to a friend and fellow actor, Nicoletta von Niebuhr (played by the Hungarian Ildikó Bánsági, who starred in Szabó's 1980 film *Confidence* and also appeared in *Budapest Tales*). Höfgens and she have known each other for a long time, and Nicoletta has just arrived in Berlin from Hamburg—she is someone like himself, and he probably knows the response she will give him. Significantly, it is not his lover Juliette's advice he has sought, for Juliette not only knows him well but wouldn't allow him to get away with his self-justifications. Nicoletta, on the other hand, advises him to accept the job. "Will you help me?" he asks her. She will. The next thing we see is Juliette being escorted out of her apartment by two men in black leather coats, who hand her a passport and a train ticket to Paris.

Höfgen thrives as Director of the State Theater, playing his role with gusto. He has a huge office, from where he oversees the running of the theater down to the work of the cleaning women, whom he charms with a combination of strictness—no shirking, he tells them—and generosity, giving them money for coffee. He has a secretary and wears a three-piece suit and horn-rimmed glasses, as befits a successful arts administrator. Höfgen clearly enjoys this new role and shows a degree of self-irony about his performance; on arriving at the office one morning, he announces to his secretary: "New suit, new shoes, new Director!" We recall what he had told Juliette back in Hamburg: he is an actor, and an actor is a mask, even when he is off stage. Sartre, in *Being and Nothingness*, devotes a couple of famous pages to the description of a café waiter who performs his job to such perfection that he is the very image of a café waiter. For Sartre, this is a version of mauvaise foi, bad faith, if the waiter actually thinks of himself as a "thing," nothing other than a café waiter, the way an ash tray is nothing but an ash tray. But if he were aware of his performance *as* a performance expected of him, then he would actually be *playing* at being a café waiter and having fun.[19] Höfgen seems to be having fun as director and even allows himself to mock the regime he now serves when he is alone with his friends Nicoletta and the communist Otto Ulrich. He complains to them that every actor he hires must now be blond, "no matter his ability," and that most of them lack talent. "They" won't let him do Schiller, and all the good contemporary authors have emigrated or else refuse to publish, so what's left for the State Theater? Shakespeare! "The regime has discovered Shakespeare as an author of the people [*ein völkische Autor*]," he announces, mocking one of the Nazis' favorite adjectives: *völkisch* was the opposite of "cosmopolitan," a notion associated with "plutocrats" and Jews. Obviously, Höfgen is here acting, for the benefit of his friends, the part of an independent thinker not beholden to those in power. But later, he will serve up to journalists exactly the same words with no irony whatsoever. *Hamlet*, he will explain, is a *völkisch* work, and the main character is not a "neurotic" as critics have thought, but a "man of the North who does not hesitate to kill," an "energetic and resolute hero."

We could say that for the journalists too, Höfgen is "just acting" —but can "just acting" remain without consequences in the real world? That is exactly the question that Höfgen's ex-wife Barbara confronts him with when they meet in Paris, shortly after he becomes Director of the State Theater. He is there on an official visit representing the government, but he meets in secret with both Juliette and Barbara. He and Juliette have a lovers' reunion, and as they lie in bed she begs him to remain in Paris. His response—it comes as a real shock to the viewer—is to ask her to stop writing to him. At that point, Juliette gives up. Barbara, however, whom he meets in a café later, challenges him with arguments: "You're more than an actor now. Theater is important to the regime," she pleads, and his presence in Germany has political meaning. He replies that he is "married to the theater" and that "someone has to save our values for a better world." Besides, he can help people from his position. "Empty words," she retorts. "You are deceiving yourself: even if you help a few people, it's only an elegant gesture to your friends. You legitimize the regime and become a partner in crime." On the street afterward, Höfgen hesitates for a moment and then descends into the metro. That descent is symbolic.

Indeed, the very next scene emphasizes that Höfgen is now fully in the Devil's hands—and like Faust in the first part of Goethe's play, he is rewarded with many pleasures. The scene is a party at Höfgen's new villa in the fashionable suburb of Grünewald, with Höfgen and his new bride Nicoletta celebrating their wedding. The General shows up with his usual retinue, just long enough to gulp down a stein of beer (we are reminded of Juliette's earlier taunt that she cannot imagine Höfgen ordering beer) and do a quick tour of the house: "Beautiful! Just in my taste," he says approvingly while inspecting the furnishings. After the General leaves, a half-dozen Mephistos wearing Höfgen's signature black cape and white mask suddenly show up and start dancing around him, singing a gratingly cheerful popular song about Grünewald. The effect is grotesque, like a Walpurgisnacht. Höfgen's role in this devils' dance is obviously that of Faust.

The high point (but we should call it the low point) of Höfgen's self-deception occurs the following morning when we see him and Nicoletta sunning themselves in deck chairs in the garden. "Do we deserve all this?" he asks reflectively and then launches into a reply: Yes, they do deserve this, because as artists, they "can and should rise above what happens in the world. No matter how filthy the world is, true art will always remain pure and true." Art is independent of politics: this is what he has been saying, to himself as well as to his wife Barbara, ever since Hitler became Chancellor. The claim may have made a certain sense in January 1933, but now it appears as willful ignorance, another definition of Sartrean bad faith.

Höfgen's willful ignorance extends not only to his own involvement with Nazi power but also to the nature of that power itself. This is demonstrated in the very next sequence, when Höfgen learns that his friend Otto Ulrich—who has been trying to organize a clandestine resistance movement in the theater— has been arrested. Höfgen rushes to the General's office to plead Ulrich's case. He has done so once before and succeeded, but this time he is received with a brutal rebuff. Höfgen has barely pronounced Ulrich's name when the General cuts him short: "Is this what you came for? Let me give you a piece of advice: Keep your nose out of this business so that you don't get crushed like a bug. Who do you think you are?" The fact that he speaks calmly makes the General's words all the more menacing. He screams only once: "Get out, *Schauspieler!*" By calling him a Schauspieler, an actor, the General echoes Höfgen's own view of himself—but in his mouth, that epithet is a brutal reminder: in the real world of Nazi power, Höfgen is a nobody, a mere actor. The Nazis' bullets, unlike those on stage, kill for real.

Höfgen rushes to the General's fiancée, his fellow actor Lotte, who informs him while brushing her hair in front of a mirror that Ulrich is dead. "Suicide, they say." Höfgen, as if in a daze, repeats the word "suicide." He seems shocked, as if this were his first encounter with the Nazis' ruthlessness. But he is now well into the period of Nazi rule (Szabó gives no indication of what year it is— it must be 1935 or 1936), and only someone who has willfully shielded his view from the reality of the regime could be so oblivious. Höfgen has yet another reason to know better because he has seen even his old enemy Hans Miklas, an actor he had had fired on account of his Nazi views back in Hamburg, arrested and suddenly declared "dead in an automobile accident" after Miklas starts protesting against the regime. In fact, it is Höfgen who denounces Miklas to the General, after Miklas seeks his signature on an anti-government petition. Some critics think of this as a willful betrayal on Höfgen's part, but that's not clear in the film. Rather, it appears that Höfgen thinks Miklas is acting as a Nazi provocateur in asking him to sign the protest, since he has always known Miklas as a convinced Nazi. He calls the General in order to protect himself and seems surprised when Miklas is hauled off by the SS and murdered the very next day. (Interestingly, in Mann's novel Höfgen plays no role at all in Miklas's death: Miklas is murdered because he goes around publicly insulting the new elites, first among them "Fatty," the General. Szabó's version may be seen as one more indication of Höfgen's unwillingness to face the real-life consequences of his actions.)

Höfgen's shock and revulsion at Ulrich's "suicide" don't last long. Aided by the ever-compliant Nicoletta, he concludes that "Ulrich knew what he was risking" and goes right back to his work as a *Schauspieler* and theorist of Nazi theater. After expounding his views about the *völkisch* Hamlet to journalists, we see him taking his triumphant bows in the role, along with Nicoletta as Ophelia, who is costumed as a blond Brunnhilde with long peasant braids.

And so, finally, we come to the scene of the General's birthday party with which Klaus Mann's novel began and which now finds its correct chronological place on Höfgen's road of degradation. The scene is lavish, a grand piece of cinematography. Höfgen is shown at the height of his prestige and power, waiting at the foot of the staircase in the Berlin Opera House, while couples in formal dress dance to the strains of Liszt's Mephisto waltz in the grand hall. His mother is present to see her son's success, and Szabó himself plays a cameo role as one of the guests who comments on the lavishness of the party. When the General and Lotte make their entrance, the guests form an honor guard as the couple crosses the hall, smiling to the assembled crowd like royalty. Höfgen watches them impassively—Szabó lingers over his face in close-up for a full twenty seconds, but it presents itself as a mask: we cannot know what he is thinking. He then gives a laudatory birthday greeting to the smiling tyrant whom he calls a "friend of the arts."

The very last scene of the film—the one most commented on by critics, for good reason—occurs right after the party, close to dawn, when the General and his retinue arrive with Höfgen at a huge, Coliseum-like structure. This scene is one of Szabó's inventions, for the novel ends quite differently. The General has called Höfgen away from the party, specifically in order to show him this work: the newly constructed amphitheater on the grounds of the Olympic Games that were to be held in the summer of 1936. Looking around him, the General exults: "This is *real* theater! *I* will be the one staging performances here!" (The audience may recall Leni Riefenstahl's highly theatrical film about the Olympic Games, *Olympia*, released in 1938.) We see the two men's faces next to each other, but Höfgen's expression is hard to read. The General continues: "Don't blink, Hendrik. Look history in the eye. We shall rule Europe and the world. We are building a thousand-year Reich!" Just as Goethe's Mephisto tells the truth about who he is, the General here states clearly who he is and what regime he represents. By telling Höfgen to look history in the eye, he underlines Höfgen's willful turning away from reality until then.

The General also confirms that he has indeed learned a lot from Höfgen the actor, just as he once told him. The Nazis, as we know (following Walter Benjamin's analysis), perfected the art of political spectacle, glorifying war itself as a work of art.[20] Here, the General displays his own theater of cruelty. First, he demonstrates the echo of the arena by bellowing Höfgen's name over and over; then he orders Höfgen to move into the center, where he is caught between two powerful spotlights that blind him. "How does the limelight make you feel?" his tormentor taunts him. "This is the real light!" Höfgen shields his eyes and tries to run out of the paths traced by the spotlights, but they keep following him. Looking utterly bewildered and disheveled for the first time (his hair is always carefully combed), he utters a small cry: "What do they want from me? I'm only an actor." His face with its anguished look fades into white as the closing credits roll.

How are we to interpret this very powerful ending? Does Höfgen finally understand the meaning of the pact he had entered into and assume his share of responsibility? Or is he still unable to "look history in the eye," whether his own history or that of Nazified Germany? If one opts for the first interpretation, one may see the scene as an epiphany, or as one critic put it, a "hopeful sign to the audience that, however late it may be, it is never too late to attain consciousness, to see things clearly and to recognize evil for what it is."[21] Personally, I am less sanguine that Höfgen finally sees clearly; his anguished cry at the end suggests confusion and self-justification instead of enlightenment. If there is an epiphany, it occurs in the spectator: the ending produces a sense of catharsis, like that of a Greek tragedy.

Responsibility in the Rearview Mirror: *Taking Sides*

The question of self-knowledge must have haunted Szabó himself because twenty years after making *Mephisto*, he made yet another film about an artist who faced crucial choices in Nazi Germany, which he thought of as a "sequel to *Mephisto*."[22] *Taking Sides*, first shown at the Toronto Film Festival in September 2001 (on the morning of September 11, which explains, according to Szabó, why the film received so little critical attention despite its stellar cast[23]), is an English-language film with a scenario by the British playwright Ronald Harwood, based on his play by the same title. Like *Mephisto*, it focuses on the career of a historical figure, who in this instance is explicitly named: the world-famous conductor Wilhelm Furtwängler. Unlike *Mephisto*, however, which advances step by step along Höfgen's itinerary, *Taking Sides* is entirely retrospective and has fewer fictional elements. The action starts after the war, when the Allied de-Nazification commission is conducting an investigation of Furtwängler's activities during the war, to determine whether he should be allowed to resume his career. In addition to being the conductor of the Berlin Philharmonic, Furtwängler had been appointed to honorific positions by the Nazis and had played a concert for Hitler's birthday; he was also known as an antisemite, although he claimed to have helped some Jewish musicians during the Nazi years.

The American investigator, Major Steve Arnold (Harvey Keitel), who is Jewish and an insurance investigator in civilian life, knows nothing about classical music and has never heard of Furtwängler, whom he refers to as a "bandleader." But he has seen British footage from the Bergen-Belsen concentration camp, showing corpses being shoveled into mass graves (this is one of the first scenes in the film), and he is determined to bring the conductor to trial as a Nazi collaborator. For him, it makes no difference that Furtwängler was a great musician. As he tells another American officer, the young German-Jewish immigrant David Will (Moritz Bleibtreu), "butchers, shopkeepers and conductors are all the same" in a criminal investigation. Will, however, has been placed on the case by another Allied body specifically for the purpose of ensuring that the defendant is granted all his rights; in addition, the young man grew up in Germany, in a music-loving family that venerated Furtwängler.

The title of the film refers, in one sense, to the running debate between Arnold and Will about the respect owed to a celebrated artist who has not been proven guilty of a crime, even if his behavior during the Nazi period was less than fully honorable. In another, equally important sense, "taking sides" refers to the debate between Arnold and Furtwängler himself (Stellan Skarsgård), who is interrogated by Arnold in three extended meetings (Figure 8). At their very first encounter (during which Arnold goes out of his way to humiliate

Figure 8 Taking Sides, *2001. MBP, Maecenas, Paladin Production, and Studio Babelsberg, in association with Jeremy Isaacs Productions, TwanPix, Satel, BR, ORF, and France 2 in cooperation with Canal+.*

Furtwängler by making him wait, forcing him to stand and then to switch seats into an uncomfortable chair), Arnold confronts the conductor with the crucial question: Why did he not leave the country in 1933, when he could easily have found work abroad, like some other great German conductors? In other words, why did he not "take a side" against Hitler? But Furtwängler refuses to be intimated. The other conductors, such as Bruno Walter, were Jewish, so they had to leave, he tells Arnold. He, on the other hand, could not leave his country. He then lists all the reasons we are familiar with, having heard them from the mouth of Hendrik Höfgen. Art should remain above politics. He didn't want Hitler and Goebbels to have the monopoly on culture but wanted to defend true German culture from the inside. By staying in Germany, he could help people who were vulnerable (he presumably helped several Jewish orchestra members). As to why he had played a concert for Hitler's birthday in 1943, he says it was one time he could find no excuse to beg out: like Höfgen, he "could not refuse."

The rest of the film is essentially an expansion of this first encounter: Arnold becomes increasingly aggressive and bullying, but he also uncovers some unpleasant facts about Furtwängler, such as his antisemitic statements, while Furtwängler continues to assert that he was seeking to maintain "liberty and humanity" by means of his art. Here it is the American major who insists on looking history in the eye (he keeps returning to the footage of the corpses at Bergen-Belsen) and who tries to puncture Furtwängler's view that he acted out of noble motives, but Furtwängler gives as good as he gets, repeating his own version and refusing to back down. Both Keitel and Skarsgård give outstanding performances, the former embodying moral outrage and the latter claiming the privileges of artistry.

Szabó portrays Furtwängler as a great artist and begins the film with a gorgeous performance of Beethoven's Fifth Symphony in a baroque church, conducted by Furtwängler during the war (the sound of bombing is heard in the background). At the same time, the film grants legitimacy to Arnold's moral passion, despite his lack of respect for "high culture." In the opening performance in the church, the camera shows us many Nazi officers in the audience, with rapt expressions on their faces, thus forcing us to ask ourselves what the possible relation between a love of great music and Nazi atrocities could be. More pointedly, when Furtwängler declares in their last meeting that "music is greater than Auschwitz," Arnold shoots back: "They played Beethoven at Auschwitz." As is well known, Jewish musicians in the camp were forced to play while others went on work details where many died. Furtwängler's response is pathetic: "How was I to know what they were capable of?" After that, he finally admits: "Yes, it would have been better if I had left." But this appears more like a statement of resignation than of self-understanding or repentance. At their earlier meeting, Arnold had accused him of "not understanding anything," and we cannot be sure that Arnold is wrong. But when Furtwängler leaves the office, his shoulders drooping, David Will puts on a recording of the Fifth Symphony conducted by him and turns the volume up, so that Furtwängler can hear it as he descends the stairs. In a voiceover, Arnold informs us that although Furtwängler was charged and brought to trial, he was acquitted and resumed his career. (He died a few years later, in 1954, but was never again allowed to conduct in the Unites States.)

Szabó ends the film in a way that seems to justify the acquittal, though perhaps not to exonerate Furtwängler: he shows documentary footage from a concert that the real-life Wilhelm Furtwängler conducted during the war, after which Goebbels went up to him and shook his hand—but by zooming in on the image of the handshake and magnifying it, Szabó discovered that the conductor had a handkerchief in his hand on which he wiped his fingers after shaking Goebbels's hand.[24] That gesture, presumably showing Furtwängler's revulsion and replayed several times, is the last thing we see in the film. But it does not wipe away the questions the film raises.

Today, Furtwängler's greatness as a conductor is up for discussion by musicologists; some claim that his focus on expressiveness, his indisputed talent for wringing emotion out of musical performances, made him "sloppy" in some of his renderings.[25] Nor is there any doubt that he was a convinced German nationalist who called German music "the greatest artistic achievement of all peoples of modern times" and who considered the "influence of Jews in cultural life" as "demoralizing."[26] He dismissed Arnold Schönberg's atonal music (Schönberg was Jewish) as "biologically inferior."[27] It is also true, however, that he never committed any crimes during the Nazi period. The worst that can be said about him (and Steve Arnold actually says it in the film) is that by his collaboration with the regime he provided cover for the Nazis' crimes. Hitler declared him to be his favorite conductor. But Szabó's emphasis is less on the man himself than on the questions he embodies: about the dilemmas that confront talented individuals who must choose how to respond to unjust state power, and about the stories they (but also any one of us who may be in a similar position) may tell themselves to justify their actions. Alex Ross's judgment about Furtwängler would no doubt be accepted by Szabó: "In the end, these recordings [made by Furtwängler during the war] make it disconcertingly clear that humanity is a neutral condition, capable of encompassing beauty and horror in the same instant."[28]

After all this, have we arrived at no more than a banal relativism? "We too could become collaborators with evil, so we should not judge others too harshly"? No, Szabó does not suggest that we could all become Nazis, or that we should withhold judgment about individuals who collaborate with evil regimes. But he shows us the gray zones we must not overlook in our judgments. Neither Höfgen nor Furtwängler, as portrayed by Szabó, is a Nazi ideologue or an outright criminal. These talented men act not out of ideological conviction but out of moral cowardice, egotism, and self-deception. They have huge personal ambitions, coexisting with genuine artistic talent and professional commitment. Theirs are traits that all of us can recognize, even those of us who lack their talent. While we may be impelled to examine our own ethical compromises and self-deceptions after viewing these films (that would be Szabó's hope, for sure), we can comfort ourselves with the thought that not living under an evil dictatorship—at least not at present—we do not have to face their stark choices.

The Parvenu's Dilemma: Loyalty and Alienation in *Colonel Redl*

"The film is about a man who wants to belong to privileged circles, classes, strata, where one has advantages, and for this reason he betrays, everyday, his world, his past, his family, his class."[29] Szabó's characterization of the protagonist of *Colonel Redl* corresponds in a striking way to Hannah Arendt's definition of the parvenu, a figure she identifies chiefly with certain Jews in their relation to the privileged classes but that one can find, she says, in any society where "defamed people and classes exist."[30] The parvenu, in her analysis, is a member of such a defamed people or class, a pariah who, by dint of ambition and talent, succeeds in leaving his origins behind but who as a result experiences a constant state of tension and ambivalence, with a "bad conscience for having betrayed his people."[31] The tragedy of the parvenu, as Ágnes Heller noted in her own exploration of this type, is that he cannot feel at home or be authentically himself anywhere: having learned to mimic the ways of the privileged classes (the parvenu "must become a master of mimicry," Heller says), he is nevertheless not fully accepted by the privileged, since they are aware of his origins, which he cannot fully hide in any case; but having abandoned and denied his origins, he cannot return to them either.[32] True to her interest in existential choices, Heller emphasizes that the parvenu's fate is actually a choice: not all those from modest or oppressed backgrounds who attain great heights fit the psychological profile of the parvenu. Arendt and Heller both use the male pronoun in describing the type, but they would no doubt agree that women too can be parvenus, with some variations in their stories. Arendt's intense interest in the nineteenth-century *salonnière* Rahel

Varnhagen, the subject of her first book, was due precisely to Varnhagen's complicated relation to Jewishness.[33]

Heller, like Arendt, recognizes that Jews are not the only parvenus in the modern world, even if they embody the type in its most painful version, since a Jewish parvenu must deny not only his family and class but also his religion. Heller stresses that the era of the parvenu" is limited in time, since the type can exist only in a stratified society in which the crossing of social boundaries is nonetheless possible. While Arendt does not put it in those terms, she too sees the parvenu as a historical figure who came into being after the political emancipation of the Jews in Europe, which opened the way for Jewish assimilation to Christian society. According to Heller, the "age of the parvenu" is the period between the early nineteenth century (as per the Napoleonic dictum of "careers open to talent") and the mid-twentieth, when presumably class stratification became irrelevant. Yet we continue, even today, to see individuals from marginalized or socially devalued backgrounds who seem to embody the type in all of its psychological complexity. Szabó put his finger on a major aspect of the parvenu's psychology when he defined his Redl as a man "ashamed of who he is," for he "considers himself and his kind of little value, even worthy of contempt."[34]

I say Szabó's Redl because the historical personage after whom the film is named has only surface traits in common with the protagonist of Szabó's film. The historical Alfred Redl (1864–1913), a member of the General Staff of the Imperial and Royal Habsburg Army and head of military counterintelligence at the time of his death, became the center of a spy scandal after his suicide in May 1913. Apparently, he had been selling information to the Habsburgs' arch enemy, Russia, for at least a decade, needing money to support his luxurious lifestyle and his love affairs with young officers. Portrayed as a talented social climber and a debt-ridden homosexual living way behind his means, Alfred Redl became the subject of numerous books and films, as well as of a play by the British playwright John Osborne (*A Patriot for Me*, 1965), from which Szabó and his co-screenwriter Peter Dobai borrow a few scenes. (They credit Osborne's play as one of the "inspirations" for the film.) Yet Szabó was right to insert a disclaimer at the beginning, according to which "the story of Colonel Redl [as told in the film] is not based on authentic documents. All the actions

of the characters are entirely invented." Although he bears the same name as
the historical Alfred Redl, the protagonist of Szabó's film is a fictional character
whose story diverges in crucial ways from that of the historical person; more
importantly, his inner life is accorded the kind of attention and portrayal that
only fiction allows.

Szabó's Redl is not a Jew, although he is sometimes taken for one or accused
of being one by others; but he is the child of a defamed class, to use Arendt's
terminology. The son of a poor railway worker and the grandson of Ukrainian
and Hungarian peasants from the edge of the Empire, the eastern province of
Galizia, Redl is stamped as marginal both geographically and socially.[35] (The
historic Redl came from a slightly higher class and his father was Austrian,
not Ukrainian.[36]) But he is an intelligent child, who earns the admiration of
his teacher in elementary school by writing a heartfelt poem of praise to the
Emperor Franz-Joseph. The teacher arranges for the boy to be admitted to the
Imperial and Royal (*Kaiserlich und Königlich*, the terminology in use since
the "compromise" of 1867, which made Franz Joseph Emperor of Austria and
King of Hungary) Cadet Academy, where he becomes a classmate of boys
from aristocratic families whose way of life he admires and seeks to emulate.
He grows up to be a skilled officer totally devoted to the Army and to the by
then aged Emperor. Unlike some of his aristocratic classmates, who can allow
themselves to be more lax in their devotion, Redl is a steadfast, even rigid
loyalist to the Empire.

By his ambition and talent and his desire to shine, Redl resembles Hendrik
Höfgen, and resembles him physically as well, for the role is played by the
same actor, the outstanding Klaus Maria Brandauer. But unlike Höfgen, who
never fully espouses the values of the Nazis whose approval he courts (he is,
after all, "just an actor," as he says), Redl believes in the benevolence of the
Empire and genuinely admires, even loves the Emperor, to whom he feels
personally indebted. When his father dies, not long after the boy enters the
cadet academy, the school's director offers him train fare and time off to go
home for the funeral, but young Redl chooses not to, because it would mean
missing the school's celebration of the Emperor's name day. Hearing this, the
director, a Colonel, appears almost shocked. In the next scene, we see Redl
sitting with his classmates in the school's ornate church, looking with rapt

attention at the officiating prelate who declares that Franz Joseph is now all of these boys' godfather. The viewer has no difficulty concluding that the boy who chose not to attend his father's funeral so that he could pay homage to a royal substitute is showing signs of identity trouble.

A striking aspect of Szabó's film is the attention he devotes to his protagonist's childhood, which is when identity troubles begin. About twenty minutes (out of 140) are devoted to Redl's early years, and they set the stage for what is to come, providing important insights into the inner life of the talented, ambitious, deeply self-alienated child who will grow up to be Colonel Redl. These sequences also allow Szabó to display once again his extraordinary ability to direct child actors; the performance of Gábor Svidrony, who plays Redl at around age nine, is as impressive as that of Klaus Maria Brandauer.

The film begins with an extended close-up of Redl's face as an adult, while the opening credits roll to the sound of the triumphant Radetzky March, celebrating an earlier Habsburg victory. The face could be a photograph, but very slight movements around the mouth indicate that this is in fact a "live" close-up, although we don't know exactly where or when it occurs. In alternating shots, we see a large yellow building which turns out to be a train station, sometimes half hidden by puffs of smoke from a train. The disclaimer about this not being a story based on documents brings the credits to an end, but we continue to see a succession of isolated shots as the film proper begins. A middle-aged man in uniform salutes by the train tracks; a woman in peasant dress draws water from a well and smiles sweetly at the camera, which then pulls back to show the name of the station in two languages: GLUCCHOWICE-GLUNNAU. We soon understand that these are Alfred's parents, the stationmaster and his wife, and that the camera occupies the place of the boy—or maybe the place of the man, if these are memory images recalled by the adult Redl. The lack of dialogue or other sounds reinforces the idea that these are visual memories. We next see four young girls standing by a window, blowing bubbles, then running in the yard, chasing a dog and yelling: Alfred's sisters. The camera moves indoors, to the stationmaster's cramped lodging, and we have more isolated scenes in quick succession: the father soaking his feet in a basin, the family around the dinner table, sitting close to each other in the light of a gas lamp (as in a painting by the seventeenth-century French painter Georges de la Tour, according to the scenario[37]), then the mother and the girls getting ready for bed in the family's bedroom: the mother blows out the lamp and smiles. On the wall, there hangs the photo of an elderly man in an army uniform, shown now in close-up: Redl's grandfather. There is also a framed picture of Jesus.

By putting Redl in the camera's place in these shots, Szabó communicates several ideas at once. These are subjective images, probably memories recalled later, of Redl's family when he was a child. The smiles of his mother and the playfulness of his sisters indicate a happy family, but we also see how poor they are, sharing a single bedroom above the train station. Redl's absence from all these scenes indicates that he is the observer (or the rememberer) and that we are seeing everything through his eyes, but it also suggests a distance between him and his family, thus foreshadowing the separation and downright denial that will define his relation to them as an adult. The visual absence of the boy's body continues for three more scenes, this time with dialogues, which involve not only the family but the larger environment. Redl, in class, reads his ode to the Emperor, but we don't see him—the camera is turned toward the class and the teacher, an elderly man who stands in front of a crucifix and a portrait of Franz Joseph. "Very good, my boy!" he exclaims. "Maybe you'll become a great poet of our fatherland." In the next scene, the teacher introduces Alfred to the Prefect and asks him to recommend the boy for admission to the cadet academy—but we still don't see the boy himself. Finally, he is ready to leave (still invisible), and his mother packs his clothes into a suitcase as she gives him parting advice: "Always stand straight, Alfred, like a man. We'll be so proud of you. Never forget that your grandfather was a peasant—and you're going to be educated with rich people. Always be grateful to the Emperor." Alfred's whole future is sketched out in the mother's words, but the life she happily anticipates for her son will not include any space for her.

The first time we see Redl himself occurs more than five minutes into the film, during training exercises with other boys at the cadet academy. They do pushups and then hop around a large courtyard with their hands behind their heads, barely distinguishable from one another. It's as if Redl's bodily presence did not really exist until he found himself in an environment far removed from the family in which he spent his first years. In the academy, he is part of a collective, wearing the same school uniform as the others. At first it's hard to tell him apart from his classmate Kubinyi (György Rácz), with whom he jousts in a different exercise; when Kubinyi's wooden lance breaks, the two boys are made to run the gauntlet together as punishment, barechested, while their classmates rain blows on them. They put an arm around each other's shoulders as they run: their shared drubbing has created a physical bond between them.

We soon discover that Kubinyi is not just any boy, but Baron Christoph von Kubinyi, the scion of a Hungarian aristocratic family. Kubiny and his slightly older sister Katalin (Dóra Lendvai), characters invented by Szabó, become the most important figures in Redl's life; this fact becomes evident in the sequence devoted to the boy's visit, during a school vacation, to the Kubinyi family's ancestral home. From the moment the carriage carrying the two boys stops in front of the mansion, greeted by servants and by Kubinyi's grandmother (Mária Majláth), a grande dame who often speaks French to her family, we can see that Redl is at once enchanted and full of anxiety in this new environment. He and Christoph wear their school uniforms throughout the visit, which seems to efface the class difference between them, but as both Redl and the viewer are aware, that difference is enormous. At the dinner table, with its white damask cloth and elegant silver and china (a striking contrast to the table we saw earlier in Redl's home), the boy keeps looking sideways at his friend to make sure that he is handling his knife and fork correctly (Figure 9). When Kubinyi's grandfather (Tamás Major) asks him, kindly but pointedly, to explain which part of His Majesty's "vast empire" he comes from, Redl stammers that he was born in Galizia. "Polish?" asks the grandfather. "My . . . my father is Ruthenian (Ukrainian), with a bit of German blood, I think," the boy replies, with an anxious look; then he continues, gaining confidence as he speaks: "I believe my mother's grandfather was Hungarian. Yes, Hungarian. They were Hungarian nobles and rich, before they lost everything. Luckily, later His Majesty helped them and gave them a position in the Civil Service." It seems clear to us, and probably to his hosts as well, that the boy is making up this story as he goes, but the grandfather expresses satisfaction: "So you have some Hungarian blood in your veins." At this, Redl relaxes and smiles. "My mother used to sing a Hungarian song about hills and fields," he says, then suddenly starts singing. The camera

Figure 9 Colonel Redl (Oberst Redl), *1985. Objektív Stúdió, Manfred Durniok Produktion für Film und Fernsehen, in association with ORF, ZDF, and MOKÉP. Copyright National Film Institute Hungary—Film Archive.*

pulls back to show the grand dining room, the family in formal attire, the servants standing at attention behind the table, all of them listening to the boy singing a simple folk song (in correct Hungarian) about a peasant girl and her suitor: it seems terribly incongruous, absurd even. When he finishes, the grandmother says to Christoph, in French: "He is very nice." "He doesn't speak French, grandmother," Kubinyi replies, in French, as the camera rests in a close-up on Redl's face. He looks bewildered, not knowing what is being said about him.

Szabó's use of close-ups in this scene is masterful, allowing us to deduce the boy's shifting feelings, from anxiety to self-confidence and pleasure, then back again. In a later scene, while Katalin plays Chopin on the piano and her brother turns the pages for her, Redl, in a show of helpfulness, goes to fill the grandfather's coffee cup from the silver samovar on the buffet, but once the cup is full, he is unable to shut off the faucet and coffee spills all over the floor. The family doesn't notice his difficulty, but we see his face expressing dismay, then panic, as he struggles with the knob. Finally, he wails softly: "Could you please help me?" The butler and two other servants rush in to remove the samovar and wipe the floor, and one of the servants, a young woman, smiles at Redl in sympathy, but he looks down, avoiding her gaze, ashamed.

Szabó has often explained the importance of the actor's face and its cinematic equivalent, the close-up, in his films. Unlike a novel, where the narrator can describe what a character thinks or feels, a film must convey interiority by visual means, "from the outside." In *Colonel Redl*, as Edward Plater has pointed out, Szabó does not use literary devices like voiceovers, dream sequences, or flashbacks to allow us to enter Redl's mind but employs, instead, "action, dialogue, and outward appearances."[38] This can be said, of course, about most films, and it is also true of some literary works, Hemingway's short stories being prime examples, but the exploration of individual states of mind through the close-up is Szabó's signature technique. The expressivity of the actor's face is paramount, according to Szabó, for "the moving picture has made it possible to present human emotions, thoughts in their movement, change. It has given the possibility to show the birth of a thought, to follow its shaping."[39] The close-up, a collaboration between the actor and the director—who decides where to place the camera in order to obtain the desired effect—allows just such an unfolding of thoughts and emotions to take place.

In his 2019 interview with András Szekfü, Szabó expounded at some length on the importance of the camera's placement: "Even a millimeter can make a difference in whether we see or don't see the light in [the actor's] eyes." And he told a lovely anecdote about Ingmar Bergman in this regard: When he asked one of Bergman's favorite actors, Erland Josephson, what Bergman told him and the other actors in order to make them perform so exceptionally well, Josephson replied: "Bergman doesn't tell us anything, but he is the only director I know who always places the camera in such a way as to show exactly how good we are."[40] The close-up calls on the viewer's contribution as well, for the viewer is asked to decipher the meanings of the actor's expressions. This is beautifully brought out in the last scene of Redl's visit to the Kubinyi family, when we see them all assembled in the salon after the samovar incident. Kubiny's sister has finished playing the piano and sits in an armchair holding her coffee cup; suddenly, she spills its contents on her white dress, in a deliberate gesture that echoes, visually, the boy's earlier mishap. Redl, understanding her action as a sign of solidarity, smiles in relief.

It's after that visit to the Kubinyi estate that the boy chooses not to go home for his father's funeral; he also starts to take piano lessons at school and to learn French. It is not too much of an exaggeration to say that Redl falls in love with the Kubinyis—not only with Christoph but with his whole family and way of life. Some commentators have suggested that Redl and Kubinyi are lovers, indeed that the whole Habsburg Army was full of gay officers.[41] But the homosociality that characterizes all-male groups is not synonymous with homosexual behavior. In the film, Kubinyi (played as an adult by the German actor Jan Niklas) is shown to be enthusiastically heterosexual, despite his emotional bond with Redl. Redl himself, differing markedly both from the historical Alfred Redl and from the character in John Osborne's play, comes across as a repressed homosexual, literally buttoned up in his uniform ("the uniform is his armor," as Szabó put it[42]), until the final plot twist when he allows himself—very briefly—to give in to his desire for a young man he is introduced to. In the meantime, he engages in sex with women and even marries a young woman from a distinguished Viennese family; while he clearly does not desire her, he apparently fulfills his conjugal duty and she becomes devoted to him. His own devotion, however (to the extent that he can devote himself to anything other than the Army), is to another woman, Kubinyi's married sister Katalin (Gudrun Landgrebe), who becomes his long-term mistress and confidante and is genuinely in love with him. She even offers to run away with him to America at one point. Katalin is the only person with whom Redl can at least partially let down his guard. "I have nobody I can embrace, just you," he tells her after their first tryst. But he admits, when she asks him as they lie in bed, that he was "thinking of somebody else" while making love to her: her brother Christoph. Redl's sexuality, we are made to understand, is as stunted as the rest of his emotional life.

As for Christoph himself, Redl's bond with him is deep, long-lasting, and ultimately doomed to fail. Kubinyi is a dashing young officer who frequents the officers' brothel and takes his military responsibilities somewhat lightly, in contrast to his plebeian friend, but while their relationship is not exactly reciprocal, he does show loyalty to Redl. On their first posting to a seaside town on the Adriatic coast, when another officer in the bar of the brothel remarks snidely to Kubinyi that "This Redl was born in Lemberg" (Lvov, in

Galizia, suggesting his low social class), Kubinyi fires back that he is Redl's friend and practically challenges the offender to a duel. Kubinyi, a favorite of the prostitutes at the brothel, is the model on whom Redl hopes to base his own sexual activity with women—but here as in other aspects of his life, Redl has to force himself to learn what comes naturally to his friend. In one outstanding scene, he "goes upstairs" with a prostitute whom Kubinyi has momentarily jilted, and peppers her with questions about him. Why are all the women so crazy about Kubinyi, he wants to know. "Because he loves doing it," she answers. (The prostitute is played by the young Dorottya Udvaros, who would return in Szabó's later films.) "Can you teach me?" Redl asks her. "That's not something that can be taught, it comes on its own. You're born with it," she replies. The parallel with aristocracy, which one is also "born with," is obvious. But Redl persists: Is Kubinyi slow or fast, tender or rough? What does he like to do? He's rough, she replies, then asks, "And what do you like to do?" Instead of answering, Redl walks over to an internal window after hearing moans on the other side and looks through the semitransparent curtain at Kubinyi and his partner, naked, tumbling around in the bed. "Look and learn," the prostitute tells him, "Your big brother knows how to do it." After that, Redl strips her naked and they too engage in vigorous sex. But on his way down the stairs afterward, looking satisfied with himself, Redl is stopped by another officer, a stranger, who kisses him on the mouth. Redl does not react, simply looks back at the officer as he opens the door to leave.

The break between Kubinyi and Redl occurs not over sex or sexuality but over the Monarchy. While Kubinyi becomes more and more outspoken in his contempt for the "senile" Emperor and affirms his own Hungarian nationalism (he is still outraged at the brutal suppression of the 1848 Revolution by the same Emperor's troops), Redl remains rigid in his loyalty to the Empire and to the person of Franz Joseph himself. As he tells his lover Katalin, the Emperor has made mistakes and some reforms are needed, but he will do his utmost to "preserve and protect the Monarchy." We are now around 1900, in the waning years of the Empire, when increasing demands for independence from its diverse ethnic groups, as well as external pressures from Russia and other potential enemies, are threatening the Habsburgs' hegemony in Central Europe. "No wonder people hate you," Katalin responds to him. Redl is clearly out of step with the times, still believing in the Empire that allowed him to become who he is (or would like to be), at a time when many others are already seeing its end, or at least its transformation.

The end of Redl's friendship with Kubinyi occurs during their posting in Galizia (Redl's birthplace), where Redl is promoted to the rank of Commander of the garrison. One evening, after Kubinyi makes yet another deprecating remark about the Emperor to a group of officers, Redl lurches at him in a fury and throws him to the ground. Kubinyi, fighting back, exclaims, "Who do you take yourself for, switchman?" This allusion to Redl's father, the stationmaster, stops Redl in his tracks. He backs off and leaves the room, looking embarrassed. The next day, when he knocks on Kubinyi's door to make amends, the latter dismisses him contemptuously. Their friendship is over. Their emotional bond persists, however, for both of them.

Paradoxically, Kubinyi the rebellious Hungarian nationalist and indifferent soldier ends up on the Imperial General Staff, in charge of Hungarian affairs. But the paradox is only apparent, for his position makes sense if we consider the deeply ingrained class snobbism that characterized Habsburg society and institutions.[43] While Redl's upward trajectory seems to bear out the regime's proclaimed egalitarianism ("careers open to talent"), Kubinyi's aristocratic family connections are a much surer guarantee of success, especially at a time when power relations in the Empire itself are shifting. The Crown Prince, Franz Joseph's nephew Archduke Franz Ferdinand, impatient to begin his own rule, cannot be wholly displeased with an officer who expresses disdain for his aged uncle. The Archduke (played by the great German actor Armin Müller-Stahl) comes across as a ruthless, politically savvy autocrat-in-waiting who eventually engineers Redl's downfall. This is another place where Szabó's film differs significantly from the historical record, which shows no involvement at all on the part of Archduke Franz Ferdinand in Alfred Redl's story. Peter G. Christensen calls Szabó's portrayal of Franz Ferdinand a "libel," since he appears as the arch villain of the film. According to Christensen, Szabó "creates sympathy for the Dual Monarchy [by presenting] Franz Ferdinand as a bigoted, evil man working against the Emperor's liberal regime."[44] But in my reading, Franz Ferdinand is shown by Szabó to be not so much an enemy of the Dual Monarchy as its last, logical representative. He is the bare-knuckled version of autocratic state power, while the aged Emperor appears as its more benign face, but basically, they represent the same system. As Dagmar Lorenz puts it, "Oppression is the pillar on which this social fabric rests: of the poor by the rich, of one ethnic group by another, women by men, gays by heterosexuals."[45]

The framing of Redl by the Archduke proves necessary because Szabó's Redl is not actually a traitor. How could he be, given his undying gratitude to the regime and to the person of the Emperor? But his very loyalty makes him, once he becomes the powerful head of military counterintellligence, a potential target of the Archduke's plotting. The Army has become too soft and undisciplined and needs to be shaken up, Franz Ferdinand tells Redl after summoning him to his office. And what better way to do that than by creating an "Affair" that will put fear into the men and show clearly "who the enemy is"? In short, Redl must find a spy within the Army, an enemy in its ranks to make an example of. Redl sets to work and quickly finds five possible candidates for the internal enemy role. But they are all aristocrats, and what's more they come from areas that have to be treated with care, the Archduke explains to him. The spy cannot be Austrian or Hungarian (the Monarchy's unity must be preserved), or Czech or Serb or Croat (too rebellious, too unstable), or a Jew (remember Dreyfus, plus the Rothschilds are essential to the Empire's finances). That leaves just one ethnic group, the Ruthenians. "Look for a duplicate of yourself, Redl," the Archduke instructs him.

The close-up on Redl's face shows that he suddenly understands. "The Archduke has me in his plans. The bullets are whistling past me," he informs his wife despairingly in the very next scene. To his relief, he does find a "duplicate" in Galizia and rushes to arrest him, but the man manages to commit suicide first. The Archduke's response is categorical: "A dead duplicate is no duplicate. Find another one, quickly." Redl actually has another possibility in mind and wishes to interrogate his former friend Kubinyi, but the Archduke sweeps away that idea: "*I* decide who is a traitor. Kubinyi is not your duplicate," he says somewhat cruelly. His manner here recalls the General in *Mephisto*, in the scene where he dismisses Höfgen as a "Schauspieler." At the end of their meeting, as if to reveal his hand, the Archduke observes: "Look here, Redl, the Emperor Waltz isn't danced anymore." He predicts that a war is coming, "maybe after an assassination. A small, local war." He is partly right, but the assassination will be his own. As to the scope and duration of the coming war, even a ruthless and politically savvy autocrat can be wrong about some things.

After that meeting, things move fast. Redl, now fully aware of the Archduke's machinations, expresses his disillusionment to his lover Katalin. "The Archduke is planning a military coup—he no longer believes in the old Monarchy," he exclaims bitterly. "Do I admit that I've been on the wrong side all this time? I can't prevent what's brewing up. What I wanted to defend doesn't exist." From there it is but a step to suicidal self-sacrifice. Redl allows himself to be trapped into a brief love affair with a handsome young Italian—his first real homosexual encounter in the film, which produces some unforgettable images: Redl and Velocchio (László Gálffi) on horseback in a snowy wood, the one in his uniform, the other in his black cape against the white, or the two of them leaning against a tree (Figure 10); Redl and Velocchio improvising a piano duet based on Papageno's and Papagena's love aria in *The Magic Flute*; Redl looking relaxed and happy for the first time, as he watches Velocchio asleep naked in his bed. But the idyll lasts only one day. The next day, after forcing the young man to admit, at gunpoint, that he was sent (he says he doesn't know by whom) to seduce Redl and pry military secrets out of him,

Figure 10 Colonel Redl (Oberst Redl), *1985. Objektív Stúdió, Manfred Durniok Produktion für Film und Fernsehen, in association with ORF, ZDF, and MOKÉP. Copyright National Film Institute Hungary—Film Archive.*

Redl recites, quasi-ironically, a whole list of precise facts about the Army's weapons to the youth and sends him on his way.

Redl's betrayal is absurd, for as he well knows, the secrets he gives out are already known to the person who set up the young seducer. In one sense, Redl's gesture can be understood as yet another sign of his loyalty to the regime. The Empire needs a traitor for a show trial, so Redl provides one: not just a duplicate of himself, but the original. In another sense, however, Redl's gesture can be understood as a sign of defiance, a middle finger raised to his ruthless boss the Archduke. This second interpretation seems to be borne out by the fact that after he is placed under arrest in a hotel room, in a sequence that begins with his being trailed on an eerily empty street by men in bowler hats, evoking the surrealist images of René Magritte and the mood of Kafka's *The Trial*, he refuses to cooperate with the Archduke's plan.[46] According to the plan (communicated to Redl by the Archduke's emissary, who is none other than Christoph von Kubinyi), Redl will plead guilty in a public trial, after which he will receive a light sentence. Kubinyi, invoking their old friendship, urges him to "behave properly" and accept this new role. But for the first time since he entered the cadet academy, Redl rejects the order of a superior: he was framed and is innocent, he insists. Also for the first time, he cracks a joke: "Betrayal has become the national pastime," he tells Kubinyi with a smile.

We next see a whole parade of other visitors, among them Redl's wife and his mistress Katalin, who both urge him to cooperate. "Tell them what they want to hear," Katalin says. But Redl remains adamant. The only visitor who tells him to fight the charge is his old friend and fellow officer Dr. Sonnenschein (András Bálint), a Jewish army doctor who has his own identity issues. We will find a Sonnenschein family and the question of Jewish identity at the center of Szabó's 1999 film, *Sunshine*.

Is Redl's refusal a sign of enlightenment, a belated realization that he has indeed been on the wrong side during all his years of loyalty to a regime that considers him, and others like him, as expendable inferiors? I would not go so far. Redl remains, throughout the film, virtually opaque to himself, devoid of self-reflection and willfully forgetful of his origins. During his posting in Galizia, he makes no effort to contact his family. When his older sister, dressed in peasant garb, shows up in his office one day, wanting simply to see him and bring news of his mother and sisters, he asks her how they knew he was there. A neighbor's son, a soldier, told them, she says. Redl's sole response is panic: he stuffs bills into her hands and tells her he can give her more money, but she must never come back. "This is a barracks, not a post office," he screams, almost totally out of control. The poor woman is appalled.

Even before his sister's visit, Redl loses control and screams in two other incidents: one night when a dog follows him down a deserted street, barking, he ends up shooting the dog in panic and runs away; shortly after that, when a Jewish man in a caftan approaches him in the local restaurant to invite him to Shabbat dinner, at the same time as a Roma woman who wants to tell his fortune, he screams at them both: it's as if he were afraid of being tainted by the Gypsy and the Jew, the two emblematic figures of pariahs in Central Europe at the time (and even today, in some places).

If these incidents suggest cracks in his armor, the cracks become even more evident after he leaves Galizia. As the head of counterintelligence in Vienna, one of his first actions is to look at his own dossier, which shows him how the regime views him: "Admires power. Expresses gratitude to the Habsburgs. Doesn't see his family in Lemberg. Pretends to be an aristocrat." In a touch of self-irony, he adds his own assessment to the list: "Insincere." Later, when he returns to Galizia to arrest the man who commits suicide, he asks his driver to go by the house where he was born, and the camera tracks over the well and the windows where his sisters blew bubbles as girls, now all devoid of people. As the car pulls away, we see his face through the window, inscrutable but sad. Later, back in Vienna, he tells Katalin about a dream: "My father was on my shoulders, pressing me into the earth." Later still, just before his arrest, he enters a church and hears an organ playing. Approaching the votive candles, he sets fire to a photograph he holds in his hand; a close-up shows that the photo is of a well-dressed young girl and a boy in cadet uniform, probably Katalin and Christoph. Is it his lifelong infatuation with them that he is trying to destroy? He starts to pray: "Our Father . . ." but is unable to go on. "Maybe I should have tried this earlier," he mutters as he leaves the church.

While these scenes suggest a degree of self-reflection and even of regret on Redl's part, they come too late to make any difference in his life, and if Redl's belated refusal to cooperate with the Archduke's plan suggests resistance, it is ineffectual. Redl cannot win against the Empire, even in the latter's waning days. The uneven match between a rebellious individual and a repressive regime is also emphasized in Szabó's next film, *Hanussen*, whose hero—yet another performer, a soothsayer who gains notoriety by correctly predicting the Reichstag fire of February 1933—is hauled off by Nazi thugs to a forest and unceremoniously shot after he tries to assert his autonomy. (I will not discuss *Hanussen* in detail here, as it repeats the themes explored more successfully in the other two films of the German trilogy.)

If Redl won't go to trial, then he must be made to commit suicide, the General Staff decides. In a gesture of power and cruelty, the Archduke orders Kubinyi to deliver the suicide weapon, Redl's own service revolver, to his former friend. After Kubinyi accomplishes his errand, with no acknowledgment of his presence by Redl, he leaves Redl's room and falls down in a faint in the corridor. The Empire could wreak havoc, Szabó suggests, even with the lives of aristocrats.

The very last images of *Colonel Redl* take us beyond this single story to the collective realm of History, which can upend the lives of Emperors as well as of their subjects. Szabó splices into black and white historical footage an image of the Archduke (i.e., Müller-Stahl) riding in his open carriage when a bullet hits him, while the triumphant Radetzky March, now sounding terribly ironic, plays on the soundtrack once again. As historical footage of First World War cannons and marching soldiers fills the screen, the camera comes to a stop on the face of a very young soldier before the closing credits roll. A whole generation of Europeans will be destroyed in this conflagration, the image suggests.

When asked by an interviewer in 1987 how he would define the world of Central Europeans, a constant preoccupation of his, Szabó replied: "the world of a man living under the permanent pressure of history."[47] Redl's story, like that of Hendrik Höfgen, was potentially repeatable throughout the twentieth century and beyond.

Notes

1   Lantos's statement is in the "Special Features" section of the DVD of the film, where we also see Szabó calling it a "soufflé": *Being Julia* (2005).

2   Personal conversation, Budapest, October 20, 2017. Like all my conversations with Szabó after the first recorded interview in 2006, this conversation took place in

Hungarian. After each meeting I wrote extensive notes in English, from which this and all the other quotations (except those from 2006) are drawn.

3   On the making of the German trilogy, see Cunningham, *The Cinema of István Szabó*, 55, 66, 75; and Marx, *Szabó István*, 259–315.

4   Imre, "White Man, White Mask," 411.

5   Benke, "Művész a hatalom csapdájában." [Artist in the trap of power]. It should be noted that the publication where this article appeared is financed by the Orbán government and that the article appeared in the wake of a nasty attack on Szabó by the government's intellectual spokeswoman Mária Schmidt, who protested against the awarding of a Lifetime Achievement Award to Szabó by the Hungarian Film Academy, on account of Szabó's past as an "agent." See https://www.civilhetes.net/schmidt-maria -tiltakozik-szabo-istvan-kituntetese-miatt

6   Hughes, "István Szabó and the 'Gestapo of Suspicion,'" 14.

7   Mann, *Mephisto*, 3. Other page numbers will be given in parentheses after the quotation.

8   See Weiss, *In the Shadow of the Magic Mountain*, 125–8, 259–60. Because of lawsuits by Gründgren or his heir (after Gründgren's death in 1963), *Mephisto* was forbidden from publication in Germany for many years, but in 1956 it nevertheless appeared in East Germany and in 1981 was finally published by Rowohlt Verlag in West Germany. Szabó had been given a copy of the East German version by the producer Manfred Durniok, who produced Szabó's film.

9   Weiss, *In the Shadow of the Magic Mountain*, 49–55.

10 Kertész, "Heureka."

11 Personal conversation, December 14, 2017. See also Zsugán, "Mephisto," 87; and Davies, "An Interview with István Szabó," 70.

12 See Mann, *Mephisto*, 48–55. The preceding quote is on p. 55.

13 Lorenz, "Ethnicity, Sexuality, and Politics," 265.

14 Fitzsimmons, "'Scathe Me with Less Fire,'" 20.

15 Hughes, "István Szabó and 'The Gestapo of Suspicion,'" 17.

16 Hirschman, *Exit, Voice and Loyalty*.

17 For comments on all three excerpts, see Christensen, "Collaboration in István Szabó's *Mephisto*," 23–5.

18 Goethe, *Faust*, Part I, trans. A. S. Kline, vv. 1338–1344. Consulted online: https://www .poetryintranslation.com/PITBR/German/FaustIScenesItoIII.php. The German original is:

Ich bin der Geist, der stets verneint!
Und das mit Recht; denn alles, was entsteht,

Ist wert, daß es zugrunde geht;
Drum besser wär's, daß nichts entstünde.
So ist denn alles, was ihr Sünde,
Zerstörung, kurz, das Böse nennt,
Mein eigentliches Element.

19 Sartre, *L'Etre et le néant*, 99–100.

20 Benjamin, "The Work of Art in the Age of Mechanical Reproduction," 241–2.

21 Margolis, "Nur Schauspieler," 86.

22 See Szekfü, *Igy filmeztünk 2*, 268.

23 Personal conversation, November 13, 2019. The film's stars are Harvey Keitel and Stellan Skarsgård.

24 Szekfü, *Igy filmeztünk 2*, 269.

25 Ross, "The Disquieting Power of Wilhelm Furtwängler, Hitler's Court Conductor."

26 Quoted in Walton, "Furtwängler the Apolitical?."

27 Ross, "The Disquieting Power of Wilhelm Furtwängler."

28 Ibid.

29 Davies, "An Interview with István Szabó," 68.

30 Arendt, *The Origins of Totalitarianism*, 66.

31 Ibid.

32 Heller, "A parvenük kora." [The Era of the Parvenu] The phrase about "master of mimicry" is on p. 119.

33 Arendt, *Rahel Varnhagen*. The book was first published in 1957, but Arendt had already completed it in the 1930s in Paris after fleeing Germany in 1933. See Barbara Hahn's Introduction to the current edition.

34 Preface to the published version of the screenplay by Szabó and Peter Dobai, 1984; quoted in Marx, *Szabó István*, 290.

35 See the fine analysis by Cernahoschi, "An Empire of Borders."

36 For basic facts about Alfred Redl's life, see Fisch, *Spy of the Century*.

37 The scenario was published in Hungarian in 1984, but the version I was able to consult appeared in French, in the journal *L'Avant-Scène du Cinéma*, no. 348 (March 1986).

38 Plater, "István Szabó's Film of Inner Conflict and Political Prophecy," 43–4.

39 Davies, "An Interview with István Szabó," 72.

40 Szekfü, *Igy filmeztünk 2*, 259.

41 Lorenz, "Ethnicity, Sexuality, and Politics," 270 and *passim*. Lorenz mistakes another
    actor for Kubinyi in a scene where an officer kisses Redl on the mouth, and she sees
    signs of homosexual desire for Redl even in Kubinyi's grandfather (a civilian), as well
    as in Redl's nemesis, the Archduke Franz Ferdinand. Thomas Warchol, for his part,
    refers casually to "Redl's Jewish lover," the army doctor Sonnenschein, although the
    film shows nothing more than a scene of drunken camaraderie between the two men
    (Warchol, "Patterns of Central European Experience in István Szabó's Trilogy and
    Sunshine," 670). John Osborne's play also suggests that homosexuality was widespread
    in the Habsburg Army.

42 Preface to the published version of the screenplay (1984); quoted in Marx, *Szabó
    István*, 290.

43 On the waning years of the Empire, see Romsics, *Hungary in the Twentieth Century*,
    chap. 1; and Mason, *The Dissolution of the Austro-Hungarian Empire, 1867-1918*.

44 Christensen, "Szabó's Colonel Redl and the Habsburg Myth," 5.

45 Lorenz, "Ethnicity, Sexuality, and Politics," 273.

46 I thank Csaba Horváth for pointing out to me the Kafkaesque mood of this sequence.
    It's not clear why Redl is in a hotel room in Vienna, the city where he lives, but he
    seems to check into the hotel as a response to being trailed. The historical Alfred Redl
    was stationed in Prague and was arrested while on a trip to Vienna.

47 Davies, "An Interview with István Szabó," 69.

3

To Be or Not To Be Jewish?

Identity as Choice or as Fate

For I who am not a Jew have nothing to prove, whereas the Jew, if he decides that his race doesn't exist, must prove it.

JEAN-PAUL SARTRE, *Réflexions sur la question juive*

Just because a Jew refuses to face facts doesn't make him a Christian.

ANDOR KNORR, In *Sunshine* scenario

In the spring of 1993, during the months I spent in Budapest, I arranged to meet with Rabbi Tamás Raj, who had been elected a member of Parliament in Hungary's first free election after the fall of communism in 1990. Rabbi Raj did not think of himself as a politician and had no intention of running again, he told me, but he had wanted to show that "if tSabo here was a Jew in a yarmulke in the communist Parliament, there had to be one in this Parliament too." There had indeed been a rabbi in the communist Parliament for many years, for under the Kádár regime, religious Jews were represented by government-approved Jewish Community Bureaus and had a representative in Parliament as well. Jews in Hungary had had the good fortune not to be entirely wiped out during the Holocaust ("only" about two-thirds of them perished during the war), and up to today the country has the greatest number of Jewish citizens in Eastern Europe, about 100,000. Most of them are not religious, and many are completely assimilated, regarding their Jewishness as no more than a distant origin. "Of Jewish origin" is a quite common form of self-identification in Hungary, as distinct from being simply Jewish.

Back in 1993, I asked Rabbi Raj: "What do you think of Hungarian Jews? Are most of them somewhat ashamed to say they're Jewish?" "Well, it's certainly not like America," he replied. "People are often afraid to say they're Jewish. But the main thing is *not* to be afraid, because people can always tell and they'll hound you. Anyway, even if you try to hide you're a Jew, the others always know." And then he told me a story:

> About twenty years ago, when I was just starting out as a rabbi, I had to go from my synagogue in Szeged [a large city in the southern part of the country] to a small town on professional business. The president of the Jewish Community Bureau was supposed to meet my train, but at the last minute he fell ill and couldn't come to the station. I had no idea where I was supposed to go, but after a while I stopped a man on the street, told him I was a rabbi, and asked whether he could direct me to the Jewish Community Bureau. The man didn't know, so I asked: "Where is the Jewish neighborhood in town? Where do the Jews live?" "There's a Jew living in that house over there," the man answered, pointing to a house nearby. I started walking toward the house, but the man ran after me. "On second thought, rabbi," he said, "You'd better not go to him. You see, only we know he's Jewish. He doesn't know it."[1]

This story is almost too good to be true, so emblematic is it of the peculiarly Jewish dilemma over personal identity that characterizes what I call the "Jewish question for Jews." It is also a very Hungarian story, as we shall see.

The "Jewish Question" for Jews

The term "Jewish question" is generally associated with antisemitism, not only because the Nazis appropriated the term and claimed to have found a "final solution" to it but because even in its origin, the term contained an implicit accusation. It first entered public discourse in Germany with the 1843 publication of Bruno Bauer's book *Die Judenfrage* (The Jewish Question), followed a year later by Karl Marx's essay, "Zur Judenfrage" (On the Jewish Question). While Bauer and Marx differed on a number of points, the question they both dealt with was that of assimilation, or the status of Jews in Christian society, which became an issue after the emancipation of Jews in Europe, starting at the end of the eighteenth century. While neither Bauer nor Marx was an avowed antisemite (Marx was an assimilated Jew whose family had converted to Christianity), their views about Jews reinforced antisemitic stereotypes. Bauer claimed that even acculturated Jews did not really want to be fully "absorbed" into the Christian mainstream, clinging to their religion; the inassimilability of Jews to the national cultures in which they lived, due to their fundamental Otherness and clannishness, has been a long-standing trope of antisemitic discourse. Marx, for his part, claimed that Jews, or more exactly, Judaism as a religion, represented the essence of capitalism (commerce, egotism) and as such was inimical to a just society.[2] Hannah Arendt has argued that Marx was expressing here the resentment of Jewish "rebel" intellectuals toward the moneyed Jews in Germany who separated themselves from fellow Jews and were too close to those in power.[3] Whatever his intention, Marx's essay confirmed the age-old stereotype of the greedy Jew whose sole interest is money.

For antisemites, the "Jewish question" was (and is, for it has not disappeared even if the term itself has fallen out of use) not a question at all, but a declaration: Jews, no matter how assimilated, can never be truly French or German or Hungarian or Polish—or, for that matter, American, for in the United States too, Jews have been seen as a "problem" by antisemites, who were not afraid to express their views right up through the Second World War and are now once again expressing them without hesitation. "The Jews will not replace us" was chanted enthusiastically at the notorious Charlottesville rally of white supremacists in 2017, and overt expressions of hate speech against Jews (as well as actions ranging from swastika graffiti on synagogue walls to mass murder) have proliferated in the United States since then.

But what has been the "Jewish question" for Jews? For some, the question was collective. Theodor Herzl, arguing for the necessity of a Jewish state in his 1896 book *Judenstaat*, subtitled the book *Versuch einer modernen Lösung der Judenfrage* (*Attempt at a Modern Solution of the Jewish Question*). For

Herzl, the only solution for Jews was to become a separate nation, so in a sense his assumption tallies with that of antisemites who considered the Jews unassimilable in Europe. But for the many Jews who did not wish to leave their European homelands, the "Jewish question" was a different matter: they either denied its existence altogether, dismissing it as an antisemitic invention, or else it became for them a question of individual identity, often experienced as a feeling of estrangement both from the non-Jewish mainstream and from other Jews. This is what Hannah Arendt had in mind when she wrote that over the course of the nineteenth century, as a consequence of emancipation, "Judaism became a psychological quality and the Jewish question became an involved personal problem for every individual Jew."[4]

Hungary provides a good example. In 1917, at a time when the so-called Golden Age of Hungarian Jewry (the period between 1867, when Jews gained full citizenship rights, and the end of the First World War, which inaugurated a period of increasing state antisemitism) was already drawing to a close, the distinguished scholarly journal *Huszadik Század* (*Twentieth Century*), founded and edited by the secular Jewish historian Oszkár Jászi, ran a special issue on "The Jewish Question in Hungary." Of the sixty Jewish and non-Jewish intellectuals who responded to the survey ("Is there a Jewish question in Hungary, and if so, what is its essence? What is [its] cause? What [is] the solution?"), only a few stated that there was "no Jewish question"—these were the staunchly optimistic Jews who reaffirmed their belief in Enlightenment ideals. "According to my experience there is no Jewish question in Hungary," wrote the Director of the Budapest rabbinical seminary, Dr. Lajos Blau; "but supposing that there is, it is essentially a leftover of medieval feeling and thought in non-Jews who insist on a Jewish question.[5] Such "leftovers," Blau claimed, would disappear once people became enlightened.

The great majority of respondents, however, both Jews and non-Jews, stated that there *was* a Jewish question. According to most Jewish respondents, its "essence" was antisemitism, itself a reaction to the problems and tensions of modernity. (This response is not that different from that of the notables who claimed that there was no Jewish question except in the minds of antisemites.) Among the responses by non-Jews, the one by Jenő Cholnoky, a professor at the university in Kolozsvár, in Transylvania, stands out for its tone as well as its content. Yes, there is a Jewish question, he wrote, and its essence is in some Jews' refusal to become Hungarian, in their stubborn clinging to a "nationhood" different from the Magyars: "it's that spoiled, Germanic-dialect-speaking, orthodox, strongly Oriental-looking Jewry that in ordinary parlance is called Galizianer [Yiddish-speaking Jews from Galizia, which before World War I was part of the Austro-Hungarian Monarchy]." Such Jews, Cholnoky stated, provoked the antipathy not only of Magyars like himself, but of "every other people brought up in a Christian civilization," and he urged the Jews of Hungary to "exterminate" the characteristics of this group from their midst.[6] One could hardly find a more graphic evocation of the divide between acculturated Jews and Yiddish-speaking *Ostjuden* that haunted so much of late nineteenth and early twentieth-century *Jewish* writing about group identity than under the pen of this Christian scholar—whose own geographic marginality in relation to Hungary (Transylvania is a border region, ceded to Romania after the First World War) may have made him especially sensitive to issues of exclusion and inclusion. Jewish writers and intellectuals in Hungary, as well as in Germany, France, and England, were acutely and often painfully aware of the differences between themselves and the dirt-poor *shtetl* Jews of Poland and Russia—some of whom were their own grandparents.[7]

From the perspective of the "Jewish question" for Jews, perhaps the most interesting response to the 1917 Hungarian survey was that of the poet and artist Anna Lesznai, who insisted on the psychological aspect of the "Jewish problem." Lesznai belonged to a wealthy Jewish landowning family and participated as a rare female member in the leading modernist literary journal in Hungary, *Nyugat* (*West*). She was thus part of a successful and assimilated Jewish elite; yet she wrote in her response: "The Jewish problem exists even when a person of Jewish origin is sitting alone in his room. It exists not only in the relations between a Jewish individual and Hungarian society. The seriousness of the problem lies in that the Jew feels like a 'Jew' for himself."[8] Forty years later, more than a decade after the end of the Second World War, the French philosopher Vladimir Jankélévitch expressed a very similar idea when he spoke at a gathering of Jewish intellectuals in Paris about "Jewishness, an internal problem." Jankélévitch wrote: "It is not enough to convert in order to cease being Jewish. [. . .] there is an essential otherness that is characteristic of Jews." The "complication" of being Jewish, which prevents Jews from ever being "one hundred percent French, or Russian, or even Israeli," was, according to Jankélévitch, both a kind of malady (his word) and a kind of privilege that defines Jews' very being. While all human beings are in some way "other" than themselves, Jews are doubly so, caught in an unresolved and unresolvable dialectic between the desire to be "just like eveyone else" (assimilation) and the desire to affirm their difference.[9]

Some people might characterize such observations as evidence of "Jewish self-hatred." I prefer to speak of conflicted identity or ambivalence about group belonging, a phenomenon that concerns not only Jews but potentially any member of a stigmatized minority in a given society. It is precisely here that we encounter the figure of the Jew who does not "know that he is a Jew," while his Christian neighbors are fully aware of that fact. Although in my discussion so far I have emphasized the existential aspect of the "Jewish question" for Jews as a phenomenon occurring in many places over a long period of time, I must now zoom in on postwar Hungary as a specific place where such ignorance of one's Jewishness was possible, and indeed quite common. It is not an accident that the anecdote the rabbi recounted to me occurred in Kádár-era Hungary. Among Hungarian Jews who had survived the Holocaust, the most observant emigrated to Israel and other countries such as the United States, Canada, or Australia in the immediate postwar years (this was the case of my own family). Many others left in 1956. While a number of Orthodox Jews remained in Hungary after 1956, most of them too old to undertake emigration, the large majority of those who remained were nonobservant Jews whose families had abandoned Jewish practice already in the prewar years and who had little or no connection to the organized Jewish community. A number were committed communists, at least until they became disillusioned. When these survivors—all of whom had experienced the trauma of persecution during the war, and most of whom had lost large segments of their families—had children of their own, a great many chose to "protect" them by not informing them of their Jewish heritage, trusting to the promises of assimilation that seemed to be offered by the communist regime. In reality, the "Jewish question" for antisemites persisted even under the communist regime, in different guises. As the eminent specialist on this subject, András Kovács, has noted, the figure of the "Jewish banker" was replaced by other stereotypes, such as the "Jewish Party Secretary," but the explanatory function of the stereotype remained the same: Jews were in control and ran the country.[10]

The result was that a whole generation of Jews born after the Second World War in Hungary grew up with neither knowledge nor understanding of their family's Jewish past, including the traumas experienced by their parents. Starting in the early 1980s, by which time the Kádár regime had loosened its grip on academic research, a team of researchers headed by the psychologist Ferenc Erős and the historian András Kovács, both of them secular Jews born in the immediate postwar years, conducted more than 100 in-depth interviews with second-generation Jews, focusing on a single question: "How did you find out that you are Jewish?" They published their first article (with one of their team members, Katalin Lévai) on the subject in 1985, eliciting enormous interest in Hungarian intellectual circles.[11] They began the article by stating that their question would have been received with incomprehension in most countries in the world (the example of US secretary of state Madeleine Albright, whose Czech parents hid their Jewish origin from her, provides a glaring exception), but that the history of Hungarian Jews, both before and after the war, made the question quite comprehensible in that country. Before the war, secular Jews had "stubbornly clung" to the promises of assimilation even in the face of increasing official antisemitism, which sought to force them out of Hungarian society. After the war, the traumatized survivors had chosen to "forget" their traumatic memories rather than trying to work through them, and they were aided by the long-standing official silence of the communist regime about the specificity of Jewish persecution and about the role played by the Hungarian government in the deportation of most of Hungary's Jewish population.

By depriving their children of information about their past, even with the best of intentions, these parents prevented them from being able to choose for themselves what their attitude toward Jewishness and Jewish identity might be. As the interviews showed, eventually the children did find out, but most often they gained no understanding of what their Jewishness might mean. Even now, one interviewee stated, the question of his Jewishness comes up only in his dreams; in his waking hours, he tries to ignore it: "If I close my eyes, people won't see me. In other words, if I don't think about the problem, then it doesn't exist, and there is no such thing as antisemitism."[12]

Jews in Hungarian Cinema under Communism

In 2000, the Hungarian Jewish Cultural Association (MAZSIKE) and the Jewish monthly *Szombat* (both founded after the fall of communism, which also made possible the flourishing of overtly antisemitic organizations and publications) sponsored a conference on "Jewish Fates in Hungarian Film." Among the interesting facts that emerged from the conference, whose proceedings were subsequently published, was that while Jews played an important role in Hungarian film production from its earliest days, relatively few films, both before and after the Second World War, presented Jewish characters identified as such on screen.[13] This is not very different from the situation in Hollywood during those years, when Jewish producers and directors, including some Hungarians, were numerous, yet very few films featured stories about Jews. *The Jazz Singer* of 1927 and *Gentlemen's Agreement* of 1947 were significant exceptions.

Before the war, the prevalent antisemitism in Hungary made explicitly identified Jewish protagonists well-nigh unrepresentable (but at least there was no Hungarian equivalent of an anti-Jewish propaganda film like the Nazis' *Jew Süss*). After the war, the taboos on mentioning religion in general and on discussing the specific persecution of Jews also acted as obstacles, although in some instances Jewish characters were shown without being named as such. Thus the kindly old musician who helps the traumatized children in Géza von Radványi's important film, *Somewhere in Europe* (1948), as well as some of the children themselves, had clearly experienced persecution as Jews during the war, without the word ever being pronounced. In 1955, *Spring in Budapest* (*Budapesti tavasz*), based on a novel by Ferenc Karinthy and directed by Félix Máriássy (who a year later would become the lead professor of Szabó's class at the Film Academy), was the first Hungarian film to deal explicitly with the persecution of Jews by the Arrow Cross, Hungary's pro-Nazi party which came to power in the fall of 1944 and whose armed thugs regularly rounded up Jews in Budapest and shot them into the Danube over the coming months. Only the arrival of Soviet troops in the city in January 1945 put an end to that horrific practice.

After Máriássy's film, a long period of silence about the Holocaust ensued, even though there were glancing allusions to it in films from the early 1960s by Zoltán Fábri and János Herskó. Fábri's *Két félidő a pokolban* (*Two Half-Times in Hell*, 1961) and *Nappali sötétség* (*Darkness in the Day*, 1963) evoke the Hungarian forced labor service for Jewish men and the persecution of Jews and communists in 1944, respectively. Herskó's *Párbeszéd* (*Dialogue*, 1963), a film on which Szabó was assistant to the director, shows the heroine returning from deportation (evoked by a shot of a concentration camp) to Budapest in 1945, without ever mentioning her Jewishness after that.

A few years later, Fábri's 1967 film *Utószezon* (*Late Season*), along with András Kovács's *Hideg napok* (*Cold Days*, 1966), exemplified what Balázs Varga has called the "guilty conscience genre" regarding the Holocaust: films that suggest a reckoning (though not a very thorough one) by some non-Jewish Hungarians with their role in the suffering of Jews during the war.[14] In these films, the focus is on the Hungarians, not on their victims. It is only in the 1980s and 1990s, starting with Imre Gyöngyössy and Barna Kabay's *The Revolt of Job* (1983), that Hungarian films focusing on Jewish characters who were persecuted began to appear.

Another fact that participants in the 2000 conference agreed on was that Hungarian films past and present, including the most contemporary ones, almost never showed the everyday lives of Jews. In a concluding roundtable featuring six participants, including filmmakers as well as scholars and critics, the historian András Kovács (no relation to the filmmaker) stated flatly that Hungarian feature films have never given an authentic image of Jewish life and Jewish concerns. "And they will continue not to do so," he concluded pessimistically.[15]

István Szabó's work constitutes an important exception to these mostly correct generalizations. Already in his first three feature films, made in the 1960s during the period of silence about Jews, Szabó not only mentioned the then taboo subject of the Holocaust, as when Eva tells János, in *The Age of Daydreaming*, that her father ate snow in Auschwitz (this may have been the first time that the word "Auschwitz" was pronounced in a Hungarian feature film) but also allowed the viewer to identify at least one character as Jewish. Even more exceptionally, Szabó in these early films honed in on the existential dilemmas of Jewish identity in Hungary, a subject that never came up even in films made much later. Why did Eva not leave the country in 1956? For many reasons, she tells János, but one that immediately jumps out at us is this one: "I wanted to prove that I was a good Hungarian." Can you be both Jewish and a good Hungarian? Assimilationist Jews thought so for many decades, and still do—but they are also, of necessity, aware that a good number of their non-Jewish countrymen think otherwise. A Christian citizen does not have to prove that he is a "good Hungarian" (i.e., a genuine Hungarian, the meaning of "good" here), but a Jewish one does. No critic at the time mentioned the exchange between Eva and János, which occurs as they sit in the newsreel movie theater watching the history of the twentieth century unfold on the screen.[16] But we who see *The Age of Daydreaming* today notice it immediately. The scene takes place under communism, way back in history; but it rings all too familiarly today, when Hungary's prime minister tirelessly promotes the idea that Hungary is a Christian country, indeed that all of Europe is Christian, even while protesting that he is not an antisemite or an Islamophobe.[17]

In *The Age of Daydreaming*, Szabó touched on the taboo subjects lightly, in what I have called a "parenthetical" fashion that would pass muster with the censor. In *Father*, his second film (released in 1966), he returned more insistently both to the touchy subject of the Holocaust and to the even touchier subject of Jewish identity in Hungary. In one scene, Takó, the young male protagonist, is hired along with several of his college friends to be an extra in a film that shows Jews wearing the yellow star, being herded by Arrow Cross thugs across the iconic Chain Bridge in the middle of the city. (This scene is itself somewhat astonishing, since there were no actual feature films being made in Hungary at the time, in the late 1960s, that would have shown such a scene.) The young people look slightly sheepish as one of the director's assistants pins the yellow star on their chest. But the director is not happy with the scene: "Look tragic! Start over!" he yells through a megaphone as the crowd trudges across the bridge. Then, he suddenly calls out to Takó, telling him to change costumes. Off with the yellow star, on with a black leather jacket and hat: Takó is now among the Arrow Cross. This can be understood as a sly commentary on the fakery of filmmaking ("Films cheat," Szabó often likes to say), but it also has a deeper resonance. How do we define a Jew? Is there a difference between a Jew and a "true" Hungarian, let alone a racist Hungarian? A few years ago, one of the most vocally antisemitic members of the far-right party Jobbik discovered belatedly that his grandmother was a survivor of Auschwitz—she had hidden her tattoo by wearing only long-sleeved dresses. The young man left the party and became a practicing Jew.[18]

Right after the filming scene, Takó and his friends are shown sitting pensively in a café on the Danube bank. "Aren't we glad we missed all that?" one asks. "I have no idea what my father was doing in 1944," says another. Then, we see Takó and one of his friends, a young woman named Anni, walking along the Danube bank, not far from where the Jews had been shot into the river twenty years earlier (Figure 11). Today there is a small memorial there, but in the 1960s only people's memories made the association. No doubt because of the filming they had just participated in, Anni suddenly confides to Takó, in an anguished monologue, that her father had been killed in the Nazi camp at Mauthausen but that she never talks about it: "For years I denied that my father died in a Nazi camp. I'd make up stories rather than admit I was

Figure 11 Father *(Apa)*, *1966. Mafilm 3. Copyright National Film Institute Hungary—Film Archive.*

Jewish. I'm Hungarian, no? Simply Hungarian. I don't know where I belong! I'm ashamed of belonging to those who were killed. I always have to prove something!" she wails. Takó, sympathetic but not knowing how to react, tells her that his father, a doctor, had saved Jews in the hospital where he worked. Then he tries to kiss her, but she runs away from him. "Don't try to be nice! I don't want to be pitied!" she cries.

In the words of these two female characters, Eva and Anni, Szabó presents a dramatic version of the Jewish dilemma about identity—the "Jewish question" for Jews expressed in its personal, individual form. Another female character, Klári in *Lovefilm*, provides the most graphic account of Jewish persecution during the war when she tells the story of how she escaped after being shot into the Danube in December 1944 (the bullets didn't reach her). Unlike Eva and Anni, who were children at the time and have grown up with the burden of the "Jewish question," Klári was a young woman who could make choices, and after she survived the shooting she chose to leave Hungary, never to return. We are not told about her life since that traumatic event, nor do we know how she relates to Jewishness while living in France, but the fact that she tells her story composedly, without tears, suggests that she does not regret her choice to leave Hungary. Beneath her calm manner, her sense of outrage and injury is palpable, and she evidently finds a certain satisfaction in reminding her listeners—who are Hungarians, and one of whom, Jancsi, is also Jewish or "of Jewish origin"—about that history.

The male characters in these early films who have Jewish backgrounds and were children during the war are more reticent than the women about their relation to a possible Jewish identity—so much so that one can speak of repression in the Freudian sense: the suppression of painful knowledge about one's past, which then manifests itself in the form of symptoms. Joshua Hirsch has persuasively analyzed *Father* in those psychoanalytic terms, but he may be overstating the case in seeing in the film a "posttraumatic autobiography" of Szabó himself.[19] In *Father*, Takó appears to be Christian: when his father, a doctor who died in the last days of the war and was hastily buried on the grounds of the hospital where he worked, is reburied in a more solemn ceremony years later, it is in a Catholic cemetery with a priest officiating. But there are hints at various points in the film that his family was originally Jewish. Takó's mother, for example, tells the young boy when they see newsreels of Arrow Cross members being executed after the war that "they were bad people, they killed many—they even wanted to kill us and they arrested Father, but he escaped." The fact that she says "they wanted to kill us," including her and the boy, indicates that they were Jewish, or considered as such by their persecutors. The Arrow Cross hunted mainly Jews, and certainly only women and children who were Jews. The child pays no attention to that detail in the mother's statement, however; instead, he fantasizes that his father was a member of the Resistance, confronting the Arrow Cross in hand-to-hand combat!

We can surmise that Takó's mother was one of those well-meaning parents who after the war hid the details of the family history from her son. Later, when he is a young man, he asks her one day whether she and his father had ever thought of leaving Hungary. She replies that they had, but at first his father had been reluctant, and then it was too late. "Your father was such a patriot," she tells him. She leaves unsaid exactly what that means, or meant, and Takó does not ask. But more than thirty years later, Szabó returned to the figure of a Jewish convert and Hungarian "patriot" who refuses to leave until it's too late in the unforgettable character of Adam Sors, in *Sunshine*.

Meanwhile, in *Lovefilm*, the third in the early trilogy (1970), we know that the protagonist Jancsi comes from a Jewish family, or from a family defined as Jewish by the authorities, because he had to be hidden for a while during the Nazi occupation of 1944. One of the first sequences in the film is a memory flashback showing the boy walking with his mother anxiously down a street, on their way to the hospital where he is hidden until a non-Jewish neighbor (his friend Kata's mother) comes to get him. The word "Jew" is never pronounced, nor does Jancsi's mother wear the yellow star, so it is left to the viewer to figure out exactly why they are hurrying down that street and why the boy has to be hidden. We also don't know where his mother goes after she delivers him to the hospital—presumably she is hidden by Christian friends, as happened to a number of Budapest Jews, but the film is silent about it. The subject of Jancsi's Jewishness never comes up again in the film, not even in the excessively reticent way it is broached in the flashback scene. As is often the case with repressed traumatic memories, that scene is triggered by a later trauma, itself a memory flashback in relation to Jancsi's present: sitting in a train on the way to France around 1966, he remembers a moment during the 1956 uprising when he was stopped by two men who demanded to see his identity card while he was riding his bicycle down a deserted street. After they let him go, the camera follows him from the back, then suddenly switches to the backs of the boy and his mother as they walk down a similar deserted street more than a decade earlier.

That Jancsi's family origin is indicated in a flashback within a flashback shows just how deeply buried the question of Jewish identity is; one may even wonder why Szabó included that scene of the boy and his mother at all. Does Jancsi never think about what happened to him during the war, or about what it means for his sense of who he is now? Evidently not, and that may be the point. The film here replicates the repression of trauma and of the Jewish identity that provoked it, which characterized the coping strategy of Jewish Holocaust survivors who remained in Hungary after the war. As Joshua Hirsch points out, Szabó's narrative strategy in his first feature films had a powerful precedent in the works of Alain Resnais, who (in films such as *Hiroshima mon amour* and *Last Year in Marienbad,* among others) "spoke about traumatic history and memory while at the same time speaking about the very difficulty of speaking about them."[20] One can assume that Jancsi will not tell his children, if he has any, of his Jewish background— but it's also quite possible that after 1990, he, like other child survivors, will have a change of heart and mind and will decide to affirm his Jewishness, at least culturally if not by religious practice. Most Jews in Hungary who affirm their identity today are secular, and most live in Budapest.

As for Szabó himself, one skates on thin ice by calling his early films examples of filmic autobiography, whether "repressed" or not. There are many autobiographical elements in these films: the doctor father who dies at the end of the war, the parents who converted to Catholicism before their son's birth, and the age of the protagonist, which is identical to Szabó's; but given Szabó's reluctance to speak of his early childhood, in particular of what happened to him in 1944–5 (he was hidden in an orphanage for several months, he told me in my 2006 interview with him), and given especially his dislike of being called a "Jewish filmmaker" or a "Hungarian Jew" (he was brought up a Catholic, he told me, and it's essentially others who "showed" him who he was), I prefer not to analyze his films from an autobiographical perspective. His aversion to being called a "Jewish filmmaker" is due to the fact that, as he explained to me in 2017, he makes "films for everybody, not just for a restricted public." When I asked him whether a "Jewish filmmaker" is understood to make films only for Jews, he replied: "Yes, and not only in Hungary—everywhere in Europe, it means that."[21] One may wonder whether the same thing could be said of the United States, where the films of Woody Allen (until his recent exclusion over issues of sexual misconduct) are certainly not considered to be exclusively for Jews. But then, Allen is also widely known and loved in Europe.

There is no doubt that Szabó's portrayals of Jewish characters ring true to most Hungarian Jews, as well as to anyone who has studied the long history of the love-hate relationship between Jews and Hungary. As he told me in 2006:

> Hungary has a special position in central Europe. If you think of Hungarian Jewish people in Australia, in America, or wherever, they're always very happy to speak Hungarian. I ask myself what is behind this love for the Hungarian language on the part of Jewish people? We never say that we're Jewish, we say we're Hungarian! This hate-love relationship: hate because of what happened, and love because there's love.[22]

Of course it's not fully accurate to say that Hungarian Jews never say they're Jewish, but Szabó did put his finger on a particularly sore spot. The great Hungarian Jewish writer Imre Kertész, whose deportation to Auschwitz and other camps as a teenager marks all of his works, expressed similar feelings about the Hungarian language, about Hungary in general, and even about his Jewishness: he felt alienated among Jews as much as among Hungarians.[23]

Jewish Identity and Its Vicissitudes in *Sunshine*

A full three decades and an epochal change in European political history went by between Szabó's first Hungarian trilogy and his 1999 film *Sunshine*, which one admirer has called a "grand totality" about Jews in Hungary and which can less hyperbolically be called Szabó's masterwork on the subject.[24] *Sunshine* is an English-language film (shot in Hungary, as usual, and immediately dubbed into Hungarian) with English-speaking stars, most notably Ralph Fiennes, who plays three different roles as the son, grandson, and great-grandson of a Jewish patriarch. Szabó explained in an interview after the film's release in Hungary that the financing came entirely from outside the country (the producer, Robert Lantos, was a Hungarian emigré living in Toronto), and in such cases "the language is determined by the one who pays."[25] But *Sunshine* is a very Hungarian film, even if some hostile critics tarred it with the label of "Hollywood." The story was conceived by Szabó, the screenplay was cowritten by him and the American playwright Israel Horovitz, and at least one early version of the scenario I have seen is in Hungarian.[26] More importantly, this film returns to many of the themes and character types that Szabó had explored in earlier works.

In one sense, however, the critics who called it "Hollywood" were right: *Sunshine* is a big-budget film, epic in scope and ambition, sumptuous in its cinematography and mise en scène, with a glittering cast in addition to Ralph Fiennes: Rosemary Harris, Jennifer Ehle, Rachel Weisz, and William Hurt play major roles, for which several of them won prizes. While the film's critical reception was mixed in the English-speaking world (some critics found the three roles played by Fiennes too schematic and repetitive) and was downright conflicted in Hungary, where fierce debates about it waged in the press for weeks, it remains one of Szabó's best-known works to contemporary audiences on both sides of the Atlantic.[27]

Sunshine is the story of four generations of a Jewish family in Hungary, told by its last descendant, whose voiceover narration begins and ends the film and enters regularly throughout. Although the voiceovers are not emphasized and few critics commented on them, they designate the film as a personal narrative, a story told by a specific individual who is also a participant in it. Ivan Sonnenschein was not yet born when the story begins, but we are reminded by his voiceovers that this is his family's history as he sees it. (Szabó had already used some voiceover narration in his first films, but not as systematically.) Despite Ivan's mediating presence, however, the film's dominant narrative mode is that of the large-scale historical epic. Events are shown chronologically, with no flashbacks; only the occasional insertion of black and white archival footage of historical events (some of them altered by

Szabó to show his fictional characters in the crowd) interrupt the visual flow of the narrative—though not its temporal flow, for these insertions are in their chronological place, usually accompanied by Ivan's voiceover narration, which often sounds like a history lesson. This is one sign that the film is intended for viewers who may not be familiar with the facts of modern central European history—Szabó's "kowtowing" to his Anglo-Saxon audience, according to Hungarian critics who found fault with the film. But the importance of *Sunshine* lies not in its narration of history; its true subject, and the reason it caused so much discussion in the Hungarian press after its release, is the collective experience of Jews in modern Hungary.

This experience is encapsulated in the existential choices made by the film's main characters at crucial moments in their lives, which coincide with significant moments in the country's history. Szabó explores the consequences of those choices, which of course could not be known in advance by those who made them. Historical fiction, especially in film, which is constrained by the time limit, necessarily involves some simplification. Complexity and nuance are sacrificed in favor of repetitive patterning that makes the history intelligible to a large public. The question one must ask is not whether a historical film shows all the nuances and competing interpretations of historical events as analyzed by historians, but whether it succeeds in accurately depicting the lived experience of a set of individuals that the viewer comes to care about, against the background of larger historical movements that are accurately depicted overall. In this, *Sunshine*—like *Doctor Zhivago*, another large-scale historical epic that some critics faulted for simplifying history—largely succeeds, even in the opinion of professional historians.[28]

The first generation of Sonnenscheins has a relatively easy path, in terms of choices. Emmanuel Sonnenschein, while still a boy, leaves his native village (probably in northeastern Hungary or Galizia) after his father, the local tavern keeper, is killed by an explosion in his distillery, and makes his way to the capital. While no exact dates are mentioned, we are evidently in the last third of the nineteenth century, after the revolutionary flames of 1848 have died down and Hungary has entered a period of economic and cultural flowering under the Austro-Hungarian Monarchy (1867–1918). Emmanuel, a poor devout Jew, takes with him to Budapest the precious black notebook that contains his father's secret recipe for a liqueur. By the time the story begins in earnest—when Ralph Fiennes makes his appearance as Emmanuel's young adult son Ignatz—Emmanuel has become rich through his distillery, which produces the tonic he calls "A taste of sunshine." *A napfény ize*, an exact translation of that phrase, is the film's title in Hungarian; "sunshine" is also the literal meaning of Sonnenschein. Emmanuel Sonnenschein's path has been that of economic success, made possible by the opportunities opened up to Jews in Hungary after they gained full civil rights in 1867.

Historians have often described the "assimilationist contract" that linked the liberal nobility to Jewish industry and finance in the period of the Austro-Hungarian Monarchy. The liberals, inspired by the ideals of the Enlightenment as well as by Magyar patriotism, sought to modernize a backward, quasi-feudal country and to create a unified nation despite the number of minority ethnic groups scattered over its large territory. The "assimilationist contract" gave Jews, especially those living in Budapest, an opportunity to participate fully in the liberals' modernization project, and in the creation of a modern Hungarian identity and culture. While they constituted only a small minority of the population, Jews represented a large proportion of the country's businessmen and entrepreneurs, and eventually of its professional and intellectual class (lawyers, doctors, journalists, and writers). In return, as the historian András Kovács explains, "Hungarian Jews were expected to demonstrate total loyalty to the Hungarian state, to accept the political hegemony of the nobility, and to strive for complete assimilation within the Hungarian community."[29]

In fact, complete assimilation was not required, if by that one means giving up the practice of the Jewish religion and all connections to Jewishness. In the decades before the First World War, Jews could freely choose to belong to the Jewish community (there were three different denominations to choose from, ranging from strict Orthodox to what today is called Reform), and at the same time to actively participate in Hungary's economic and cultural life. Emmanuel Sonnenschein appears to have made just such a choice. He presides over a weekly Friday night dinner with his family, and his home in the middle of the city is full of beautiful furniture and objects, including Jewish ritual objects (such as silver candlesticks for Shabbat candles) lovingly lingered over by Szabó's camera. At the same time, Emmanuel (David de Keyser) often hums Hungarian folksongs, even at the Sabbath table; and at the feast after the wedding of Ignatz and his cousin Valerie (Jennifer Ehle), which takes place in the late 1890s in the great Dohány Street synagogue of Budapest, the first dance by the happy couple is a slow csárdás to the tune of one of Hungary's best-known folksongs, "Spring Wind" (*Tavaszi szél*), played by the Roma band that Emmanuel has hired for the celebration. This song becomes a musical leitmotif in the film, along with Schubert's *Fantasia in F Minor for Four Hands*, which the young lovers often play together and whose melody accompanies the family's evolution throughout the following decades. Szabó thus bows both to the high culture of Central Europe that so many Jews on the road to assimilation adopted as their own, and to Hungary's folk traditions, which many Jews also identified with.

Emmanuel's sons, Ignatz and his younger brother Gustave (James Frain), face more complicated choices than their father. Both become educated professionals, Ignatz a jurist and Gustave a doctor. This too is part of Emmanuel's success and a source of pride: his sons do not follow him into business but rise even higher. Ignatz is appointed as a district court judge and is soon known to his superiors for his integrity and his unfailing dedication to the Empire. In this, as well as in his personal loyalty to the Emperor Franz Joseph, he resembles Szabó's Colonel Redl, but in a higher echelon: he does not need to learn table manners. Soon he is summoned by his superior, the Minister of Justice, who offers him a promotion as a judge of the Central Court. The only problem, he tells Ignatz, is that a Central Court judge cannot have a name like Sonnenschein: "Please choose a more Magyar-sounding name. This is not an order, merely a piece of advice. In the end, the choice is up to you." Here then is the first of the younger Sonnenscheins' life-changing choices. Ignatz consults his cousin and lover Valerie, who is also like a sister to him since they were brought up together, and then discusses the question with the whole family around the dining table. "Does this mean you want to abandon the faith?" his father asks him. Ignatz protests: "No, I swear, I would never."

Magyarizing one's name in the period before the First World War did not have the same anxious connotation (hiding one's Jewishness for fear of persecution) that it would acquire during the 1930s and during the postwar period. Change of name was practiced not only by Jews but by other ethnic minorities in Hungary—Slovaks, Croats, and Germans—who wanted to affirm their loyalty to the nation. For Jews, who had acquired their Germanic names in the eighteenth century under the Habsburg Emperor Joseph II, Magyarizing their name was a sign of patriotism as well as of belief in the promises of assimilation. It did not necessarily imply a renunciation of Jewish self-identification or of Jewish practice, although Jews in Budapest generally practiced a Reform brand of Judaism in opposition to the Orthodox practice of most provincial Jews. By changing his name when he does, Ignatz, who is accompanied in this enterprise by his brother Gustave and by Valerie, is not giving up his Jewishness but rather affirming his Hungarianness.

The new name the Sonnenschein trio chooses, after some searching, proves to be prescient: Sors means "fate" in Hungarian as well as in Latin, Ignatz is pleased to declare. It's somewhat startling to discover, as I did only recently, that Sonnenschein was the family name of Leopold Szondi (1893–1986), a Hungarian Jewish psychoanalyst (he changed his name in 1911) who fled the Holocaust in Hungary in 1944 and gained worldwide fame that same year as the inventor of the technique of *Schicksalanalyse* ("fate analysis"). The technique is based on the Szondi Test, a psychological projective test that remained in wide use all over the world into the 1970s and is still used in some settings. The test comprises a set of forty-eight portrait photographs from the late nineteenth century, purporting to show individuals with diagnosed mental illnesses (including "homosexuality"); the patient taking the test is asked to examine each portrait and express an opinion about it. The purpose of these tests, administered over several sessions, is to recognize and confront the patient's "familial unconscious" and discover a "hidden ancestor." This allows the patient, according to the theory, to "integrate disavowed unconscious aspects . . . in becoming a true person with a destiny (*Schicksal*) that was to some extent freely chosen."[30] Szabó obviously knew about Szondi, and about "fate analysis," when he chose both the old and the new names of the Jewish family in *Sunshine* (the name Sonnenschein had already occurred in *Colonel Redl*, in the character of the Jewish Army doctor who is Redl's friend), though it is doubtful that he would adopt all of Szondi's views about family inheritance, not to mention the classifications of mental illness that Szondi—like other psychiatrists of his time—subscribed to.[31]

The fate that Ignatz, Valerie, and Gustave choose—or more exactly, hope for—by changing their name is that of a "happy" assimilation as Jews in Hungary, a fact that Szabó emphasizes by their delighted laughter as they run down the stairs after leaving the registry where they signed their new names for the first time. Soon after this, at Ignatz and Valerie's wedding, the Cantor's Hebrew chanting in the synagogue, followed by the Hungarian folksong at the wedding feast, seems to confirm that hope. (Szabó asked an actual rabbi to perform the wedding ceremony in the synagogue, and by a nice coincidence it was none other than Tamás Raj, who had told me the anecdote with which I started this chapter.)

But cracks in the assimilationist mirror in which the young people see themselves begin to show quite quickly. Soon after his wedding, Ignatz, now a Central Court judge, obliges the Minister of Justice by finding a legal way to delay a corruption trial that would have benefited the Minister's political enemies. We recognize here the political intrigues of the declining Habsburg Empire that Szabó had already explored in *Colonel Redl*, but this time with a twist that is reminiscent of *Mephisto*, since Ignatz is accused by his wife and his brother of collaborating with a corrupt regime. Just as Höfgen's lover Juliette, in *Mephisto*, confronts him when he first accepts to become a spokesman for the Nazis, Valerie confronts her husband in their first big quarrel: "Ignatz, you are selling your soul. Who are you trying to please?" He responds angrily: he must try to please everyone, starting with Valerie and her "lovely Hungarian heart," as well as the Emperor, the Minister, his brother Gustave, who wants to turn the world upside down (Gustave, whose work as a doctor brings him in daily contact with the suffering poor, is a Socialist and a strong critic of the Empire), as well as his father, who wants to keep the world exactly as it is! The viewer is invited to sympathize with Ignatz—the Empire, after all, was not Nazi Germany and did offer great opportunities for advancement to men of talent, including many Jews, but Szabó also shows that Ignatz allows himself to be used by those in power, who make his advancement possible and who are counting on his gratitude.

This is of course true of many ambitious individuals making their way in a hierarchy: compromises may be asked of them that will confront them with difficult moral choices. Szabó, however, makes it a point to frame the issue specifically as it affects Jews. When the Socialist Gustave attacks the Empire as hopelessly corrupt and accuses his brother of collaboration, Ignatz screams at him that he should be grateful to a regime that has allowed a "Jew like him" to become a doctor. "I believe in my right to assimilate to the country I love," he proclaims. Gustave, in turn, accuses Ignatz of blindness: Can't he see that he will never be accepted by the powerful and will always be treated with suspicion? Only the workers and the exploited are true allies of the Jews, he says. Popular antisemitism in Hungary was quite rampant, so Gustave is exhibiting a certain ideological blindness of his own in saying this (Figure 12).

Valerie, who is present at their confrontation, accuses them of behaving like "rabbis fighting over the Torah." As for herself, she rejects both of their arguments: she wants simply to be "like a wildflower, growing exactly where it belongs." She feels at home in her country, which she loves, and that's enough for her, she says. Szabó clearly considers Valerie as an important figure. She is the only member of that generation who is present until almost the very end of the film (Jennifer Ehle is replaced about halfway through by Rosemary Harris), and she is also the only member of the family who chooses an artistic vocation: she becomes a photographer. Although we are told by the voiceover narrator that she has a successful career between the two world wars, we only

Figure 12 Sunshine, *1999. Alliance Atlantis, Serendipity Point Films, Kinowelt, Robert Lantos Production, Bavarian Film, Telefilm Canada, ORF.*

ever see her taking photographs of the family, not professionally. Still, she functions as a mouthpiece for what might be called the aesthetic view of life: even as an old woman, having undergone much suffering, she affirms that the search for what is beautiful endows life with value. According to some critics (including my own earlier analysis), Valerie constitutes the moral center of the film and comes closest to Szabó's own position.[32]

It is also true, however, that Szabó's treatment of the female characters in this film, including Valerie, is somewhat marginal in relation to his main theme. Women play important roles as wives or lovers (and provide great opportunities for the female leads, including not only Ehle and Harris but Rachel Weisz and Deborah Kara Unger); and Valerie, in addition to her artistic vocation, displays a strong ethical sense, as her argument with Ignatz about his kowtowing to the powers that be indicates. But the female characters as portrayed by Szabó are curiously uninvolved with the major subject of this film—which may in fact be the point. They don't compromise themselves morally or ideologically because they remain in the private realm of the family or else in the aesthetic realm, refusing to engage in politics. In an interview with a Hungarian woman journalist after the film's release, Szabó stated: "Women stand with two feet on the ground. . . . They are much closer to nature, to every part of nature, including blood, than men. . . . For that very reason, they are less likely to fall prey to the attractions of ideologies and of history, they are more able to safeguard their identity than men."[33] This is clearly meant as a compliment but can also be seen as a sexist stereotype. The statement relegates women to a realm outside the public sphere in which the men in the family function and which demands ideological and historical choices on their part. The choices of the female characters involve only the men in their lives. Valerie takes the lead in her love affair with Ignatz and later leaves him for another man before returning to him when he is most vulnerable. The women in the next two generations are similarly assertive in love but lack Valerie's generosity. A wildflower, to take up Valerie's metaphor for her sense of herself, does not face any choice at all—it simply is. While Szabó proclaims his admiration for women's "naturalness," what really interests him in this film is the question of existential choices defined in ideological and historical terms, and it is the men who make them.

The two brothers are emblematic figures, representing typical but starkly opposing choices that assimilated Jews in Hungary made at the turn of the twentieth century. The loyalist Ignatz, like many Jewish businessmen and professionals at the time, remains committed to the values of liberal tolerance that he sees embodied in the Empire, even after its fall; the rebellious Gustave, like many middle-class Jewish intellectuals at the time (including the philosopher György Lukács and the sociologist Karl Mannheim), is critical of the Imperial regime and participates in the short-lived communist government led by Béla Kun that followed the defeat of 1919. (Kun was also from a Jewish family.) Szabó's portrayal of Gustave is somewhat cursory, although the character comes across as an attractive and passionate young man and a defender of the working class; he is also quite rigid, joining the Kun government as health minister and endorsing its brutal tactics as "necessary." After the collapse of the Kun regime, which was hated by many Hungarians, its participants were forced into exile, and Gustave disappears from the film for three decades. He spends those years in Paris, but the film tells us nothing about him during his exile, including any persecution he may have experienced in Nazi-occupied France.

Ignatz is given a more detailed treatment, and although some critics faulted Szabó for drawing him superficially as well, I find Fiennes's portrayal of this character both convincing and sympathetic. Valerie accuses him, after he returns home from several years of service as a military judge in the First World War, of being a man without feelings whom she can no longer love, but Ignatz as played by Fiennes is, rather, a man whose feelings are constantly held in check by conflicting obligations. As he tells Valerie in their big quarrel soon after their marriage, he feels he must please too many people at once; the result is that he disappoints many of them. He disappoints his father and causes his mother hysterics but pleases Valerie when he insists on marrying her, despite his parents' wishes; he disappoints his patron the Minister of Justice but pleases his family when he refuses to run for Parliament in a safe seat the Minister offers him; he disappoints his brother when he refuses to serve as a judge in the Kun regime (whereupon the regime puts him under house arrest) and disappoints the Horthy government that follows, when he refuses to hand out punitive sentences to former communists who remained in the country— whereupon he is forced into early retirement and dies not long after, a broken man.

Above all, Ignatz disappoints himself. In a brief but telling scene that takes place on the Balkan front during the war, he attends a service in the local synagogue after learning of his father's death back in Budapest. After the service, one of the other worshipers, who has recognized him as an officer despite his civilian clothes, runs after him and identifies himself as the Town Clerk. "Is the Major Jewish?" he asks. Ignatz doesn't answer (the answer is obvious, since he was just in the synagogue) but asks him what he wants. "Several officers are being court-martialed this week, and I thought the Major would like to know that one of them is Jewish," the man replies. "I am an officer of the Emperor," Ignatz tells him stiffly and walks away as the man looks after him, his face falling. Once he reaches his room, Ignatz looks at himself in the mirror and spits at his image.

Is he spitting at himself for having betrayed his father's memory by refusing to identify himself as Jewish, since his father was a devout Jew? Or for having behaved rudely to a man who meant well, despite his illegitimate request? Or does he regret having gone to the synagogue in the first place? We cannot know, but we understand that Ignatz is a conflicted man, and his internal conflicts invade even his most intimate relations. After the war is over and he returns home, Valerie informs him that she is leaving him because she cannot "live without love." His response is to keep repeating "But I do love you!" as he grabs her and rapes her. Afterward, he starts to cry and begs her forgiveness. (Valerie does leave, but returns when she learns that he is under house arrest.)

If Ignatz's fate has elements of both grandeur and tragedy—he is a man destroyed by his rigid loyalty to a flawed regime that he idealizes, but whose proclaimed values of liberal tolerance are admirable—the fate of his son Adam is tragic without grandeur. Adam (played by Fiennes) and his older brother István (Mark Strong) come of age in the 1920s, at a time when virulent nationalism and antisemitism were rampant in Hungary. One reason for this was the country's humiliating defeat in the First World War, which resulted in Hungary losing two-thirds of its territory; another reason was the backlash against the Commune of 1919, led by Béla Kun, which became identified in the popular imagination with Jews because of the large number of assimilated

Jewish intellectuals (like Gustave in the film) who had participated in it. Bullied and attacked by his own schoolmates as a Jew who doesn't belong to "the nation," Adam takes up fencing and becomes a champion saber fencer, eventually winning a gold medal for Hungary in the 1936 Olympics. In the process, he also becomes a rigid Hungarian patriot who is unable to see what is clear to others: Hungary is no longer a country where a Jew can feel at home. After his first training as a fencer in the Jewish fencing club, Adam is told that in order to be a national champion he must gain admittance to the Officers' club, which has the best fencers. But Jews cannot be members of that club, so Adam converts to Catholicism without hesitation, along with his brother and his brother's fiancée; he marries another Jewish convert he meets in the catechism class on the way to conversion.

Szabó's (and Fiennes's) portrayal of Adam is somewhat heavy-handed, since he is not shown as having any conflicts over his choices. Indeed, once he becomes a Catholic, he starts to disparage Jews for caring only about money, like the character in a well-known Jewish joke.[34] When the head of the Jewish fencing club begs him to remain with them instead of joining the Officers' club and offers him large sums of money in exchange, Adam rebuffs him and then remarks scornfully to his sister-in-law: "These Jews, they think they can buy anybody." After his Olympic victory in Berlin, he is approached by the Hungarian-American representative of a Jewish fencing club in New York, who offers him a position and urges him to emigrate, given the dire situation of Jews in Europe; this scene takes place after Szabó's camera has lingered over the Nazi dignitaries and the swastikas plastered all over the Olympic Stadium, which Adam's trainer at the Officer's club (a non-Jewish aristocrat) notices with some anxiety. Adam, however, has seen nothing at the Olympics but his and his team's victory. He categorically rejects the American's offer: "Hungary is my homeland. I will never leave it," he asserts angrily, provoking the other man to reply: "You're blind. Leave the country before it's too late" (Figure 13).

This scene echoes not only Adam's earlier encounter with the head of the Jewish fencing club in Budapest but also the scene where his father Ignatz rebuffs the Jewish town clerk with "I'm an officer of the Emperor." Adam's rigid loyalty to his antisemitic "homeland" appears a great deal more problematic than his father's loyalty to the Empire, however. When he returns to Budapest

Figure 13 Sunshine, *1999. Alliance Atlantis, Serendipity Point Films, Kinowelt, Robert Lantos Production, Bavarian Film, Telefilm Canada, ORF. Copyright ISL Film Kft, Kinowelt Filmproduktion GmbH, Screenventures XXIX Productions Ltd. and DOR Film.*

with his triumphant teammates, where a cheering crowd awaits them and he is the center of everyone's attention, he makes a speech whose unintended irony is all too obvious: "We fought for our magnificent Motherland, which will live forever!" Even his loving wife tells him afterward, with a slight tinge of mockery, that sometimes his Hungarian patriotism is "a bit much."

Two years later, after the first anti-Jewish law—which deprived most Jews in Hungary of civil rights—is passed by the Hungarian Parliament, Adam is thrown out of the Officers' club by one of his Olympic teammates, an avowed antisemite, who has become the club's chief. When Adam protests that as an Olympic champion he and his family are exempt from the law's exclusions and that all he wants to do is fence, his presumed comrade—who has been openly hostile to him from the start—tells him: "Fine. But you won't fence with us." Then, turning the knife in the wound, he adds: "You'd never have been awarded your gold medal but for the fact that two of the judges were Jews." Despite this blatant rejection and the government's outright persecution, however, Adam persists in declaring that "it's all temporary." This makes even his usually passive brother remonstrate with him: "For God's sake, Adam, open your eyes. Don't delude yourself. You're afraid to see what they are and you're afraid they'll see what you are." This pretty much sums up the extreme lack of introspection that is Adam's dominant trait. Unlike his father, who manifested at least a glimmer of inner conflict over his rigid loyalty to the Empire, Adam clings to his blindness as if it were clear sight.

This leads to the most dramatic scene in the film, which takes place during the Second World War, when Adam and his teenage son are prisoners in a Hungarian forced labor camp. The exact year is not specified, but forced labor service for Jewish men started in 1941, when Hungary was already engaged in the war on the side of the Axis powers, and continued through 1944, after the Nazis occupied Hungary and began the systematic deportation of Jews. The forced labor camps allowed Jewish men who survived them to escape deportation, but the treatment of prisoners by Hungarian gendarmes ranged from harsh to homicidal. Adam falls victim to a sadistic guard who singles him out because he is wearing a uniform jacket from the Officers' club (he is technically entitled to it as an Olympic champion) as well as a white armband which designates him as a convert. "Who are you, Jew?" the guard asks him. "Adam Sors, an officer in the Hungarian army and Olympic gold-medal winner," Adam replies. The guard has him stripped naked and savagely beaten, and asks the same question again and again, but even as he faints from the increasing torture, Adam continues to repeat that he is Adam Sors, Olympic champion. (The fate of Adam is modeled on that of the Hungarian fencing champion Attila Petschauer, a Jewish convert to Catholicism who was beaten to death in a forced labor camp.[35]) The guard then has him strung up on a tree and doused with cold water; he gradually turns into an ice statue, refusing onto death to call himself a Jew. Meanwhile, his son (our narrator, Ivan) and the other prisoners stand by, helpless.

Ágnes Heller, who devoted two separate articles to this film, noted that Adam is not so much a Jewish martyr as a martyr of assimilation, since he is willing to die for his belief that he is not a Jew but a full-fledged Hungarian. In Heller's opinion, Adam is the very embodiment of the parvenu who denies his origins as he seeks entry into a society that rejects him, but he attains tragic status by his stubborn clinging to the lie about his life, which becomes a form of resistance to the violence inflicted on him.[36] More is involved here, however, than simply self-deception. Adam believes, without ever actually formulating that belief but clearly acting on it, that he can choose himself— or, to use a more recently trendy term, to fashion himself—as a certain kind of human being: a Catholic, a Hungarian patriot, and a fencing champion. Heller considers this belief a delusion, given the history of Jew hatred that has persisted in Europe for 2,000 years. That assimilation is a delusion is one of the arguments she advanced in her book on the "insolubility" of the "Jewish question."[37] But she also recognized, as did Sartre in his reflections on identity, that in a free society one should be able to choose to be or not to be Jewish—or Catholic or any other religion. What makes Adam's fate tragic is that he lives in a time and a place where Jewishness is not a choice but a fate imposed on individuals through violence, by a murderous regime. Admittedly, we may feel contempt for a man who denies his origins, especially if he started out life in a stigmatized group, but do we have the right to judge him in an absolute way? However we answer that question (I say No), one thing is certain: we do not have the right to force him into accepting, let alone affirming, a religious identity that he refuses. Any regime that arrogates that right to itself is by definition a dictatorship or an Inquisition.

In Szabó's film, the most elusive relation to Jewishness and identity, as well as the most challenging one to convey in a historical context, is that of Adam's son Ivan. The son of two Jewish converts to Catholicism, Ivan apparently grows up with no religious identification (we never see any member of his family going to church after their conversion), but he is labeled a Jew in forced labor while still a teenager and is made to watch the brutal murder of his father for affirming that he is Hungarian. At the end of the war, he returns to the family apartment, now threadbare, to find the two other survivors of the family: his grandmother Valerie, who survived the Budapest ghetto, and his uncle Gustave, who has been called back to Hungary by the Communist Party. Gustave's return, along with that of the faithful family servant Kató (played by the iconic Hungarian actress Mari Töröcsik), who managed to hide some of the family's furnishings in her village during the war, allows Szabó to circle back to the family's happier days under the Monarchy. "Wasn't it wonderful to grow up in this house, Gustave!" Valerie exclaims. Gustave, in turn, reminds her that he had always been in love with her. They play

Schubert together on the piano, just as she and Ignatz had done when they were young.

Ivan, however, has no such anchor of identity. He is a very young man whose crucial experience in life until now has been one of helplessness. When Gustave, ever the activist, asks him what he and the others did while his father was being tortured ("How could thirteen guards hold back two thousand people?"), Ivan responds, sobbing: "Nothing. They were armed. I could do nothing." Gustave then advises him to join the police and hunt down his father's killers. We are now around 1946 or 1947, during the few years after the war when Hungary had a fledgling democratic regime, with competing political parties; many former collaborators and war criminals were being tried and executed, including the leader of the infamous Arrow Cross, Ferenc Szálasi (executed on March 12, 1946). This was also the time when many Jews in Budapest, grateful to the Soviet Army for having liberated them, joined the Communist Party. Some also joined the special police force charged with rooting out war criminals, which later became the feared and loathed secret police, AVO.[38] The officer who interviews Ivan as a police candidate, Andor Knorr (played memorably by William Hurt), tells him after hearing about his father: "You've come to the right place. We're going to get every one of those fascist bastards." Knorr, we eventually learn, is a survivor of Auschwitz who grew up in a Jewish orphanage and joined the Socialist Party while still a teenager. For good measure, Szabó also has him recall that he was arrested by the Arrow Cross and shot into the Danube in October 1944—a startling historical error, for deportations to Auschwitz occurred in the spring of 1944 and the Arrow Cross came to power that fall, but Auschwitz survivors did not return to Budapest until well after its liberation by the Soviet Army in January 1945.

Szabó puts into Knorr's mouth a condemnation of Hungary's collaboration with the Nazis that did not fail to offend some of *Sunshine*'s Hungarian viewers: "They [the war criminals] can't fob it off on the Germans. It [the deportations] was organized and carried out by Hungarians. Nice, ordinary Hungarian people did the dirty work. And who came up with the anti-Jewish laws in the first place? Parliament." Knorr is correct, and Szabó's inclusion of those words in the dialogue was a quasi-polemical act, for Hungary has still not officially recognized, let alone apologized for, the Hungarian government's role in the persecution of Jews during the war. After the film's release in Toronto, some members of a Hungarian-American group (now defunct), the Hungarian Lobby, wanted to organize a boycott in protest, and one particularly outraged viewer called the film a "clumsy, biased and openly anti-Hungarian work" that served the interests of "immoral, nation-destroying, foreign" elements.[39] More significantly, as far as denial of responsibility is concerned, in July 2014 the Orbán government created a sculpted memorial in the middle of Budapest, which shows Hungary as a female victim of the German eagle. This whitewashing of Hungary's collaboration with the Nazis prompted a huge outcry by historians and liberal groups and received wide coverage in the international press.[40] Almost immediately, a makeshift but very powerful counter-memorial went up in front of the official one, consisting of a long row of suitcases and placards showing the names of Jewish victims of deportation.

The dialogue between Ivan and Knorr when they first meet points to the challenges that Szabó faced in recounting Ivan's story. How could a large-scale narrative film meant for an international audience even begin to portray, in less than an hour of film time, the complexities of Hungary's political history in the post–Second World War period, let alone the choices that confronted Jews in Hungary during that time? Ivan's choice to join the police in 1946 out of a desire to avenge his father's murder makes sense and is emphasized in the dialogue with Knorr. But it's less easy to explain Ivan's evolution after the Communist Party takeover a couple of years later, when the dictatorial regime of Mátyás Rákosi began (Rákosi was from an assimilated Jewish family), not to mention Ivan's choices after Rákosi was deposed in 1953. These were the years that saw attempted reforms, then the 1956 uprising and its failure, followed by the repressive early years of the Kádár regime and the eventual "thaw" of the 1960s.

Szabó's solution was to focus on a few key moments and to emphasize the repetitive nature of some of Ivan's choices when compared to those of his father and grandfather. Like his grandfather Ignatz, who staunchly defended the Empire and was rewarded by it, Ivan becomes for a time a loyalist of the Rákosi regime (at least outwardly, for we never see him discussing, let alone defending the regime in private) and receives numerous decorations as a police officer.

Again like his grandfather, he becomes the protégé of a highly placed official in the regime, the "Comrade General" who expects him to do his bidding. In one gorgeously filmed scene of the kind Szabó excels at, showing a huge crowd in a gala at the Opera House, we see Ivan mount the podium, dressed in his uniform with its row of medals, in front of a giant portrait of Stalin. Delivering birthday greetings to the Soviet dictator, he shouts his prepared lines: "We must find all fascist comrades and destroy them. Comrade Stalin has shown us the way!" (Figure 14).

Whereas Ignatz actually believed in the beneficence of the Empire and could defend his belief in arguments with his brother, Ivan's loyalty to the Rákosi regime seems to depend exclusively on the promise of hunting down his father's murderers. By the early 1950s, however, when the Opera House scene takes place, the hunt for fascists had been replaced by the hunt for internal enemies of the regime. This process had already begun with the show trial and execution of László Rajk, a highly ranked member of the Party who was accused along with several others of being a "Titoist spy" and executed in September 1949. (Rajk is often identified as Jewish, but actually he came from a Seventh-Day Adventist family; some of his codefendants were Jews, however,

Figure 14 *Sunshine, 1999. Alliance Atlantis, Serendipity Point Films, Kinowelt, Robert Lantos Production, Bavarian Film, Telefilm Canada, ORF. Copyright ISL Film Kft, Kinowelt Filmproduktion GmbH, Screenventures XXIX Productions Ltd. and DOR Film.*

and were questioned about being Zionists.[41]) A viewer not versed in postwar Central European history is left uninformed about these developments, however, and even the historical voiceover narration that accompanied earlier segments is absent during the sequences that take place during these years. We therefore have no guidance either to Ivan's inner feelings and thoughts or to the larger historical context. Instead, Szabó relies on repetitive patterning to advance the story.

This is most evident in a key sequence involving Andor Knorr, which becomes a turning point in Ivan's evolution. The sequence begins when his "protector," the Comrade General, summons Ivan to his office and informs him that "we've discovered a monstrous conspiracy backed by Israel," a Zionist plot to overthrow the Socialist state. The leader of the conspiracy, he informs Ivan, is none other than Andor Knorr. At Ivan's incredulous response, the Comrade General tells him that "we have films of Knorr speaking to Israeli agents." Earlier, Szabó had devoted a lengthy scene to Ivan's interrogation of a filmmaker who had made fake documentaries about Russian atrocities on the Eastern front for the Horthy regime, so we can surmise that the films about Knorr's betrayal are also fakes. (The contemptible filmmaker, played by the Hungarian actor Péter Halász, returns in several later scenes as well; he is obviously of some importance to Szabó, who told me in 2017 that he had thought of devoting a whole film to that character.[42]) Then, as if to reveal the real intent behind the accusation, the Comrade General embarks on a long rant against the Zionist conspirators, "these Jewish gentlemen" who, unlike himself and other communists from the working class, "have never held a hammer. They say there are antisemites in this country, but whose fault is that? The Jews have all the jobs. More came back from the camps than those who went there!" Ivan's job is to "drag these bastards in and indict every one of them. Keep Jews off your team," the Comrade General instructs him.

Once again, Szabó is making (perhaps too heavy-handedly, for the Comrade General's rant is unusually blunt) a historically accurate point, or even two of them: popular antisemitism persisted in Hungary after the war, and soon Hungary and other communist regimes, which had been friendly to the new state of Israel, turned against it and started purging highly placed Jews from their ranks on charges of "Zionist conspiracy."[43] The trial and execution of Rudolf Slansky and several other Jewish Communist Party members in Czechoslovakia in 1952 is the best known of these antisemitic show trials. In Hungary, the much-feared head of the AVO itself, Gábor Péter, who was from a Jewish family, fell victim to a similar purge in early 1953, though he was never executed and was released six years later.[44]

One can wonder why Szabó has the Comrade General assign the task of finding "Zionist agents" to a young man whose father, as he well knows, was murdered in a Jewish forced labor camp. Is this quasi-sadistic gesture a loyalty test? In one version of the scenario that didn't make it into the film itself, when the Comrade General tells Ivan to keep Jews off his team, Ivan responds: "I can't be sure of who is Jewish." To which his boss replies, in a line straight out of Sartre's *Antisemite and Jew*: "A Jew is whoever others consider a Jew." And then he adds, as a thinly veiled threat: "You are not considered as one, for the moment."[45] The implication is not only that Ivan's status (Jew or not Jew?) could change, independently of any choice on his part, but also that his performance in carrying out the assignment will be decisive. While this bit of dialogue did not make it into the actual film, Ivan's response in the film is clear enough: he stumbles out of the Comrade General's office to the nearest toilet, where he vomits. We cannot be sure of exactly what provokes his revulsion. Is it the prospect of having to interrogate a man he admires, and whose integrity he believes in? Or is it the antisemitic rant he has just witnessed and that seems to have been addressed specifically to him? What exactly is his relation to Jewishness?

Szabó devotes a full ten minutes of screen time to the "Zionist conspiracy" episode, out of a total of around sixty minutes in Ivan's segment of the film. Ivan interrogates Knorr (now a prisoner) twice, in extended scenes. During their first encounter, he follows the script he has been given: "When did you meet with Zionist agents to plot the overthrow of the Socialist state?" Knorr scoffs at the question: he has never met any Zionist agents. Has he heard of Zionism? Ivan asks. Yes, of course, Knorr replies. One of his friends in the orphanage went to Palestine before the war, but he stayed in Hungary and joined the Young Socialists instead. Then he was deported to Auschwitz. "Were there any Zionists in Auschwitz?" Ivan asks. In answer to the absurd question, Knorr can only look at him pityingly. Ivan then bursts out: "Why do

Jews have to get involved in everything? Wasn't Auschwitz enough for you?" Knorr's response could almost be a quote from the work of Imre Kertész, who in addition to his novel *Fatelessness* devoted several essays to the question of the Holocaust's meaning for European culture. In Kertész's view, the Holocaust was not just a Jewish tragedy but a European one. As he writes in one major text, "Auschwitz was European man's greatest trauma since the cross."[46] His Christian allusion was no doubt part provocation, part confirmation of his point. For a survivor like himself, Kertész insisted, Auschwitz was a permanent presence. "Whatever I think about, I'm still thinking about Auschwitz. Even if apparently I'm speaking about something else, even then I'm speaking about Auschwitz."[47] Szabó has Knorr say to his young interrogator: "Even you will never be free of Auschwitz. Auschwitz was our baptism. Auschwitz doesn't make a better or worse man out of you. It gets burned into your brain." In their second meeting, Knorr asks him: "Who benefits from this? Or have we just gone back to antisemitism as a solution?"

Ivan does not respond to Knorr, but from that point on, his relation to his patron the Comrade General deteriorates fast. "How the suffering of Jews seems to touch you," the latter tells him caustically, when he expresses doubt about Knorr's guilt and mentions that he survived Auschwitz. Later, after Ivan reports (knowing he will provoke fury) that in his opinion Knorr is innocent, the Comrade General bursts in on him while he is taking a shower and berates him, in a scene that bears a disturbing resemblance to his father Adam's torture: like Adam in the forced labor camp, Ivan stands stark naked, dripping with water, in front of a short man in uniform who screams insults at him; and also like Adam, Ivan defies his tormentor and sticks to his ground. The Comrade General replaces him with another interrogator, who will have no compunctions about trying to beat Knorr into a confession. Knorr will die under torture.

Clearly, Szabó intends the "Zionist conspiracy" episode to be a turning point in Ivan's evolution and also to provide the motivation for his later choices. The episode becomes a hinge for Hungarian history as well, for right after the shower scene Ivan's voiceover narration resumes. He explains that after Stalin died in 1953, power relations in Hungary shifted as well: the Comrade General was arrested and Knorr was posthumously rehabilitated and given a new burial, at which Ivan was asked by Knorr's family to give the eulogy. His speech by the graveside is at once a confession, an indictment of the Stalinist regime, and the record of a conversion: "Andor Knorr, one of your murderers has come to say goodbye to you," Ivan begins. "We believed we were going to make the world a better place for people, but ended up making it much worse." And then: "I'm saying goodbye to you but also to myself. I watched while my father was killed, and did nothing. And then I watched them do the same to you. I make a promise to you, to do everything in my power to punish those who have turned ideals into crimes."

As we might expect, this speech does not go over well with his new boss at the security police, even in the more reformist times after Stalin's death. Ivan tells us in voiceover that he resigned from the police right after Knorr's funeral and started exploring the regime's crimes, in order to try and overcome his "crippling guilt." Soon it's the 1956 uprising, and we see Ivan in a crowd of protesters where someone reads verses from the great Hungarian revolutionary poet Sándor Petőfi. Ivan climbs up on a pedestal near the Petőfi monument and gives a spontaneous speech ("Communism is crumbling. We must have no fear!") and then leads the crowd in attacking a Soviet tank. He is arrested and jailed for several years, emerging from prison just around the time, in the early 1960s, when the Kádár regime started allowing greater individual freedom to citizens as long as they did not try to intervene in politics.

If all this seems a bit much to squeeze into a short amount of screen time (the multiyear events I summarized in the preceding paragraph take up only nine minutes), that is part of the aforementioned narrative challenge in this segment of the film. Moreover, instead of merely facing choices similar to those faced by his father and grandfather —chief among them being whether, or for how long, to collaborate with a repressive regime—Ivan is slated to be the one who eventually breaks out of the repetitive pattern of accommodation and failure. His story is meant to end on a positive note. Szabó therefore had to find a way to motivate Ivan's choices so that they appear believable to the viewer. While Ivan's sudden turning against the totalitarian regime that he has served for several years may appear somewhat contrived, as does his heroic leading of the crowd in the attack on the tank, Szabó seeks to provide adequate motivation for them by the detailed account of the

Zionist conspiracy episode, which unfolds over just a few weeks or months in historical time but occupies around the same amount of screen time as the whole decade that followed it.

Ivan's pattern-breaking choice consists in abandoning the name his grandparents and great-uncle had chosen two generations earlier and taking back the family's Germanic name: Sonnenschein. This action—whose shock effect is indicated by the astonished response of the woman in the government office who registers the new name—is itself motivated by a previous sequence in which Ivan's grandmother Valerie, who has been his unfailing source of comfort and practical wisdom, suffers a stroke; when she is asked her name at the hospital, she replies that she is Valerie Sonnenschein and resists Ivan's attempt to correct her, repeating her original name. After she dies, he wakes up one night from a nightmare, having dreamt that he has no face. His response to this dream is to start over from scratch: he throws out the family's old furniture and its entire archive of papers and objects, including the famous recipe book for the "taste of sunshine" tonic that he and Valerie had searched for in vain just weeks earlier—it falls to the ground, unnoticed by him, as he empties a box of documents. Also thrown out are piles and piles of daily newspapers whose front pages evoke Hungary's painful twentieth-century history.

In the end, only the grand piano and a table and chairs are left in the freshly scrubbed apartment. But Ivan does manage to find and keep at least one small part of the archive: a letter written by his great-grandfather Emmanuel to his son Ignatz when the latter was about to embark on his career as a judge. "Never allow yourself to be driven into the sin of conceit," Emmanuel wrote to his son. "Trust no one, examine all things for yourself. If life becomes a struggle for acceptance, you will always be unhappy. Never give up your religion, it is a solid boat that can stay balanced and carry you to the other shore," and so on. These words of wisdom, which are accompanied by a close-up of Emmanuel Sonnenschein, are further reinforced, in what I think is an excess of redundancy, by close-ups of Ivan's father and grandfather (who have the familiar face of Ralph Fiennes), who read various portions of the letter. If we were so inclined, we could see in this little sequence a confirmation of Peter Szondi's *Schicksalanalyse*, with Ivan discovering his "hidden ancestor" in the figure of his great-grandfather (Figure 15).

Figure 15 Sunshine, *1999. Alliance Atlantis, Serendipity Point Films, Kinowelt, Robert Lantos Production, Bavarian Film, Telefilm Canada, ORF. Copyright ISL Film Kft, Kinowelt Filmproduktion GmbH, Screenventures XXIX Productions Ltd. and DOR Film.*

The next scene shows him at the office for changes of name, after which he walks with a lighthearted step down a crowded pedestrian street—but suddenly we find ourselves in post-communist Budapest, more than two decades later, and Ivan's final voiceover informs us: "By the time I finished this story, the third tragic misadventure of our century was over. After the Monarchy and the fascist years, the communist regime also went up in smoke." He informs us that by taking back the family's old name, he found the solution to his identity crisis: after leaving the government office, "For the first time in my life, I walked down the street without feeling like I was in hiding. I knew that the only way to find meaning in my life, my only chance in life, would be to account for it." Following the tried and true Proustian model, the film we have just seen is Ivan's accounting, proof of his accomplishment as the author of his family story. Curiously, the young Ivan of the 1960s is shown walking down a pedestrian street in Budapest that was created much later, potentially causing some confusion about when this last scene takes place. But walking behind him in the crowd, unnoticed unless you look for him, is István Szabó himself, a man in his sixties, the actual author of this film.

It was Ivan's change of name that caused the controversy among Hungarian intellectuals (though not among the public, for the film was a huge commercial success in Budapest) when the film was released in the dubbed Hungarian version. The negative critiques, in addition to taking potshots at Szabó for having made a "Hollywood-style" film, focused on what they took to be the film's "message": Jewish assimilation in Hungary is, and has always been, a failure; the only solution for Jews is to do as Ivan does in the film, take back their Jewish names, and with it, their Jewish identity. But this message is dangerous, these critics argued, because it sets Jews apart and plays into the hands of antisemites, who have always considered Jews as "different."[48] Those who defended the film interpreted Ivan's gesture differently: Ivan does not, in fact, proclaim a Jewish identity for himself at the end, they said. What he proclaims is his desire to "breathe freely," without having to conform to others' expectations of him. The true subject of the film, according to this view, was not Jewish assimilation and its problems but the modern search for identity, for in modern times individuals are constantly confronted with existential choices. The Jews simply provide the sharpest version of this search, so in that regard, "We are all Jews," wrote one critic who identified himself as a non-Jew but who still felt that the film told his story.[49] Szabó himself expressed a similar interpretation in interviews. According to him, Ivan's taking back the Sonnenschein name was not a sign of a newly proclaimed Jewish identity but a sign of his respect and admiration for his grandmother Valerie, who had sought to find beauty in life despite the destructiveness of history.[50]

What is striking about both of these ways of interpreting the film's ending is how personally implicated the critic himself or herself felt about the film. "This is not about literary or cinematic solutions, it's about our life," wrote the journalist Anna Földes, stating that she felt "sad and puzzled" after leaving the movie theater, for according to her Szabó presents the "worst possible" solution to the search for identity: providing fodder for antisemites. Iván Vitányi, who adopted a totally different interpretive position, still agreed that the film was "about our life," since even as a non-Jew he felt the film told his story.

As for me, I was deeply moved when I saw *Sunshine* for the first time, in Paris in the summer of 2000; after multiple viewings since then, I am still moved by it. It was the film that made me want to write about Szabó, and that set me on the path toward writing this book.[51] But it is not my family's story. My father, the oldest child and only son of poor Galizian Jews, born in 1910, when that part of Poland was still part of the Habsburg Empire, grew up as a devout Orthodox Jew in Budapest and was never faced with the kinds of choices that the men of the Sonnenschein/Sors family faced. The idea of changing his name, let alone converting to Catholicism, would never have crossed his mind. And even I, his unbelieving daughter ("I've never been much of a believer," the aged Valerie says to Ivan after he is released from prison), still made sure that both my sons had their bar mitzvahs. Yet, aside from the visual beauty of Szabó's film and its gorgeous use of music, what drew me and moved me to write about it almost immediately was the family story and the collective History it tells, which appear to me (despite occasional heavy-handedness in the telling) to be authentic and compelling—and courageous too, for Szabó expressed some difficult truths about Hungarian history, truths that to this day are considered taboo by many Hungarians.

As concerns the film's ending, in my view Ivan's decision to take back his family's original name may not be a declaration of religious identification on his part, but there is no doubt that his name identifies him to most Hungarians as a person "of Jewish origin," to use the common euphemism. Szabó is not sending a "message" about Jewish identity, however. If there is any message in the film, it concerns personal freedom, or what Sartre called authenticity. In *Antisemite and Jew* (*Réflexions sur la question juive.* 1946), Sartre argued that Jews—he was thinking of French Jews he knew, most of whom had abandoned any kind of Jewish practice— should not try to hide their Jewish origins, especially since others will still consider them as Jews. Rather, they should affirm themselves, as if to say: "This is where I come from. Deal with it." This is of a piece with Sartre's views about other social outcasts, such as Jean Genet, who defiantly identified himself as a homosexual and a thief after being labeled that by others.[52] At the same time (and this is just one of the knotty interpretive problems posed by *Antisemite and Jew*), Sartre envisaged and hoped for a time, after the triumph of socialism, when antisemitism would disappear and Jews would become simply ordinary Frenchmen. They would also cease being Jews.[53]

The invocation of individual freedom and authenticity is of course a highly individualistic way of looking at things. But as Szabó so convincingly shows in his film, the flame of individual freedom, and hence of existential choice, can be extinguished quite quickly by the winds of History. In a wide-ranging interview he gave to a Hungarian journalist a few weeks before the film's release in Budapest, Szabó expressed the optimistic belief that after the suffering inflicted on Hungarians, both Jews and non-Jews, by twentieth-century ideologies, people would no longer accept a "flag-waving search for enemies" as the way to affirm the nation's rise.[54] Yet in today's Hungary, prime minister Viktor Orbán and his supporters are constantly waving the flag and searching for enemies, both inside and outside the country. Thus far, Jews have not been targeted as a group, but some Jews, notably the Hungarian-American philanthropist George Soros, are singled out for demonization.[55] Szabó's hope for a national community not built on the traditional "us versus them" dichotomy is very far from being realized, and not only in Hungary.

Notes

1 I first wrote about my meeting with Rabbi Raj in my memoir *Budapest Diary*, 185–7, from where this passage is adapted.

2 Marx's essay, which includes excerpts from Bauer's book, is in Marx, *Selected Writings*, 1–26.

3 Arendt, *The Origins of Totalitarianism*, 64.

4 Ibid., 66.

5 Hanák, ed., *Zsidókérdés asszimiláció antiszemitizmus*: [Jewish question, assimilation, antisemitism], 21.

6 Ibid., 58–9.

7 The classic work on this subject is Aschheim's *Brothers and Strangers*.

8 Quoted in Fejtő, *Hongrois et juifs*, 209–10.

9 Jankélévitch, "Le Judaisme, problème intérieur," 55–6. The preceding pages on the "Jewish question" were adapted from some of my own writings on the subject, notably in *The Némirovsky Question*, 22–7.

10 Kovács, *A Kádár rendszer és a zsidók* [The Kádár regime and the Jews], 21–2.

11 Erős, Kovács, and Lévai, "Hogyan jöttem rá, hogy zsidó vagyok" [How I found out that I'm Jewish].

12 Ibid., 134.

13 Surányi, ed., *Minarik, Sonnenschein és a többiek* (Minarik, Sonnenschein and the others). I am grateful to Louise Vasvári for bringing this book to my attention.

14 Varga, "Hiányjel" [Ellipsis], 31.

15 Surányi, *Minarik, Sonnenschein és a többiek*, 133. For a more recent survey that reaches similar conclusions, see Feigelson and Portuges, "Screen Memory: The Jewish Question."

16 Eva even escaped the attention of a much more recent critic, Tamás Halász, who presented a thorough survey (save for that omission) of "Jewish motifs" in Szabó's films at the 2000 conference. Halász points out, interestingly, that Szabó's oeuvre is strikingly coherent, with certain motifs and characters recurring, "as if he had made just one film" (Halász, "Az illustrációktol a nagytotálig" [From illustrations to grand totality]), 110.

17 Viktor Orbán's most combative, and explicit, expression of racism to date occurred in a speech he gave in Romania on July 23, 2022, in which he ridiculed "the West" for promoting the idea of a "mixed race society" and stated, in the name of Hungary and other Central European countries, that "we do not want to become peoples of mixed race." The full text of the speech is online: https://bukarest.mfa.gov.hu/rou/news/speech-by-prime-minister-viktor-orban-at-the-31st-balvanyos-summer-free-university-and-student-camp-23-july-2022-tusnadfuerdo-baile-tusnad

18 This story was reported by major news outlets in the United States and England and was also the subject of a long article in *The New Yorker*: Applebaum, "Anti-Semite and Jew: The Double Life of a Hungarian Politician."

19 Hirsch, *Afterimage*, 111–13 and 120–8.

20 Hirsch, "István Szabó," 6.

21 Personal conversation, October 20, 2017.

22 Suleiman, "On Exile, Jewish Identity, and Filmmaking in Hungary."

23 I discuss Kertész's complicated attitudes toward Hungary and the Hungarian language in detail in my essay, "Writing and Internal Exile in Eastern Europe."

24 Halász, "Az illustrációktol a nagytotálig" [From illustrations to grand totality].

25 Szabó, "Hulljék mázsákban a popcorn" [Let popcorn flow by the ton], 2. The article is signed "blanka."

26 Hungarian scenario of *Sunshine*, at Hungarian National Film Archive Library. See Note 45 in the following.

27 *Sunshine* won the Canadian Genie prize (Canada's version of the Academy Awards) in 2000 for best film and was nominated for a Golden Globe in the same category; all the major actors were nominated for prizes, and Ralph Fiennes won for the best actor at the Europa (Berlin) film festival; Jennifer Ehle and Rosemary Harris shared the Satellite prize for the best supporting actress.

28 See, for example, Deák, "Strangers at Home," 30–2. While Deák, a noted Hungarian-American historian, mentions one or two small details that Szabó got wrong (e.g., the Emperor would never shake the hands or touch the shoulder of a commoner, as happens in the film), he finds Szabó's overall account accurate.

29 Kovács, "Jews and Politics in Hungary," 50.

30 Bergstein, "Photography in the Szondi Test," 224. This article is an excellent introduction to Szondi's method and theories.

31 Szondi's work is still being carried on, by the Szondi Institute Foundation in Zurich and by the Swiss Association for Fate-analytical Therapy (Schweizerische Gesellschaft für Schicksalsanalytische Therapie—SGST), as well as the International Szondi Society (Internationale Szondi-Gesellschaft).

32 See, for example, Haraszti, "Hivasson esztétát!" [Call an aesthetics specialist!]. My previous analysis of *Sunshine* appeared in my book *Crises of Memory and the Second World War*, ch. 5, where I discuss the women characters in the film in greater detail. My discussion of *Sunshine* here owes much to that chapter but is also a revision of it.

33 Szabó, "Itt vigyázni kell" [Here one must be careful].

34 Cohen and Gruen, poor Jews, pass by a church which advertises that converts that day will be given $200 in cash. Gruen goes inside and emerges a few hours later, looking pleased with himself. When Cohen asks him, excitedly, "So, did you get the $200?," Gruen replies: "You Jews, you care only about money!"

35 Deák, "Strangers at Home," 31.

36 Heller, "A parvenuk kora" [The Era of the Parvenu], 134, and "Megjegyzések és ellenmegjegyzések Szabó István filmjéhez" [Notes and Counternotes on István Szabó's film], 10. Heller admired the film overall even while expressing some reservations.

37 Heller, *A "Zsidókérdés" megoldhatatlansága, avagy Mért születtem Hébernek, mért nem inkább Négernek?* [The Insolubility of the "Jewish question," or Why was I born a Hebrew, why not a Negro instead?].

38 See Romsics, *Hungary in the Twentieth Century*, 272–3. Also Karády, "Some Aspects of Jewish Assimilation in Socialist Hungary, 1945-1946," 73–132.

39 These words were included in an e-mail from one Károly Dombi to the head of the Hungarian Lobby, Béla Lipták, and were part of a dossier on the film (at the Hungarian National Film Archive Library) prepared by the left-leaning daily *Népszabadság* in January 2000. (*Népszabadság* was done away with not long after Viktor Orbán's party won a landslide victory in the Hungarian elections of 2010.) The story in *Népszabadság*, by Gábor Miklós, reported that the proponents of the boycott demanded an apology from the film's producers and creators.

40 See, for example, Fehér, "Hungarian Sculptor Defends Monument to Victims of Nazis" and Mark MacKinnon, "Statue in Budapest based on Second World War Evokes Dark History."

41 For the information on Rajk, I thank István Rév, a professor of history at the Central European University and a specialist in the period. For the accusation of Zionism against some of Rajk's codefendants, see the news report from the Jewish Telegraphic Agency dated September 21, 1949, https://www.jta.org/archive/issue-of-zionism -injected-into-hungarian-spy-trial-one-defendant-says-he-was-zionist

42 Personal conversation, July 2, 2018.

43 On the change in Soviet policy toward Israel, See Herf, *Israel's Moment*, 458–60.

44 On Gábor Péter, see the obituary in the *New York Times*, https://www.nytimes.com /1993/04/12/obituaries/gabor-peter-86-dies-led-hungarian-police.html

45 This scenario, in Hungarian, is titled "Revised Fourth Draft" and dated May 25, 1998; Hungarian National Film Archive library, catalogue number Q3046, p. 139. For Sartre's famous statement, see *Réflexions sur la question juive* [Antisemite and Jew], 83.

46 Kertész, *Gályanapló* [Galley Diary], 36. Kertész repeated this statement in several other works, including his autobiography, *K. dosszié* [K Dossier]. Neither book has been translated into English, but they exist in French and German, among other translations.

47 Kertész, *Gályanapló*, 36.

48 Földes, "Sors Út" [The way of fate or Sors's way]; György, "Sorsválasztók" [Those who chose their fate or Those who chose Sors].

49 Vitányi, "Miröl szól *A Napfény ize*?" [What is the subject of *Sunshine*?].

50 Szabó, "Hulljék mázsákban a popcorn," 2.

51 My essay, "Jewish Assimilation in Hungary, the Holocaust, and Epic Film: Reflections on István Szabó's *Sunshine*" appeared in *Yale Journal of Criticism* in 2001 and was eventually revised for inclusion in *Crises of Memory and the Second World War*.

52 Sartre, *Saint Genet, comédien et martyr*.

53 Sartre, *Réflexions sur la question juive*, 178ff. For more on Sartre's problematic book, see the special issue of *October*, Hollier, ed., "Jean-Paul Sartre's *Anti-Semite and Jew*."

54 Szabó, "Itt vigyázni kell" [Here one must be careful].

55 The Orbán government led a veritable witch hunt against Soros in the run-up to the 2018 elections, and Orbán was still mentioning Soros as the "enemy" in his July 23, 2022, speech (see Note 17). For a detailed first-person report on the anti-Soros campaign of 2017–18, see Suleiman, "A Letter from Budapest," *Tablet Magazine*, March 14, 2018, https://www.tabletmag.com/sections/news/articles/a-letter-from -budapest.

4

Living Together?

The Idea of Community after Communism

Here one can be misunderstood in six different languages.

ZOLTÁN SZÁNTÓ, in *Meeting Venus*

Suicide is not the solution.

EMMA, in *Sweet Emma, Dear Böbe*

"In our age, there is no such thing as 'keeping out of politics.' All issues are political issues," wrote George Orwell in his famous essay on "Politics and the English Language."[1] Orwell wrote this in 1946, after one of the biggest historical upheavals the world has known. The Second World War not only upended the totalitarian regimes of Hitler and Mussolini but also prepared the way for the Stalinist takeover of Central Europe. As long as political life goes on, every end is also a beginning, and this is nowhere clearer than in periods of radical regime change. The new regime arrives promising a whole new life and world (or else the restoration of an older one it idealizes, as happened in France after Napoleon), while those who have lived under the regime that has just been overthrown rush or struggle to adapt to the change.

In the daily life of individuals, it is often on the symbolic level that radical change is first experienced: new vocabularies, new names, new emblems.

In Szabó's film *Father*, we know that a major historical change has occurred when we see the plaque on the façade of Takó's elementary school replaced by another one: what was a Benedictine *gymnasium* is renamed a State Elementary School. A similar exchange, but in reverse, occurs in Szabó's 1992 film *Sweet Emma, Dear Böbe* (*Édes Emma, drága Böbe*), where the communist plaque outside a school is replaced by one bearing the traditional Hungarian emblem of the crown of St. Stephen. No words are necessary to explain the significance of these changes in nomenclature, which speak for themselves.

A more extended example of the way language accompanies and sometimes even anticipates historical upheaval is found in the great modernist writer Dezső Kosztolányi's novel *Édes Anna* (Anna Sweet). The novel, part of the canon of Hungarian literature, was published in 1926 when the authoritarian Horthy regime was already well established. But the moment that interests Kosztolányi occurs seven years earlier, immediately after the downfall of the short-lived communist regime led by Béla Kun, which itself followed the collapse of the much longer-lived Habsburg Empire. The action of the novel begins on July 31, 1919, the day that Kun fled the country to the Soviet Union; the first chapter, one-page long, is titled "Béla Kun Flies Away." We see the nobleman Kornél Vizy in his apartment in the building he owns, reacting to the news that Kun is gone. It appears that the Commune has fallen, but Vizy is still in a state of uncertainty. When he hears a knocking at the door, he fears the worst, but it's only the house superintendent, who addresses him as "Méltósàgos úr," Your Honor. Vizy responds by calling him "Ficsor elvtárs," Comrade Ficsor. The superintendent has reverted to the pre-Commune honorific for addressing a gentleman, while the aristocrat uses the term that was obligatory for everyone just a day earlier. But Ficsor is not happy to be called Comrade, because the times are changing and it will be best for him if his past as a supporter of the Commune is forgotten. The "rascals" have fallen, he informs Vizy, and the good old red-white-and-green national flag is once again flying over Castle Hill.

The seriocomic implications of this exchange are not lost on the narrator, who comments: "Thus they conversed with world-historical politeness, taking turns in giving advantage to the other."[2] The narrator's irony captures beautifully the state of uncertainty in which people find themselves during this moment of transition. While the actual plot of the novel, featuring the eponymous Anna Sweet (Édes, sweet, is her family name), appears to be only tangentially related to the historical moment that is foregrounded in its opening pages, it is in fact deeply imbricated with it. Anna, a girl from the countryside who is hired by the Vizys and works for them as a "model" maid, ends up committing a gruesome double murder. But despite her violent action, Anna's most salient characteristic, Kosztolányi suggests, is her defenselessness. Despite her great efficiency as a servant, she is a victim: poor, uneducated, and inarticulate, with no sense of her own agency, as if it were natural that others should decide her fate. By a horrible irony, her senseless act of violence may be the only action she accomplishes entirely on her own, although she can hardly be called its agent, since it appears opaque and incomprehensible even to herself.

It would be too simple to attribute an ideological thesis to Kosztolányi's novel. Anna's action is not attributable to a single cause or system, whether communist or capitalist or quasi-feudal (as Hungary was in the 1920s). But Kosztolányi does show how individual lives are imbricated in collective history and in language. Anna's status as a maid, a *cseléd*, makes it difficult for her to attain full personhood; the way her employers treat her is clearly dehumanizing. The question that this novel asks, implicitly, is: What constitutes a community, a safe space for human development, in a time of sudden historical change when everyone feels vulnerable and seeks to act only for their own preservation?

The collapse of communism in Eastern Europe, which actually occurred over a period of several years in some countries (notably Poland and Hungary), but which is more commonly associated with the sudden fall of the Berlin Wall on November 9, 1989, was another moment of radical change, which completely transformed the political and economic world system that had been created after the Second World War. The Cold War, the Iron Curtain, communism in Central Europe, and the Soviet Union itself were all swept away in what seemed like a few days.[3]

To be replaced by what? The answers to that question throughout the 1990s wavered between hope and disillusionment. The hope was that democracy would take hold in the former Soviet bloc countries, whose members would eventually join the larger European community, which itself was being transformed from an economic alliance (EEC) to a firmer union, the EU. The Maastricht Treaty, the first of several treaties that sought to cement the European Union, was signed in 1993; by the end of the decade, inhabitants of member states could travel freely across each others' borders, attend each others' universities, and work where they wished; soon a number of them would also share a common currency, the Euro, a sign of the promises of economic globalization. In 2004, eight former communist countries, including Hungary, Poland, and the Czech Republic, became members of the EU (though not of the Euro zone).

Cosmopolitanism, an age-old idea whose value had fluctuated over the centuries (Goethe was proud to call himself a citizen of the world and Kant theorized the notion, but two centuries later, "rootless cosmopolitans" were hounded by the Nazis and their ilk), once again gained currency in the writings of thinkers as disparate in other ways as Jacques Derrida, Jürgen Habermas, and Martha Nussbaum.[4] Cosmopolitanism, all the theorists agree, is an alternative to nationalism but can also exist in productive tension with it, as long as nationalism is conceived of not as a narrow-minded chauvinism but as a sense of collective belonging to a place and a culture. This is how Ernest Renan envisioned nationalism in his seminal essay, "What Is a Nation?" (1882), and it also figures in Benedict Anderson's conception in his book a century later, *Imagined Communities*. Allegiance to the world—what Habermas envisions as a "cosmopolitan community of states and world citizens" and what Anthony Appiah calls simply "kindness to strangers"—does not necessarily exclude love of one's country.[5]

But other events of the 1990s and later, starting with the brutal civil wars and genocides of the former Yugoslavia and continuing with the seemingly endless migrant crises culminating in the Syrian crisis of 2015 and Hungary's construction of a barbed-wire fence along its southern border, undid the early optimism. Nationalism of the worst kind, feeding on fear and loathing of "others," became a powerful force once again, not only in Eastern Europe but in the West as well. And the promises of globalization in the economic sphere also turned out to be double-edged. Inequalities multiplied, not only among nations but also within: some people grew enormously rich, installing gold-plated bathroom fixtures in their multiple properties, while others struggled to put food on the table. The French economist Thomas Piketty has demonstrated in great detail the extent of such inequalities in our time and their deleterious effect on capitalism itself, since they tend to foster political instability and violence.[6]

Today, the world is still struggling with the hopes and disillusionments that followed the fall of the Wall, and it even appears that we are regressing to a period before the Cold War. In February 2022, for the first time in more than eighty years, Europe saw the invasion of a sovereign country by its aggressive neighbor, who then engaged in the indiscriminate bombing of cities and civilian populations and whose Army committed war crimes in the towns and villages it invaded.[7]

In the first years of the 1990s, István Szabó made two films that speak to the issues of hope and disillusionment I have outlined. *Meeting Venus* (1991), Szabó's first English-language film, supported by international financing and a generous budget, and *Sweet Emma, Dear Böbe* (1992), a Hungarian film made on a shoestring budget, were conceived and written very close to each other. Szabó has said that the scenario for the latter was mostly written when he interrupted that project to make *Meeting Venus*, pressed by the film's British producer.[8] He shot *Sweet Emma, Dear Böbe* in 1991, before *Meeting Venus* had even opened in Hungary. One can think of these two films as complementary, quasi-simultaneous versions, or visions, of post-communist Europe, the one cautiously optimistic, the other close to despairing.

"A Metaphor for Europe"? Passions and Music in *Meeting Venus*

Meeting Venus is a story of artistic collaboration in the new Europe. A Hungarian conductor, little known outside his native country, has been invited by a European opera company based in Paris, Opera Europa, to conduct an international cast in a one-night performance of Wagner's *Tannhäuser* at the Paris Opera. Much rides on this single performance, for it will be telecast simultaneously to twenty-seven countries, opening up the possibility of international fame for the conductor Zoltán Szántó (Niels Arestrup). The time is *c.* 1990, after the fall of the Wall but before that epoch-making event has fully registered in people's consciousness or gained their confidence. Thus the East German tenor, Schneider (Marian Labuda), whose recordings Szántó is familiar with, corners the Maestro in a hallway on the first day of rehearsals to ask for his help. He explains that he used to work in a factory and was discovered by a famous conductor while singing in the chorus; he now owns a garage run by his wife, which he has kept because "singing is not safe business." He wants Szántó's help so that he can move to a cheaper hotel than the one provided by Opera Europa, using the surplus money to buy cans of car paint to take back home. "You understand this, since you too are from the ex-East," he tells Szántó, whose face registers a mixture of amusement, dismay, and a touch of contempt. This is one of many instances in the film where Szabó's oft-proclaimed preference for close-ups to indicate complex inner states of feeling is put to use.

The Maestro himself, however, is not above feeling like a man "from the ex-East." When he arrives at Charles de Gaulle airport and has his Hungarian passport scrutinized extra carefully by French officials, he feels humiliated. In an internal monologue addressed to his wife in Budapest, he says "Nothing has changed, they still treat us badly." When he is singled out to have his bags searched by French customs, he feels like a man who enters a drawing room with "shit on his shoes." But then the customs official finds his conductor's baton in its velvet-lined case and asks: "Music?" Szántó says yes, and the respectful response of the official puts an end to his humiliation. It's as if the word "music" were a shibboleth to overcome national animosities; the hope that art can transcend both national and personal differences will be the dominant theme of the film from this moment on.

Meeting Venus raised high hopes for international success among its backers, which included the American giant Warner Brothers. Its producer was the highly esteemed British filmmaker David Puttnam, who had known Szabó since 1982 when they first met at the Academy Awards ceremony in which Puttnam's *Chariots of Fire* won the Oscar for best film and *Mephisto* won for best foreign film. Puttnam and his team aimed, with *Meeting Venus*, for commercial success among an "upmarket" mainstream public, counting on the appeal of opera for many Europeans and on the star power of Glenn

Close (who plays a world-renowned Swedish diva Szántó falls in love with) in the United States.[9] These hopes were not fully realized, and the film did quite poorly at the box office, especially in the United States, despite its positive reception at the Venice Film Festival and generally positive reviews.[10] It is currently available for streaming on Amazon Prime, however, which may indicate a certain staying power. Independently of financial considerations, Puttnam (who had hired the veteran screenwriter Michael Hirst to shape Szabó's screenplay in English) appears to have been fully supportive of Szabó's intellectual ambitions in making the film. These were spelled out at some length in the fifteen-page booklet that was distributed to the press when the film opened in Hungary, in November 1991. There Szabó wrote (I translate):

> All over Europe, the barriers raised by the past half century between the peoples of the continent have fallen. Finally people can get rid of their fears, and ideas can circulate freely between the former blocs. This newfound freedom must carry with it tolerance and mutual understanding. [. . .] Everything that happens on the Parisian stage of the film's Opera Europa is a representation of what is happening in today's Europe. All of the quarrels and misunderstandings among the cast are metaphors for Europe. [. . .] In Europe we must learn to live together. Despite our different mentalities, religions, and the languages we speak, we still possess something unique: it is European culture, a European soul.[11]

This may sound somewhat overblown, and the idea of a unique "European soul" was not necessarily a selling point for audiences in the rest of the world, but Puttnam wholeheartedly seconded Szabó's views. "I think this is a very courageous film," he stated on the same page. "It creates a bridge between conventions that for most people would constitute unconquerable obstacles."

The idea of the film as a "metaphor for Europe" was further developed by Szabó in a long interview with the journalist Károly Csala, which appeared at around the same time:

> We wanted to talk about what happens if people from various European countries, each with their particular mentality, life experience, [ethnic] origin, native language, prejudices, and feelings of inferiority get together

with a common goal, working to create something. So it was this "European metaphor" that excited us—to say figuratively what would happen if in today's Europe, which is full of anxiety, chauvinism, stupidity, nationalism, jealousy, and mutual animosity, these people come together in order to create something beautiful. We wanted to show that, if circumstances allowed, cooperation is possible despite everything.[12]

In this interview, Szabó also explained why he chose Wagner's *Tannhäuser* as the "something beautiful" that comes into being despite all the problems among the cast and crew. Szabó himself had directed a production of the opera in Paris some years earlier, an experience he found unpleasant because of all the bureaucratic obstacles—but he considered that fact as merely anecdotal, for there were much stronger reasons for his choice of this particular opera in the film. *Tannhäuser* tells the story of a medieval minstrel-knight (the eponymous hero) who seeks redemption but is torn between his carnal love for the goddess Venus, in whose cave he spends several years, and his spiritual love for the lady he left behind while indulging his carnal passion, the virginal Elizabeth. Szabó used this theme to point to a second metaphor operating in the film, next to the primary metaphor of the production as a microcosm of Europe. According to this second metaphor, the existential dilemmas portrayed in Wagner's opera are mirrored in the lives of the artists who come together to interpret it. "We tried to make a film in which the main characters are in the same situation as the medieval singer—each lives in a state of doubt, not knowing how to manage their life," Szabó told his interviewer. "But in the meantime, they have a common goal: to create a performance." As for the choice of Wagner, that too was deliberate, Szabó said, because of Wagner's ambiguous status in European history as a genius who "thought badly" and who had been used by a "very dark political power. "We chose him, aside from his music, because we thought that this ambivalent Wagner was a very important part of Europe, of our Europe."[13]

Meeting Venus, then, is a film freighted with significance. The question that confronts a commentator is whether the finished work lives up to its director's ambitions. John Cunningham, an astute and knowledgeable critic of Hungarian cinema and of Szabó's oeuvre, faults *Meeting Venus* on several grounds, even while granting it merit in attempting to deal with a complicated subject that is difficult to represent on screen. In his opinion, Close and Arestrup, whose stormy love affair dominates the plot (by a nice twist, Close, who plays the passionate lover in Szántó's life, sings the role of the chaste Elizabeth in the opera), lack sufficient "chemistry," and Close is too petite to play the role of a diva with the soaring voice of Kiri Te Kanawa, who sings her arias. These are highly subjective judgments, to be sure (I found the chemistry between the two actors persuasive enough), but Cunningham also raises another issue that deserves further discussion. It concerns Szabó's choice to set his Maestro up against various collectives—the chorus, the orchestra, the union of stagehands, the union of accompanists—whose demands and bureaucratic regulations hamper his attempt to create great music. In this situation, the democracy that was presumably the desired outcome of a united Europe is put into question, since the collectives—democratic institutions par excellence— are represented as enemies of art. If Szántó triumphs in the end by creating a great performance despite all obstacles, Cunningham writes, it is "a triumph for individualism and is achieved against the chorus, the orchestra and their unions," all of them collective bodies—which seems odd, he adds, for a "film director whose work is so intimately and intricately bound up with the joint labour and inputs of so many others."[14]

Aniko Imre, whom Cunningham quotes, goes even further in this direction. In her view, "democracy" in the film becomes a negative term, as when Szántó writes to his wife that "apparently due to democracy, nobody seems to care about *Tannhäuser*, except perhaps Miss Anderson [the diva, who by now is Szántó's lover]." Imre's comment on this statement is: "In comparison with the magnificent demon of Communism, the omnipresent, everyday politics of Western democracies appear irritating and sad."[15]

In fact, nowhere in the film does Szántó (or Szabó) suggest that communism was "better" than the messy Western democracy, where groups jostle for power. But Aniko Imre is right when she states that the ending of the film is "highly idealistic" (not a term of praise from her perspective), for it shows that "Wagner's music does finally create multinational love, even if only for the duration of a performance." When the stagehands' union imposes the ultimate obstacle by going on strike and refusing to raise the security curtain in the opera house at the last minute, the singers perform in front of the curtain in their costumes, concert style. "Without the interference of cheap spectacularity, the sheer power of the music—and Szántó's supreme talent—proves victorious," Imre notes. But she disapproves of this ending, for it enshrines the white male heterosexual artist, who thereby loses all his former sense of inferiority as an Eastern European and becomes a "'transnational' 'Western' man"—again, not a positive term in her critical vocabulary.[16] More sweepingly, Imre faults *Meeting Venus* for presenting a "distorted picture of the new, post-Communist Eastern Europe," one that is comforting to the West (Hollywood-style) but that ignores the plight of women and non-privileged Eastern Europeans—those who don't "speak English perfectly" and don't belong to the educated elite—in the new global economy. Curiously, Imre fails to mention Szabó's next film, *Sweet Emma, Dear Böbe*, which deals precisely with the plight of those non-privileged Eastern European figures.

Still, the issues raised by these critics are worth exploring further. Is Szabó expressing a disturbingly antidemocratic worldview in this film? And does the idealistic ending, which shows the transcendent power of music in a chaotic world of passions and conflict, merit criticism, if not outright dismissal as a facile Hollywood fantasy?

Let's start with the second question. There is no doubt that Szabó idealizes music in this film, seeing it as a kind of universal, albeit temporary or momentary "cure" for the troubles of everyday life. Nor is *Meeting Venus* the first work in which he suggests as much. The very first film he made, his black and white, seventeen-minute "graduation film" from the Film Academy, was titled *Koncert*. It is a charming film in the mood of the French New Wave, or of René Clair's brand of surrealism (in *Entr'acte*, for example). We see three young men on a tricycle, hauling a grand piano behind them along the Danube bank, and then a large mirror descending a staircase. The mirror turns out to be carried by a beautiful young woman, and when the three guys see her they run after her, leaving the piano behind. A small crowd gathers, and a few people approach the piano and start to play. The first two play badly, but the third plays very well. He is followed by a man who appears to be a composer and plays like a pro, attracting more onlookers who applaud when he finishes. After that, someone taps out the opening bars of *La Marseillaise*, followed by more applause. Then it starts to rain! A few people take off their jackets to cover the piano and start to drive it away, but at that point the three young men from the opening shots return and run after them.

That's all, that's the story: for a brief moment, in a large anonymous city, a small crowd of random individuals becomes a community, united by the power of music. *La Marseillaise*, a universal signifier of togetherness (never mind its bloody call to action), underlines the message and may also remind viewers of a famous scene in *Casablanca*, where the French anthem plays a similar role. After that brief moment, everyone returns to their daily struggles. The beauty of *Koncert*, which won a prize at an international film festival for its fledgling filmmaker, is in its concision and its lighthearted way of making a serious point: music can sometimes unite people, even if only for a little while. This is also the point of *Meeting Venus*.

Does Szabó's idealization of music, in the very early film as in the later one, make him overlook the fact that many Nazis loved Beethoven, not to mention Wagner? Of course not—he even made a film about that problem a dozen years after *Meeting Venus*, *Taking Sides* (which I discussed in Chapter 2). The ability to entertain contradictory points of view on a complicated subject is not a fault, however.

In *Meeting Venus*, the theme of music as a unifier across borders, first broached in the scene of Szántó's arrival at the Paris airport, is restated several times before its fullest expression in the film's final sequences. When Szántó arrives at the opera house later in the day for his first meeting with the cast and crew, accompanied by the manager of Opera Europa (who is Hungarian, an emigré from 1956), he starts by talking about *Tannhäuser*: his only desire is to create a beautiful performance of this great work, he says, which is really "about us. How should we live? Venus or Elisabeth, carnal or spiritual?" It is clear, however, that many of those present don't understand him well, since English—the lingua franca of the "new" Europe—is not a language they have mastered. Some people try to translate for their neighbor, while others merely look bewildered. This is when we hear Szántó say, in an internal monologue to his wife, "Here you can be misunderstood in six different languages." Szántó's fervent remarks about the opera are further deflated when the leader of the chorus interjects that they don't get paid enough, and the first violinist says it's hard to work under these conditions. But when Szántó sits down at the piano and asks various singers to sing, the atmosphere suddenly changes. Schneider, the tenor/garage owner from Dresden who knows almost no English, sings beautifully, and everyone claps, including the stagehands. Then Szántó smiles, and his face, shown in close-up, looks almost ecstatic.

The pattern of discord followed by musical cooperation is repeated several times in what follows—indeed, one could reproach Szabó for repeating it too often. One scene that works particularly well, however, occurs a few sequences later when the Hungarian secretary of Opera Europa, Jean Gábor (Moscu Alcalay), crosses swords with the German Schneider. The two men are roughly equal in size, both of them short and plump, and we have seen them in previous scenes behaving aggressively. Schneider, in particular, takes offense at the slightest hint of what he considers to be "mockery," as when the American tenor Steve Taylor asks him what it was like to sing in the GDR, where he himself could of course never sing. (Jokingly, but perhaps to illustrate the quip about being misunderstood in six different languages, Schneider, Taylor, the Italian baritone Sarto, the French stage manager Tailleur, and a couple of other characters all have the same name translated into their respective languages, and it is also Szabó's name in Hungarian.) In this particular scene, Gábor and Schneider disagree about where the latter should be standing, and Gábor starts yelling at him: "I won't take any more of your German aggressiveness!" whereupon Schneider stalks off, taunting the Hungarian with the repeated insult of "Dirty faggot!" Gábor responds by screaming "Dirty Communist Nazi!" and the two almost come to blows, while Szántó sits at the piano with his head bowed in apparent despair. But suddenly he starts to play, improvising a song: "Ugly Germans, Lazy Poles, Filthy Spaniards, how they hate each other! Catholics, Protestants, Jews!" Suddenly the mood becomes quieter, and the diva Karin Anderson (Glenn Close) joins Szántó at the piano: "Boring Belgians, Bloody British, Drunken Danes!" she sings, and he echoes her happily, laughing. Everyone claps. The moment of ugly nationalist confrontation has been defused and turned into a comic musical duet. Not long after this, Szántó and Anderson become lovers, united by their common dedication to the art as well as by their mutual attraction (Figure 16).

Figure 16 Meeting Venus, *1991. Warner Bros, Fujisankei Communications Group British Broadcasting, County Natwest Ventures. Copyright The Bountiful Company Ltd.*

By the time of the final scene of triumph at the performance, Szántó and Anderson have lived through a stormy love affair and come out at the other end, as friends—at least that is what we may surmise. She smiles at him benevolently from the stage, dressed in her virginal white costume, while he is conducting, as if to say, "This is what really matters." Meanwhile, Szántó's betrayed and angry wife (Dorottya Udvaros), at home in Budapest, watches the telecast from their bedroom and is carried away in admiration—Szabó cuts to her several times, to show the evolution of her feelings. It's as if Wagner's music and the conductor's artistry have created peace not only among the various nationals but also in the conductor's private life. Of course, this may be true only during the time of the performance, after which everyone will return to their everyday passions.

The other question, regarding Szabó's attitude toward democracy and collective bargaining, is no less complicated. The unions with their constant demands and regulations and threats of strike are portrayed as obstacles to the creation of great music that Szántó is obsessed with. Indeed, it becomes a kind of running gag in the film that just when a rehearsal gets going, it is interrupted by a coffee break or a rule about not working overtime or a new strike. Geopolitics also plays a role: the leader and union representative of the chorus berates the American tenor at one point because the United States bombed Lybia and invaded Panama (in 1989). When Szántó complains about this to the Director of Opera Europa (Erland Josephson, of Ingmar Bergman fame), the latter tells him that the union rep is "close to the Socialists," so it would be politically unwise to cross him. (In 1989 the Socialist Party was in power in France, with François Mitterrand as President.) Besides, we know from an earlier scene that the Director of Opera Europa, a Spaniard named Picabia, is himself a former communist who even claims to have been the author of the Republican anthem of the Spanish Civil War, "Ay, Carmela!" Although he is no longer a communist, he is not about to try and discipline a left-wing chorus leader. At that point, Szántó bursts out: "I hate this democracy of yours! Art is order."

The messiness of contemporary politics and the baggage of twentieth-century European history that weighs on many of the characters is a leitmotif in the film and may be hammered home a bit too insistently by Szabó. The secretary of Opera Europa is a former Romanoff princess, another member of the staff is a Russian Jewish emigré, and the manager is a 1956 Hungarian exile who "served under Horthy, Hitler and Stalin" before serving him, Picabia says with a laugh. The union representative in the orchestra is another Hungarian who left in 1956 and who was Szántó's lover when they were both students (a possible allusion to *Lovefilm*)—not to mention Schneider and Szántó himself, who still carry traces of their past as citizens of the former Soviet bloc. All this makes for a very busy scenario (made even busier by Szabó's characteristic use of short takes and lots of cuts), with dialogues whose quick historical references may escape the ordinary moviegoer. It can also give rise to some lovely moments, however, as when Schneider, the Romanoff princess, and the Russian Jewish emigré form a trio to sing a Russian folk song at the cast party—"Stalin's favorite song," Picabia tells the Maestro.

Does Szabó share his conductor's impatience with "democracy" and his love of art as order? Yes and no. He himself used the line about art in a November 1991 interview, when asked what music meant to him: "I like classical music. There is so much disorder in our lives, I see so much chaos around me, that the order and clarity of classical music almost plays the role of a kind of mental hygiene in my life."[17] This does not mean, however, that he despises democracy or collective action. On the night of the performance, demonstrators outside the opera house carry placards and chant a ditty denouncing the event's main financial backer, a company called Eurogreen, whose policies may be harmful to the environment (though the company denies this), as we learned in an earlier scene set at a press conference. Szabó juxtaposes the demonstrators with the well-dressed operagoers, including the CEO of Eurogreen, who arrives in a limousine with his wife and daughter. Nothing in the scene suggests that the demonstrators have less right to be there than the others. Eurogreen is both a large multinational corporation that attracts hostile, probably justified criticism from environmentalists, and a sponsor of beautiful music—not a comfortable idea, but a contemporary reality. Does the one negate the other? Szabó leaves that question open.

The idea of community has been a mainstay of many of Szabó's films ever since his early Hungarian works, including *25 Firemen's Street* and *Budapest Tales*, both of which feature a group rather than individuals. In *Confidence*, the community he explores is reduced to just two people in a room; although they are there for political reasons (it's 1944 in Budapest and they are part of the resistance to the Nazi occupation), they gradually fall in love and come to embody what Georges Bataille called "the true world of lovers."[18] But communities both large and small are made up of individuals, and Szabó often underlines the tension between personal and group interests. In *Meeting Venus*, the group interest is to create a beautiful performance of Wagner's opera, and at certain moments—whenever they actually make music or perform a job related to the performance—the musicians and the crew rise to the occasion. But they are also human, with personal ambitions and group loyalties outside the opera, which sometimes take precedence. The stage manager, who is responsible for raising the curtain, is clearly a lover of music, and he takes Szántó's side early on, when Karin Anderson's gorgeous rendition of an aria is interrupted by timers going off, signaling a break for the orchestra. "I'm sorry sir, they don't love music," the manager says to Szántó disapprovingly. But on the night of the actual performance, he is the one who refuses to raise the curtain: a strike has been declared and he simply cannot go against the union's decision, he explains to the Maestro.

But the Maestro himself is in a non-simple position, for (and this can be said of all artists, including the director of this film) his genuine devotion to his art is inseparable from more self-centered desires: to become famous, to earn the respect of his peers, to be paid properly for his work (another running gag in the film involves Szántó's repeated attempts to extract the payment due to him from Opera Europa), and to be loved by a beautiful woman who is not his wife. In the end, he obtains all that, which is why a hostile critic can call *Meeting Venus* a Hollywood-style film that glorifies the white, heterosexual, Western (i.e., privileged in relation to East Europeans) male. But I think it would be disingenuous to claim that Szabó "should have done it differently." The recent film by Todd Field, *Tár* (2022), features a world-famous female conductor (Cate Blanchett) whose personal life is tawdry but whose devotion to music is sublime. The latter does not excuse her moral failings; rather, it coexists with them. Human passions are violent and messy, and yet we also yearn for transcendence. That is a central insight in *Tár*, as it is in *Meeting Venus* and in Wagner's *Tannhäuser*.

Hanging On: Precarious Lives in *Sweet Emma, Dear Böbe*

If *Meeting Venus* presents a cautiously (or provisionally) optimistic vision of the new Europe after the fall of the Iron Curtain, *Sweet Emma, Dear Böbe* (*Édes Emma, drága Böbe*) appears almost as a kind of corrective. It's as if Szabó were saying: "Yes, great art can sometimes transcend national differences and act as a unifier, but there is also a harsh new reality in the lives of ordinary people affected by global changes, which cannot be overlooked." In *Sweet Emma, Dear Böbe*, Szabó returned to a Hungarian subject for the first time since the late 1970s; although he often mentioned with some pride, in interviews, that he shot all of his films, even the ones with international financing, as much as possible in Budapest, this was his first film since *Confidence* (1980) that portrayed Hungarian lives, and the first one since *Lovefilm* (1970) that focused on a contemporary situation, as opposed to a historical or an abstract one. (The only other film by Szabó since *Sweet Emma, Dear Böbe* that is similarly set in present-day Hungary is his most recent one, *Final Report*, which I will discuss later in this chapter.) As one Hungarian critic put it, "This film is about us. People who, after the regime change, breathed again but faced growing uncertainty."[19]

The people at the center of Szabó's film are two young women (female protagonists were another "first" for the filmmaker) whose lives were not easy before 1989 but become even less so after that epoch-defining date. Emma (Johanna ter Steege, who played a secondary role in *Meeting Venus*) and Böbe (Enikő Börcsök) are teachers of Russian in an elementary school in Budapest, living on meager salaries that allow them no other lodging than a room they share in a teachers' hostel on the city's outskirts. They are both from small villages in the countryside, evidently the only members of their families with some education. But after the "regime change," Russian will no longer be a required subject in Hungarian schools, so Emma and Böbe, along with many of their colleagues, must learn to teach English instead. This shift in languages, requiring a drastic reeducation for the two young women, is a powerful indicator of the new global reality that impinges on their lives. One of the first scenes in the film takes place in the schoolyard, where a group of children burn a Russian textbook and sing the Song of the Volga Boatmen, in Russian, as a mock dirge for it while their teacher, Emma, watches in consternation.

No doubt because of the word Édes which occurs in both titles, at least two Hungarian critics drew a parallel between Szabó's heroines and the provincial protagonist of Kosztolányi's *Édes Anna*. Emma and Böbe are "educated granddaughters of Anna Édes," one critic noted.[20] When I too mentioned the novel to Szabó, he vigorously protested that he never thought of Kosztolányi while making the film, but the phonetic echo is unmistakable (at least to a Hungarian viewer with some literary baggage), and despite obvious differences in the plot, Szabó's heroines too appear defenseless in the face of a sociopolitical reality over which they have no control. Szabó certainly knows the film adaptation of the novel by Zoltán Fábri, a filmmaker he greatly admires. Fábri's *Édes Anna*, starring Mari Törőcsik in one of her first major roles, was released in 1958, when Szabó was preparing to make his graduation film at the Film Academy; a few years later, it was one of the works mentioned in a long interview with Fábri that Szabó published in a widely read film journal.[21]

The sudden change in language teaching—signaling the geopolitical shift that aligned Hungary and the other former Soviet bloc countries with the global market economy, where English is dominant—contains possibilities for comedy, which Szabó suggests in an early scene where one of the teachers in the school, speaking in Russian and Hungarian with an exaggerated Russian accent, mocks the whole thing. But quite soon, we also see the situation's darker side. In two separate scenes in the film, Emma and Böbe are shown, along with other former Russian teachers (almost all of whom are women) in the English-language class, straining to adapt their body as well as their mind to the new language. The retraining, as Szabó shows, involves a completely new discipline for the mouth and the vocal organs—discipline in Michel Foucault's sense, a forcing of the body into new positions that, even if they are not meant as punishment, can seem punitive.[22] Significantly, the language that is taught is American English, not British.

In the first scene, we see Emma and Böbe struggling to pronounce English words correctly, mimicking the teacher. After some stock phrases like "Would you like some coffee"? "No, thank you," the sentences turn to typically American questions of identity: "What do you do?" This is a question one rarely hears asked between strangers in Europe, but it is often the first thing people ask when they meet each other in the United States. "I'm a teacher," the women respond in chorus. "What do you teach?" "Literature." By an ironic twist, Emma has difficulty pronouncing the word "Literature," which is precisely what defines her professional identity. In the process of attempting to retrain her body to pronounce English words, she is forced to put into question her whole way of being in the world. Technically, Emma is a language teacher, and language and literature are separate subjects in Hungarian schools. But in this instance, literature is clearly meant to define these women's professional identities, since the language drill is designed for them. (In an early version of the scenario preserved at the library of the Hungarian National Film Archive, Emma is shown at one point trying to teach Pushkin's *Eugene Onegin* to an unruly class.)

The contrast between a "disciplined"—forced—adoption of language and the innate way one inhabits one's own language is beautifully brought out in the second sequence that involves an English lesson: the challenge of the letter W, so difficult for an Eastern European to master, is here combined with a tragicomic repetition of the phrase, "What are we waiting for"? What indeed? Emma rolls her eyes, suggesting an ironic detachment, but the next thing we see is her recurrent nightmare, where she is rolling naked down a steep hill, unable to find something to hang on to—a metaphor for the sense of disorientation and helplessness produced by this new situation in her life. The scene right after that, however, shows Emma and Böbe with their women colleagues joyously laughing, no longer sitting in a classroom but in a café. Their bodies and faces, which in the schoolroom are tense, straining with effort, are relaxed, moving easily. As they joke about a hypothetical personals ad they're composing, they take delight in playing with language, creating hilarious puns and *double entendres* ("young woman teacher seeks firm, athletic man, well versed in tongues"), something they could obviously not do in English. Nor, presumably, in Russian, for that matter. When they first learned to teach Russian, they probably went through a similarly painful disciplinary process. Now, they are forced to go through another one, because the rules have changed. According to the new laws of globalization and geopolitics, they must learn to teach English or be out of a job.

It hardly needs to be said that the economic and political realignment after 1989 had major social consequences in Hungary, as in other Central European countries. Friends often told me when I was living in Budapest in 1993 that before the "regime change" people lacked many things but at least they lacked them together. After the change, differences between rich and poor became flagrant. Inequality had existed under communism as well, with Party leaders enjoying privileges closed to others. But now, gross economic inequality was out in the open. Luxury stores appeared, selling goods that were not available in earlier times, but most people now could not afford them. Inequality between social classes became exacerbated in the years after 1989, a phenomenon Szabó shows in several ways. Emma, for example, works three times a week as a cleaning lady for a family whose large, luxuriously furnished apartment is a glaring contrast to the tiny room she shares with Böbe, but the family doesn't find time to visit the old grandmother who is in a nursing home, asking Emma to do that job as well. In one powerful sequence, we see Emma and Böbe walking down the pedestrian mall on Váci Street, in the city center.

They stop and stare at store windows, knowing that they cannot buy any of the objects displayed (Figure 17). Almost mockingly, a bookstore window features a title that evokes an earlier revolutionary moment: *Who Was Rosa Luxembourg?* Clearly, not many people care about that question. Emma and Böbe are followed by a Roma woman with her children, who begs them for money: compared to her, even they appear among the privileged and they shoo her away.

In the new global economy, people themselves can become goods to be bought. After their stroll down Váci Street, Emma and Böbe sit in a café frequented by tourists, where they are soon joined by a third young woman. Two men enter, and Böbe makes eyes at them. Emma looks uncomfortable, especially when the men sit down next to them and strike up a conversation. One of them speaks Hungarian: How many languages do the women know? he asks. Many, Böbe replies. The man tells them that his friend is German but knows Russian—the friend tries to engage Emma by speaking a few words in Russian, but she doesn't respond. Böbe, however, responds with a laugh: "Just think, Russian has become a world language!" Her remark, while humorous, also indicates the new reality that after 1989 Russia too is part of the global economy.

Figure 17 Sweet Emma, Dear Böbe (*Édes Emma, drága Böbe*), 1992. *Objektív Stúdió Vállalat, Videovox Stúdió, Mafilm Audio Kft., Manfred Durniok Produktion. Copyright National Film Institute Hungary—Film Archive.*

The men invite them to order drinks and by implication to spend the evening with them. Emma refuses to participate in this exchange (free drinks and dinner in exchange for the woman's body) and leaves; Böbe, however, embraces it. This harkens back to an earlier scene, in which Emma and Böbe, spending a carefree weekend together in a country house lent by a friend, become quite tipsy and engage in an extended dialogue about what matters in life. Emma says knowledge is more valuable than power because no one can take it away from you, as her grandmother always told her. Böbe scoffs at this idea: "Bullshit," she says, "Things have changed, and it [knowledge for its own sake] is totally useless." So what does it mean to live well? Emma asks. For Böbe, it means the freedom to go out and enjoy yourself, to buy nice clothes without having to skimp; for Emma, it means liking what you do, being loved, living in a community, feeling solidarity—but at those words, Böbe becomes downright angry and calls Emma a fool. Words like "solidarity" or "community" may have had value once, she says, but they have lost it. "Don't tell me about the future! I want to live well. . . . If there is no other way, I'll find a foreigner, and goodbye!"

In the café scene, we see Böbe acting on that resolution, trying to find a foreigner who will pay. But things end very badly for her because the new system that she is hoping to exploit exploits her and destroys her: she will soon be arrested for currency fraud, drug dealing, and prostitution, one more victim of the generalized traffic in women and commodities. The commodification of women's bodies was featured in an earlier scene, where a whole lineup of professional women, mostly teachers, audition naked for roles as extras in a "film about a harem." Szabó emphasizes the humiliation they endure in trying to supplement their meager income, standing naked in front of the director and his team, who evaluate them like cattle. Of course, it is Szabó who exposes those naked bodies to the viewer, thus implicating himself in the very exploitation and commodification he is critiquing. Curiously, in interviews he gave about the film, he refused to talk about the specific exploitation of women that he shows so well; his film is not about women, he said, but about "people" (*emberek*) who struggle with the new economic reality—some of them manage to survive, while others don't.[23]

After her release, Böbe returns to the hostel and commits suicide by jumping out of a bathroom window. Emma, devastated, runs down to her as she is dying and whispers in a broken voice that "this is not the solution." But even though she rejects suicide, Emma does not find much of a solution either: in the film's final shot, we see her standing in a subway underpass, hawking newspapers, like the young vendor we saw in an earlier scene. Szabó has explained that the idea for the film first came to him when he met a street artist doing portraits for tourists, who turned out to be the drawing teacher at an elementary school—it was the only way he could make ends meet, the man told Szabó.[24] In that final shot, Emma appears traumatized, repeatedly screaming the title of the newspaper, *Mai nap, Mai nap, Mai nap*: Today's day, Today's day, Today's day, as the final credits start to roll. Not exactly an upbeat ending.

When *Sweet Emma, Dear Böbe* was released in the spring of 1992, it got mostly positive reviews and wide coverage in the press. The following year it was awarded the Silver Bear at the Berlin Film Festival as well as the European Film Award—the Felix—for best screenplay. Szabó himself gave a number of interviews in which he explained his interpretation of the film. On the one hand, he thought of it as a character study. Some people, he told one interviewer, have an inner strength that allows them to "hang on" (*kapaszkodni*) in difficult times, while others lack that strength: Emma has it, Böbe does not. In this perspective, individual strength and willpower determine whether one is able to overcome life's challenges. But Szabó also suggested a collective and historical explanation that limits the freedom of the individual:

> In my lifetime, there have been six or seven changes in regime (*rendszerváltás*), which fundamentally transformed society and the ruling classes: "Am I up or am I down?" Things change very quickly in this country. Here we've always had to start over with learning things, there are frequent windstorms, and it's very hard for people to stand on their feet.[25]

While he insists in all these interviews that his film offers no solutions, that he only wants to show the problem, he says he knows at least one thing: "Society has a responsibility to help those who are weaker. [. . .] Society cannot exist without solidarity, compassion, and assistance to those who, for one reason or another, find themselves in difficulty."[26]

But community and solidarity, as the film shows, are precisely what tend to disappear in a time of "windstorms" and uncertainty. Böbe is not entirely wrong to claim that those words no longer mean anything. Admittedly, they didn't mean much under communism either. Although the rhetoric of the communist regime, whether under Kádár or Rákosi, celebrated community and schoolchildren sang songs about it, in Hungarian memory those years too were full of windstorms and uncertainty; under Rákosi, they were years of harsh repression and police terror as well. Szabó's film does not imply that communism was "better" than the market economy that followed it—but the sins of the former don't necessarily excuse the shortcomings of the latter.

Indeed, the other major social consequence of the 1989 regime change, in Hungary and elsewhere, was that even while facing an uncertain future, people also had to struggle with what to say or even think about their past. This was true in society at large as well as in the microcosm of the school. We see it in a scene that follows the two women's dialogue about values. In the teachers' room, two of the older teachers argue about their degrees of involvement with the previous regime: "You were a Party secretary!" "Yes, but I eventually quit." "At the last minute, when she ship was sinking!" "And what about you? You got a decoration, the Ministry gave you a free apartment." An older teacher, exasperated, asks why people always have to be labeled: communist, fascist, Horthyist, Stalinist, bourgeois—she rejects them all, and her question makes clear that this kind of bickering and settling of scores is not unique to the regime change of 1989 but occurred in previous moments of political upheaval as well.

The struggle with the past involves not only professional life but even the most intimate relations, Szabó suggests. Emma is in love with the school principal, Stefanics (played by Peter Andorai, who had starred in *Confidence* a decade earlier), a married man who once thought of divorcing his wife for her. But in the new political situation, Stefanics worries about maintaining his job despite his connection to the old regime and no longer has time for love. "Yes, I once loved you, but no more," he tells Emma in a long scene of confrontation where she begs him to reaffirm their old feelings (Figure 18). He tells her that he feels cornered by the new reality, having to fight for his position. "I won't slip backward because of you," he says somewhat brutally, and his response evokes the nightmare image of Emma herself sliding down a hill, grasping for something to hang on to. Soon after that, we see them kissing passionately in his car, but there

Figure 18 Sweet Emma, Dear Böbe *(Édes Emma, drága Böbe), 1992. Objektív Stúdió Vállalat, Videovox Stúdió, Mafilm Audio Kft., Manfred Durniok Produktion. Copyright National Film Institute Hungary—Film Archive.*

is clearly no future for their relationship. After Böbe is arrested, Stefanics wants nothing more to do with her roommate: furious and still worried about his own position, he asks Emma whether she too is a "whore." Even the community of lovers has been dissolved by the "regime change," it would appear.

The film industry was not immune either, as Szabó noted in interviews at the time. Whereas under communism Hungarian filmmakers could count on full subsidies from the government, with fewer and fewer restrictions over content during the 1980s, under the new market economy they not only received fewer subsidies but had to face competition from Hollywood films, which had a great deal more appeal for the Hungarian public on the open market.[27] "[In the old days] my colleagues and I were in such a privileged position that we thought everything was due to us," Szabó explained to one interviewer. But under the new conditions, Hungarian filmmakers would have to start from scratch, finding ways to deal with the new realities, he told another.[28] Did that mean that Hungarian filmmakers had to learn to make Hollywood-style films? Szabó did not say that, but he did imply that filmmakers had to appeal to the public's taste. At the same time, he maintained a position he has reiterated more than once: no culture and no country can afford to do without a body of films in its own language.

John Cunningham considers *Sweet Emma, Dear Böbe* to be an example of a film that fulfilled two new requirements, since it was both popular with Hungarian audiences (though obviously no match in sheer numbers for Hollywood blockbusters, but that was never its aim) and in their own language.[29] It is significant, however, that the three feature films Szabó made during the decade that followed (*Sunshine*, 1999; *Taking Sides*, 2001, and *Being Julia*, 2004) were all in English, with international stars and financing from abroad. They were mostly filmed in Budapest, however, according to Szabó's custom.

"Poor Hungary": *Relatives* and *Final Report*

Shortly after finishing *Being Julia*, Szabó returned to Hungarian subjects and the Hungarian language and has not left them since. *Rokonok* (*Relatives*), released in 2006, was an adaptation by Szabó and Andrea Vészits of a novel published in 1930 by the highly respected writer Zsigmond Móricz. *Az Ajtó* (*The Door*, 2012), also cowritten by Szabó and Vészits, was adapted from the internationally acclaimed novel by Magda Szabó (no relation to the filmmaker), and *Zárójelentés* (*Final Report*, 2020) was written and directed by Szabó, who also acted as an executive producer. While all of these films were shown in film festivals in Europe (*Relatives* was also screened at the Chicago International Film Festival), only *The Door*, which stars Helen Mirren (her voice was dubbed into Hungarian) and was financed in part from outside Hungary, received international distribution or recognition. *Relatives* and *Final Report* are virtually unknown in the United States, France, and Great Britain and are not available on streaming services or DVD. One cannot lay the blame for this neglect entirely on the new economic realities of globalization, where artistic productions from small countries and in "minor" languages often have a hard time being noticed. A few films in Hungarian have done well internationally, notably *Son of Saul* by László Nemes, which won the Academy Award for best foreign film, and *On Body and Soul* by Ildiko Enyedi, which won the Golden Bear in Berlin, as well as the international hit *1945* by Ferenc Török. There is no doubt, however, that the exclusively Hungarian subjects, as well as the cast, crew, language, and financing of *Relatives* and *Final Report*, contributed to their lack of appeal for international audiences and distributors. The fact that news of Szabó's youthful entanglement with the communist secret police became known around the same time as the release of *Relatives* in 2006 may also have contributed; the scandal around Szabó's name that year eclipsed the film itself, certainly in Hungary.

Relatives, like many of Zsigmond Móricz's novels, takes place in the 1920s in a small provincial townwhere everyone knows everyone and is likely to be connected to them through kinship. As one character says right at the beginning, it's the kinship ties that have held the nation together for a thousand years.[30] But kinship is also a major source of the corruption that festers in the town, since all the government officials from the mayor on down are in cahoots with the bankers and landowners, who are their kin, while the poor tenant farmers and others in the lower classes suffer. In the novel, a young and somewhat idealistic but weakwilled official in a minor job at the City Hall is propelled into a powerful position when he is unexpectedly elected to the post of chief prosecutor because the favored candidate commits a faux-pas at the last minute, alluding jokingly to his and others' corrupt practices. Kopjáss, the new prosecutor, becomes the victim of those practices—first by allowing himself to be roped into some shady deals by various "relatives" and then by trying to assert his authority against such deals. He is outmaneuvered in the latter attempt by the mayor and the local banker and ends up committing suicide.

One can see why this subject, and Móricz's handling of it, would appeal to Szabó. While Móricz satirizes the "family ties" that allow for rampant corruption and egotism, he also deplores the absence of genuine solidarity and concern for the general good on the part of government officials. Already at the time of *Sweet Emma, Dear Böbe*, Szabó had expressed a similar worry over the absence of social cohesion in Hungarian society. "We are intolerant toward each other," he told a journalist in 1992. "The rise of hatred toward others creates a general sense of insecurity that is a cause for worry," he added.[31] By 2005, when he made *Relatives*, Hungary had become a member of the European Union, but economic inequalities and financial insecurity remained, as did government corruption. In 1994, the Socialist Party, led by former communists, was elected to head the government, but accusations of mismanagement and corruption brought Viktor Orbán's party, Fidesz, to power four years later. Fidesz had started out after 1989 as a left-leaning party of "Young Democrats," but by 1998 it was on its way toward the right and even the extreme right, where it has resided since 2010, when it won by a landslide after losing in 2006. Today, after three more elections, Fidesz's grip on power seems unbreakable. Orbán has become famous (and admired by right-wing politicians the world over) for his autocratic tendencies and his cementing of "illiberal democracy," a term he coined and cites proudly. He is also famous for presiding over a regime of unparalleled corruption, where his friends and relatives have become multi-millionaires thanks to their access to the generous subsidies of the EU.[32]

Szabó and his co-writer on *Relatives*, Andrea Vészits, remained faithful to Móricz's novel, even incorporating large bits of dialogue. It's astonishing how contemporary Móricz himself can sound to a reader today. There is a question in the novel about Hungary's need for an "American loan" and its desire to become a "European country"—in order to achieve that, Móricz has his protagonist say, Hungarians must "learn to love paying taxes" rather than looking for ways to evade them. Only by becoming a willing taxpayer can a citizen fully participate in the life of the country and the general good, the newly elected chief prosecutor explains. But the canny mayor soon puts an end to such declarations, just as he reproaches Kopjáss for using the word "truth" (*igazság*) in an interview he gave to the press. "Truth" is a dangerous word, the veteran politician instructs the apprentice, because it can be used against you later by your enemies.[33] Kopjáss thanks him for the lesson: he is not a crusader, even if he tries to assert a certain justice later and is crushed for it.

Szabó does invent one character who is not in the novel: an old beggar who appears only three times, very briefly, but who utters some of the most crucial lines in the film. The first time we see him, he is standing on the street with his cup out as Kopjáss approaches, on his way to work—but we hear the beggar's voice before we see him, before Kopjáss reaches him and drops money into his cup. "For the poor in Hungary, for poor Hungary," he keeps repeating. He thanks Kopjáss for his charity—this is obviously not the first time. After the latter goes on his way, we hear the old man's voice trailing after him: "Poor Hungary." By the time he reappears, much later in the film, Kopjáss is deeply implicated in the machinations of the mayor and the local banker (who is a distant relative of Kopjáss, a fact he keeps emphasizing after the young man rises to power). Kopjáss stops by the beggar again and gives him money, while the latter repeats his usual refrain, "For the poor in Hungary. For poor Hungary." This time, we realize that the beggar functions like a Greek chorus, uttering the truth of the play: poor Hungary indeed, when it is in the hands of men like these.

The beggar's final appearance occurs in the very last shot, when he cradles Kopjáss's dead body in his arm, in a gesture that recalls Emma bending over her dying friend in *Sweet Emma, Dear Böbe* (Figure 19). There is nobody else there, only the desolate landscape of the pig farm (a major element in the corruption plot) where Kopjáss shot himself. Holding him, the beggar mutters, again reminding us of the earlier suicide scene: "This shouldn't have happened. They tricked you." Then the closing credits begin to roll, to the tune of an irritatingly jolly pop song from the 1920s that also opened the film.

*   *   *

During one of our meetings in the fall of 2017, I asked Szabó whether he had plans for another film. Yes, he told me, and he had just finished the screenplay. It was about a doctor in Budapest, the chief cardiologist in a hospital, who is forced into retirement and returns to practice general medicine in the village

Figure 19 Relatives *(Rokonok), 2006. Objektív Filmstúdió, ISL Film, TV2.*

where he grew up, where his father had been the doctor for many years and where his mother still lives. He smiled: "After that, the plot takes off." And what was the title of the film, I asked. *Zárójelentés*, he said. "Final Report?" I asked. Yes, that was the literal meaning, he said, but the word is just a technical term for the document that's issued when a patient leaves the hospital, whether dead or alive. A discharge paper, that's all it is, he insisted—the word, and his film's title, have no symbolic meaning.

Nevertheless, it is hard to consider *Final Report*, which premiered in Budapest in February 2020, just weeks before the pandemic lockdown, as lacking in symbolic meaning. For one thing, it may be Szabó's last film. In 2021, a few months after his eighty-third birthday, he was interviewed at length on a radio program and podcast devoted to discussions with people in the "fourth quarter" of life. The interviewer asked whether he thought there was "still time left" to make another film. Szabó replied that he is thinking about it but is not sure he has the physical stamina: "One has to put in 14-hour days while making a film." The interviewer, visibly moved, responded: "You have given us a lot. Thank you for that."[34]

Final Report appears as a valedictory in more ways than one, starting with the cast that Szabó assembled. The main character, Dr. Iván Stephanus, is played by Klaus Maria Brandauer, the star of *Mephisto*, *Colonel Redl*, and *Hanussen*; the role of Stephanus's wife, an aging but still active opera singer, is played by Dorottya Udvaros, the betrayed wife of the conductor in *Meeting Venus*, who had had a small role in *Colonel Redl*; Stephanus's boyhood friend, now the parish priest in the village, is played by Károly Eperjes, who had major roles in Szabó's two preceding films, *The Door* and *Relatives*, and had also appeared in *Colonel Redl*. András Bálint, the star of Szabó's earliest films, has a small role as a friend of Stephanus and director of the hospital where the latter works, while Enikő Börcsök, who played Böbe in *Sweet Emma, Dear Böbe*, here plays a middle-aged baker's wife in the village. Perhaps most poignantly of all, the handsome Peter Andorai of *Confidence*, *Mephisto* (where he played Höfgen's communist friend Otto Ulrich, murdered by the Nazis), *Sweet Emma, Dear Böbe* (where he was Emma's love interest Stefanics), and several other of Szabó's films, here plays an old man who sits all day on a bench in the village square and who functions like the old beggar in *Relatives*, as a witness to the action. Andorai, who had been ill for several years and could no longer walk, died just before *Final Report* was released, in February 2020.

To anyone who is familiar with Szabó's earlier films, seeing these actors again, all of them looking much older, is a bittersweet experience. (Szabó pays homage to another old friend as well, the Czech director and actor Jiri Menzel, whom he had enrolled in several films for cameo roles. Menzel, who died in 2020, was too sick to act in *Final Report*, but Szabó included a scene of Stephanus at the movies, watching a comedy from the 1960s directed by Menzel.) In one scene, Stephanus and his doctor friend (Bálint) play a gentle game of tennis, which is interrupted when the doctor falls down and Stephanus rushes to his side. Luckily it's not serious, but the two men look at each other ruefully and laugh: they are old.

The indignities of old age, or what is considered as such by those around one, is a main theme in *Final Report*. Stephanus appears to be in his seventies (Brandauer was seventy-five at the time of filming) but is physically fit and clearly not ready to retire; when he announces the news of his "firing" to his adult daughter, however (she does not live in Hungary—they talk on video), she is cheerfully unsympathetic. "You can rest a bit now," she tells him. Stephanus jokes to his wife that he'll open a record store and sell his collection of great opera recordings. He is a passionate devotee of opera, and even dreams of singing himself—the film opens with a dream sequence in which Stephanus is called to attend to an opera singer who has had a heart attack on stage and winds up singing the man's role—to laughter and boos from the audience!

When his mother (Mari Csomós) suggests that he come back to practice in the village, which hasn't had a doctor in over a year, Stephanus jumps at the chance. He is very much needed, it turns out, and his waiting room is always full. But as the action advances and he becomes involved in the complicated politics of the village, where everyone knows everyone else's business and the young mayor is king, Stephanus discovers that he is powerless. His powerlessness is made clear when he rushes the village baker, who has just had a heart attack, to the local hospital, where none of the staff know him and nobody wants his opinion, even though he shouts that he's a cardiologist and they must do as he says to save the man's life. In his fury, he grabs the young

ER doctor by the collar and is unceremoniously ushered out of the emergency room, where the villager later dies.

After that defeat, Stephanus and the mayor (who has heard about the incident at the hospital, where his cousin is the chief physician) clash over the building of a spa that will use the "medicinal hot springs" of the village, according to the mayor, but the doctor considers that to be a lie, since the waters are not really medicinal. (Shades of Ibsen's play *An Enemy of the People*, which has a similar plot.) The mayor then starts a vicious campaign against Stephanus as an "enemy of the village," after digging up the story of Stephanus's arrest and cooperation with the communist secret police decades earlier, when he was a student. This is clearly Szabó's version of the 2006 scandal about his own secret police involvement. I think it would have been better left out (there would have been other ways to indicate the mayor's hostility), but if the film is indeed a valedictory, it's understandable that Szabó wanted to include it.

Eventually, Stephanus realizes that he has lost the battle; in fact, all the good people in the village have lost theirs. The attractive singing teacher, a widow, who started a successful children's chorus in the school, is driven to suicide when false rumors circulate about her presumed sex life, including an affair with Stephanus. His assistant, a woman his age who had been his girlfriend in high school and who returned to the village after retiring as a nurse, is fired and faces poverty, since she cannot live on her pension. His old friend, the village priest, had returned years earlier, abandoning a successful career in the Vatican when the parish was left without a priest, but now his parishioners have "lost confidence" in him, the Bishop informs him. This is due in large part to his close friendship with Stephanus. As the two old friends sit in a boat on a quiet pond together, fishing (a recurrent image in the film), Stephanus says: "We're too old. We have become superfluous in this new world."

The new world he refers to is today's Hungary, but it might just as well be the globe, or at least the Western world as it has developed since the fall of the Berlin Wall. This world, connected by the internet (Stephanus's daughter calls him on video from Australia) but somewhat lacking in human relations, is in many ways a prosperous one: even the Hungarian village, where pensioners struggle to get by, looks spruced up, and the mayor's plans include the building of a luxury hotel. But it is also full of corrupt officials and of ordinary people who suffer. "I write prescriptions, but they don't do any good. Hatred makes people sick," Stephanus tells his friend the priest. Community feeling, if it ever existed, is long gone, as is any sense of Christian charity; all that remains is distrust and suspicion, especially of "outsiders," which is put to use by the mayor in his hold on power.

Szabó offers Stephanus a moment of moral revenge, however: as he is leaving the village, in apparent defeat, to return to Budapest, he is called to the mayor's bedside. The younger man has had a fainting spell and Stephanus revives him with an injection. When the mayor asks him whether he is dying, Stephanus responds, "Not yet." And when he asks how much he owes him for the visit, Stephanus responds:

> You're a mean, vile scoundrel, but I'm still a doctor and I'm obliged to take care of you, whether I like it or not. One day everyone in the village will know exactly who you are—unfortunately, wicked people tend to live long, it's the good ones who die young. When you do die, I hope you go to hell.

This speech could be interpreted as the "final report" Szabó wants to leave us with. But he adds one last scene to the film: on the stage of the Budapest Opera House, the pilgrim's chorus in the last act of Wagner's *Tannhäuser* lines up to sing their finale, and Stephanus is in the front row, costumed as a penitent, singing Hallelujah (Figure 20). He has found a way to occupy his retirement years by indulging in his passion for opera and his love of singing. Throughout the film, there have been scenes of singing, either in the opera house or by the children in the chorus of the music teacher; the scenes of the chorus are among the loveliest in the film—yet another throwback to Szabó's earliest works, where he used child actors to great effect. In the final scene, Szabó suggests once again, as he had done in *Meeting Venus*, that music is a salve for many wounds. One only wishes that this concluding idea were more convincing, after all the nastiness that preceded it. Yet clearly, the final scene is important to Szabó and is of a piece with all of his thinking: art has a positive role to play, even in the worst of times.

In the 2021 interview I cited earlier, after the interviewer thanked Szabó for his work, Szabó replied: "I made films because I wanted to tell stories that had to be told and that would help people to live. To realize that they are not alone

Figure 20 Final Report *(Zárójelentés), 2020. Film Street.*

in struggling with problems." Then he told a lovely anecdote, which I offer as a conclusion to this book. More than forty years earlier, just before he made *Confidence*, he invited the female lead Ildikó Bánsági, who had appeared in one of his earlier films and would appear in several more over the years, to go with him to see Ingmar Bergman's *Scenes from a Marriage*, which was playing in Budapest. After about forty-five minutes of watching the film, Bánsági turned to him and whispered: "How does this man know me so well?" "That's what a great film does," Szabó told the interviewer. "It makes you feel that the filmmaker is telling your story."[35]

Notes

1 Orwell, "Politics and the English Language," 137.

2 Kosztolányi, *Édes Anna*, 13.

3 For a detailed historical account, see Connelly, *From Peoples into Nations*, chaps. 24 and 25.

4 Derrida, *Cosmopolites de tous les pays, encore un effort!*; Habermas, *The Crisis of the European Union*; Nussbaum, *The Cosmopolitan Tradition*; all three also contributed to *The Cosmopolitanism Reader*, ed. Garrett Wallace Brown and David Held. See also, among many others, Appiah, *Cosmopolitanism*.

5 Habermas, *The Crisis of the European Union*, xi; Appiah, *Cosmopolitanism*, chap. 10.

6 Piketty, *Capital in the Twenty-First Century*. Jürgen Habermas has pointed out that "[e]ven in the fundamentally conservative business sections of our leading daily newspapers one can find thoughtful agreement with Thomas Piketty's diagnosis." See Czingon, Diefenbach, and Kempf, "Moral Universalism at a Time of Political Regression," 13.

7 I am of course referring to Russia's unprovoked invasion of Ukraine. Documented stories about war crimes committed by the invading forces and about the bombing of civilian populations have appeared regularly in the press.

8 Marx, *Szabó István*, 332.

9 Ilott, *Budgets and Markets*, chap. 12.

10 *Ibid.* See also Cunningham, *The Cinema of István Szabó*, 88.

11 Publicity booklet, in Hungarian, on *Meeting Venus*, 11. (At the Hungarian National Film Archive library.) I assume similar booklets were distributed in English and perhaps other languages as well.

12 Csala, "Europai Metafora" [European Metaphor], 24.

13 *Ibid.*

14 Cunningham, *The Cinema of István Szabó*, 89.

15 Imre, "White Man, White Mask," 419; qtd in Cunningham, *The Cinema of István Szabó*, 89.

16 Imre, "White Man, White Mask," 421.

17 Csala, "Europai Metafora" [European Metaphor], 24.

18 Bataille, "Le monde vrai des amants." [The true world of lovers]. In Hollier, *Le Collège de Sociologie (1937-1939)*, 49–50.

19 Bölcs, "Édes Emma, drága Böbe." At Hungarian National Film Archive library.

20 *Ibid.* The other reference to Kosztolányi's novel was in Ozsvárt, "Review of 'Édes Emma, drága Böbe.'" At Hungarian National Film Archive library.

21 Szabó, "Szabó István beszelgetése Fábri Zoltánnal" [István Szabó's conversation with Zoltán Fábri]. A long excerpt appeared in Szabó, *Beszélgetések Filmrendezővel* [Conversations with the Filmmaker].

22 Foucault, *Surveiller et punir* [Discipline and Punish].

23 See, for example, Szabó, interview in *168 Óra*, February 11, 1992 (name of interviewer unknown). Clipping at the Hungarian National Film Archive library.

24 Niedzelski, "Az én dolgom szólni" [My job is to say something]. Clipping at the Hungarian National Film Archive library.

25 *Ibid.*

26 *Ibid.*

27 Cunningham, *Hungarian Cinema*, chap. 9: "The Walls Come Down: The 'System Change' and after."

28 Niedzelski, "Az én dolgom szólni" [My job is to say something] and interview in *168 Óra*, February 11, 1992.

29 Cunningham, *Hungarian Cinema*, 145.

30 Móricz, *Rokonok*, 28.

31 Szabó, Interview in *168 Óra*.

32 Orbán has recently been threatened with sanctions by the EU for fraudulent mismanagement of subsidies and for espousing antidemocratic measures (such as the takeover of universities by private, government-funded foundations and the elimination of practically all the free press in Hungary) that go against the EU's rule of law principle. At the same time, Orbán has become the darling of right-wing politicians the world over, including the United States. See Marantz, "Does Hungary Offer a Glimpse of Our Authoritarian Future?" and Suleiman, "Anti-Democratic Politics in Hungary: Viktor Orbán and 'Illiberal Democracy.'"

33 Móricz, *Rokonok*, 43–4 and 58–9.

34 Szabó, in Fodor, "Negyedik negyed" [Fourth Quarter].

35 *Ibid.*

References

Books and Articles

Adorno, T. W., Else Frenkel-Brunswik, Daniel J. Levinson, and R. Nevitt Sanford; in collaboration with Betty Aron, Maria Hertz Levinson, and William Morrow. *The Authoritarian Personality* [1950]. With a new introduction by Peter E. Gordon. London and New York: Verso, 2019.

Allen, Roger. *Wilhelm Furtwängler: Art and the Politics of the Unpolitical*. Woodbridge: The Boydell Press, 2018.

Anderson, Benedict. *Imagined Communities: Reflections on the Origin and Spread of Nationalism*. Rev. ed. London: Verso, 1991.

Appiah, Kwame Anthony. *Cosmopolitanism: Ethics in a World of Strangers*. New York: W.W. Norton, 2006.

Applebaum, Anne. "Anti-Semite and Jew: The Double Life of a Hungarian Politician." *The New Yorker*, November 3, 2013.

Arendt, Hannah. *Rahel Varnhagen: The Life of a Jewish Woman*. Translated by Richard Winston and Clara Winston. New York: New York Review of Books, 2022.

Arendt, Hannah. *The Origins of Totalitarianism*. New edition with added Prefaces. New York: Harcourt Brace & Company, 1976.

Aschheim, Steven. *Brothers and Strangers: The East European Jew in German and German Jewish Consciousness, 1800–1923*. Updated edition. Madison: University of Wisconsin Press, 1999.

Bachelard, Gaston. *La Poétique de l'espace*. Paris: PUF Quadrige, 2001 [1957].

Bán, Zsofia and Turai Hedvig, eds. *Exposed Memories: Family Pictures in Private and Collective Memory*. Budapest and New York: Central University Press, 2010.

Bataille, Georges. "Le monde vrai des amants." In *Le Collège de Sociologie (1937–1939)*, edited by Denis Hollier. Paris: Editions Gallimard, 1979.

Benjamin, Walter. "The Work of Art in the Age of Mechanical Reproduction." In *Illuminations*, translated by Harry Zohn, edited and with an introduction by Hannah Arendt, 217–52. New York: Schocken Books, 1968.

Benke, Attila. "Művész a hatalom csapdájában" [The artist in the trap of state power]. *Országút*, April 20, 2020.

Bergstein, Mary. "Photography in the Szondi Test: 'The Analysis of Fate.'" *History of Photography* 41, no. 3 (2017): 217–40.

Bölcs, István. "Édes Emma, drága Böbe." *168 Óra*, March 24, 1992.

Brown, Garrett Wallace and David Held, eds. *The Cosmopolitanism Reader.* Cambridge: Polity Press, 2020.

Burgin, Victor. "Paranoiac Space." *Visual Anthropology Review* 7, no. 2 (1991): 22–30.

Cernahoschi, Rebecca. "An Empire of Borders: Central European Boundaries in István Szabó's *Colonel Redl.*" In *Border Visions: Identity and Diaspora in Film,* edited by Jakub Kazecki, Karen A. Ritzenhoff, and Cynthia J. Miller, 61–74. Lanham: Scarecrow Press, 2013.

Christensen, Peter G. "Collaboration in István Szabó's *Mephisto.*" *Film Criticism* 12, no. 3 (1988): 20–32.

Christensen, Peter G. "Szabó's *Colonel Redl* and the Habsburg Myth." *CLCWeb: Comparative Literature and Culture* 8, no. 1 (2006). http://docs.lib.purdue.edu//clcweb /vol8/iss1/8

Connelly, John. *From Peoples into Nations: A History of Eastern Europe.* Princeton: Princeton University Press, 2020.

Csala, Károly. "Europai Metafora" [European Metaphor]. *Népszabadság,* November 2, 1991.

Cunningham, John. *Hungarian Cinema: From Coffeehouse to Multiplex.* London: Wallflower Press, 2004.

Cunningham, John. *The Cinema of István Szabó: Visions of Europe.* New York: Columbia University Press, 2014.

Czingon, Claudia, Aletta Diefenbach, and Victor Kempf. "Moral Universalism at a Time of Political Regression: A Conversation with Jürgen Habermas about the Present and His Life's Work." *Theory, Culture, Society* 37, no. 7–8 (2020): 11–36.

Davies, Ioan. "An Interview with István Szabó." *Cineaction,* no. 11 (Winter 1987–8): 66–72.

Deák, István. "Scandal in Budapest." *New York Review of Books,* October 19, 2006.

Deák, István. "Strangers at Home." *New York Review of Books,* July 20, 2000.

Dempsey, Judy. "The Past, the East Learns, is Always Present." *New York Times,* February 8, 2006.

Derrida, Jacques. *Cosmopolites de tous les pays, encore un effort!.* Paris: Galilée, 1997.

Dragon, Zoltán. *The Spectral Body: Aspects of the Cinematic Oeuvre of István Szabó.* Newcastle: Cambridge Scholars Press, 2006.

Erős, Ferenc, András Kovács, and Katalin Lévai. "Hogyan jöttem rá, hogy zsidó vagyok" [How I found out that I am Jewish]. *Medvetánc,* no. 2–3 (1985): 129–44.

Esterházy, Péter. *Javított Kiadás: Melléklet a Harmonia Caelestishez* [Revised Edition: Appendix to *Harmonia Caelestis*]. Budapest: Magvető, 2001.

Fehér, Margit. "Hungarian Sculptor Defends Monument to Victims of Nazis." *Wall Street Journal,* August 1, 2014. https://www.wsj.com/articles/hungarian-sculptor-defends -monument-to-nazi-occupation-1406910612

Feigelson, Kristian and Catherine Portuges. "Screen Memory: The Jewish Question." *Hungarian Studies* 11 (2017): 19–38.

Fejtő, François. *Hongrois et juifs.* Paris: Fayard, 1997.

Fitzsimmons, Lorna. "'Scathe Me with Less Fire': Disciplining the African German 'Black Venus' in *Mephisto.*" *Germanic Review* 76, no. 1 (2001): 15–40.

Fodor, János. "Negyedik negyed" [Fourth Quarter] [Radio]. Interview with István Szabó. *Radio Bécs,* February 26, 2022.

Földes, Anna. "Sors Út" [The way of fate or Sors's way], *Népszabadság*, February 19, 2000.

Foucault, Michel. *Surveiller et punir: Naissance de la prison* [Discipline and Punish]. Paris: Gallimard, 1975.

Gervai, András. "Egy ügynök azonosítása" [The identification of an agent]. *Élet és Irodalom*, January 27, 2006.

Goethe, *Faust*, Part I, translated by A. S. Kline, [online] https://www.poetryintranslation .com/PITBR/German/FaustIScenesItoIII.php

György, Péter. "Sorsválasztók" [Those who chose their fate or Those who chose Sors]. *Élet és Irodalom*, February 11, 2000.

Habermas, Jürgen. *The Crisis of the European Union*. Cambridge: Polity Press, 2012.

Halász, Tamás. "Az illustrációktol a nagytotálig" [From illustrations to grand totality]. In *Minarik, Sonnenschein és a Többiek*, edited by Vera Surányi, 110–23. Budapest: Magyar Zsidó Kulturális Egyesület and Szombat, 2015.

Hanák, Péter, ed. *Zsidókérdés asszimiláció antiszemitizmus: Tanulmányok a zsidókérdésről a huszadik századi Magyarországon* [Jewish question, assimilation, antisemitism: Studies on the Jewish question in twentieth-century Hungary]. Budapest: Gondolat, 1984.

Haraszti, Miklós. "Hivasson esztétát!" [Call an aesthetics specialist!]. *Élet és Irodalom*, February 25, 2000.

Heller, Ágnes. "A parvenük kora" [The Age of the Parvenu]. In *A "Zsidókérdés" megoldhatatlansága* [The Insolubility of the "Jewish question"]. Budapest: Múlt és Jövő Kiadó, 2004.

Heller, Ágnes. *A Philosophy of Morals*. Oxford: Basil Blackwell, 1990.

Heller, Ágnes. *A "Zsidókérdés" megoldhatatlansága, avagy Mért születtem Hébernek, mért nem inkább Négernek?* [The Insolubility of the "Jewish question," or Why was I born a Hebrew, why not a Negro instead?]. Budapest: Múlt és Jövö, 2004.

Heller, Ágnes. "Megjegyzések és ellenmegjegyzések Szabó Istvàn filmjéhez" [Notes and Counternotes on István Szabó's film]. *Múlt és Jovő*, August 8, 2001: 1–12.

Herf, Jeffrey. *Israel's Moment: International Support for and Opposition to Establishing the Jewish State, 1945-1949*. New York: Cambridge University Press, 2022.

Hirsch, Joshua. *Afterimage: Film, Trauma, and the Holocaust*. Philadelphia: Temple University Press, 2000.

Hirsch, Joshua. "István Szabó: Problems in the Narration of Holocaust Memory." *Journal of Film and Video* 51, no. 1 (Spring 1999): 3–21.

Hirsch, Marianne. *Family Frames: Photography, Narrative, and Postmemory*. Cambridge, MA: Harvard University Press, 1997.

Hirschman, Albert. *Exit, Voice and Loyalty: Responses to Decline in Firms, Organizations, and States*. Cambridge, MA: Harvard University Press, 1970.

Hollier, Denis, ed. "Jean-Paul Sartre's *Anti-Semite and Jew*." *October*, no. 87 (Winter 1999).

Hughes, John W. "István Szabó and the 'Gestapo of Suspicion.'" *Film Quarterly* 35, no. 4 (Summer 1982): 13–18.

Ilott, Terry. *Budgets and Markets: A Study in the Marketing of European Film*. London: Routledge, 1996.

Imre, Aniko. "White Man, White Mask: Mephisto Meets Venus." *Screen* 40, no. 4 (1999): 405–22.

Jaehne, Karen. "István Szabó: Dreams of Memories." *Film Quarterly* 32, no. 1 (Fall 1978): 30–41.

Jankélévitch, Vladimir. "Le Judaïsme, problème intérieur." In *La Conscience juive, données et débats*, edited by Eliana Amado Lévy-Valensi and Jean Halpern, 54–79. Paris: Presses Universitaires de France, 1963.

Karády, Viktor. "Some Aspects of Jewish Assimilation in Socialist Hungary, 1945–1946." In *The Tragedy of Hungarian Jewry*, edited by Randolph Braham, 73–132. Boulder: Social Science Monographs, 1986.

Kertész, Imre. *Gályanapló* [Galley Diary]. Budapest: Magvető, 1992.

Kertész, Imre. "Heureka." Nobel Lecture 2002. Translated by Ivan Sanders. *PMLA* 118, no. 3 (May 2003): 604–9.

Kertész, Imre. *K. dosszié* [K Dossier]. Budapest: Magvető, 2006.

Kertész, Imre. *Sorstalanság* [Fatelessness]. Budapest: Századvég Kiadó, 1993 [1975].

Kierkegaard, Søren. *Either/Or*. 2 vols. Translated by David F. Swenson and Lillian Marvin Swenson; vol. 2 translated by Walter Lowrie. Princeton: Princeton University Press, 1944.

Konrád, George. *A Guest in My Own Country: A Hungarian Life*. Translated by Jim Tucker, edited by Michael Henry Heim. New York: Other Press, 2002.

Kosztolányi, Dezső. *Édes Anna*. Budapest: Osiris, 2019 [1926].

Kovács, András. *A Kádár rendszer és a zsidók* [The Kádár regime and the Jews]. Budapest: Corvina, 2019.

Kovács, András. "Jews and Politics in Hungary." In *Values, Interests and Identity: Jews and Politics in a Changing World*, edited by Peter Y. Medding, 50–63. New York: Oxford University Press, 1995.

Lelkes, Éva. "Három kisfilm sikeréröl a rendezővel, Szabó Istvánnal" [About the Success of Three Short Films, with the director István Szabó]. *Film, Szinház, Muzsika*, February 15, 1963.

Lénárt, András. "Emigration from Hungary in 1956 and the Emigrants as Tourists to Hungary." *Hungarian Historical Review* 1, no. 3–4 (2012): 368–96.

Lorenz, Dagmar C. G. "Ethnicity, Sexuality, and Politics in István Szabó's *Colonel Redl* and *Mephisto*." In *Insiders and Outsiders: Jewish and Gentile Culture in Germany and Austria*, edited by Dagmar C. G. Lorenz and Gabriele Weinberger, 263–79. Detroit: Wayne State University Press, 1994.

MacKinnon, Mark. "Statue in Budapest based on Second World War Evokes Dark History." *Toronto Globe and Mail*, December 15, 2014. https://www.theglobeandmail.com/news/world/statue-in-budapest-based-on-second-world-war-evokes-dark-history/article22099406/

Mann, Klaus. *Mephisto*. Translated by Robin Smyth. New York and London: Penguin Books, 1983.

Márai, Sándor. *Memoir of Hungary, 1944–1948*. Translated by Albert Tezla. Budapest: Corvina and Central European University Press, 2005.

Marantz, Andrew. "Does Hungary Offer a Glimpse of our Authoritarian Future?." *The New Yorker*, July 4, 2022.

Margolis, Harriet. "'Nur Schauspieler': Spectacular Politics, *Mephisto*, and *Good*." In *Film and Literature: A Comparative Approach to Adaptation*, edited by Wendell Aycock and Michael Schoenecke, 81–95. Lubbock: Texas Tech University Press, 1988.

Marton, Kati. *The Great Escape: Nine Jews Who Fled Hitler and Changed the World*. New York: Simon & Schuster, 2006.

Marx, József. *Szabó István: Filmek és Sorsok* [István Szabó: Films and Fates]. Budapest: Vince Kiadó, 2002.

Marx, Karl. *Selected Writings*. Edited by Lawrence H. Simon. Indianapolis: Hackett, 1994.

Mason, John W. *The Dissolution of the Austro-Hungarian Empire, 1867–1918*. 2nd ed. London and New York: Longman, 1997.

Móricz, Zsigmond. *Rokonok*. Budapest: Szépirodalmi Könyvkiado, 1989 [1932].

Mülner, Dora. "Itt vigyázni kell" [Here one must be careful]. Interview with István Szabó. *Népszabadság*, February 8, 2000.

Nagy B., László. "Kűzdelem az árvasággal" [Struggle with Orphanhood]. *Élet és Irodalom*, December 10, 1966: 9.

Nagy B., László. "Nosztalgia és Küldetés" [Nostalgia and the Task at Hand]. *Élet és Irodalom*, October 10, 1970: 13.

Niedzelski, Katalin. "Az én dolgom szólni" [My job is to say something]. Interview with István Szabó. *Békés Megyei Hírlap*, May 9–10, 1992.

Nietzsche, Friedrich. *Ecce Homo*. Translated by Clifton Fadiman. In *The Philosophy of Nietzsche*, 809–946. New York: The Modern Library, 1954.

Nussbaum, Martha. *The Cosmopolitan Tradition: A Noble but Flawed Ideal*. Cambridge, MA: Harvard University Press, 2019.

Orwell, George. "Politics and the English Language." In *In Front of Your Nose, 1945–1950*, edited by Sonia Orwell and Ian Angus, 127–40. Boston: David R. Godine, 2000.

Ozsvárt, Tamás. "Review of *Édes Emma, drága Böbe*." *Nógrád*, April 17, 1992.

Papp, Gábor Zsigmond. "Mondani kell valamit" [One has to say something]. Interview with István Szabó, *Magyar Narancs*, May 3, 2001: 34–5.

Paul, David. "Szabó." In *Five Filmmakers: Tarkovsky, Forman, Polanski, Szabó, Makavejev*, edited by Daniel J. Goulding, 156–208. Bloomington: Indiana University Press, 1994.

Petrie, Graham. *History Must Answer to Man: The Contemporary Hungarian Cinema*. Budapest: Corvina Kiadó, 1978.

Piketty, Thomas. *Capital in the Twenty-First Century*. Translated by Arthur Goldhammer. Cambridge, MA: Harvard University Press, 2014.

Plater, Edward M. V. "István Szabó's Film of Inner Conflict and Political Prophecy: The "Poseur" in Istvàn Szabó's *Colonel Redl*." *Hungarian Studies Review* 14, no. 1–2 (1992): 43–57.

Pongrácz, Zsuzsa. Interview with István Szabó, *Filmvilág*, May 1, 1971.

Portuges, Catherine. "The Political Camera: Comparing 1956 in Three Moments of Hungarian History." In *Cinema, State Socialism and Society in the Soviet Union and Eastern Europe, 1917–1989*, edited by Sanja Bahun and John Haynes, 151–71. London and New York: Routledge, 2014.

Renan, Ernest. *Qu'est-ce qu'une nation?*. Paris: Mille et une nuits, 1997 [1887].

Rév, István. "The Man in the White Raincoat." In *Past for the Eyes: East European Representations of Communism in Cinema and Museums since 1989*, 3–56. Budapest: CEU Press, 2008.

Romsics, Ignác. *Hungary in the Twentieth Century*. 2nd ed. Translated by Tim Wilkinson. Budapest: Corvina, 2010.

Ross, Alex. "The Disquieting Power of Wilhelm Furtwängler, Hitler's Court Conductor." *The New Yorker*, May 2, 2019. https://www.newyorker.com/culture/cultural-comment/ the-disquieting-power-of-wilhelm-furtwangler-hitlers-court-conductorctor (accessed November 15, 2022).

Sadler, John and Sylvie Fisch. *Spy of the Century: Alfred Redl and the Betrayal of Austro-Hungary*. Barnsley: Pen and Sword History, 2016.

Said, Edward. "Reflections on Exile." In *Altogether Elsewhere: Writers on Exile*, edited by Marc Robinson, 137–49. Boston and London: Faber and Faber, 1994.

Sartre, Jean-Paul. *L'Etre et le néant* [Being and Nothingness]. Paris: Gallimard, 1943.

Sartre, Jean-Paul. *Réflexions sur la question juive* [Antisemite and Jew]. Paris: Gallimard, Folio edition, 1954.

Sartre, Jean-Paul. *Saint Genet, comédien et martyr* [Saoint Genet, Comedian and Martyr]. Paris: Gallimard, 1952.

Schindler, John R. "Redl—Spy of the Century?." *International Journal of Intelligence and Counterintelligence*, no. 18 (2005): 483–507.

Suleiman, Susan Rubin. "A Letter from Budapest." *Tablet Magazine*, March 14, 2018. https://www.tabletmag.com/sections/news/articles/a-letter-from-budapest

Suleiman, Susan Rubin. "Anti-Democratic Politics in Hungary: Viktor Orbán and 'Illiberal Democracy'." Scowcroft Paper, no. 20. Scowcroft Institute of International Affairs, Texas A&M University: https://bush.tamu.edu/wp-content/uploads/2021/07/Suleiman -Paper-No.-20.pdf

Suleiman, Susan Rubin. *Budapest Diary: In Search of the Motherbook*. Lincoln: University of Nebraska Press, 1996.

Suleiman, Susan Rubin. *Crises of Memory and the Second World War*. Cambridge, MA: Harvard University Press, 2006.

Suleiman, Susan Rubin. "Jewish Assimilation in Hungary, the Holocaust, and Epic Film: Reflections on István Szabó's *Sunshine*." *Yale Journal of Criticism* 14, no. 1 (Spring 2001): 233–52.

Suleiman, Susan Rubin. "On Exile, Jewish Identity, and Filmmaking in Hungary: A Conversation with István Szabó." *Kinokultura*, Special issue 7 (February 2008). http:// www.kinokultura.com/specials/7/hungarian.shtml

Suleiman, Susan Rubin. "The 1.5 Generation: Thinking About Child Survivors and the Holocaust." *American Imago* 59, no. 3 (Fall 2002): 277–95.

Suleiman, Susan Rubin. *The Némirovsky Question: The Life, Death, and Legacy of a Jewish Writer in Twentieth-Century France*. New Haven: Yale University Press, 2006.

Suleiman, Susan Rubin. "Writing and Internal Exile in Eastern Europe: The Example of Imre Kertész." In *The Exile and Return of Writers from East-Central Europe*, edited by John Neubauer and Borbála Zs. Török, 368–83. Berlin and New York: Walter de Gruyter, 2009.

Surányi, Vera, ed. *Minarik, Sonnenschein és a többiek* [Minarik, Sonnenschein and the others]. Expanded edition, Budapest: Magyar Zsidó Kulturális Egyesület and Szombat, 2015.

Szabó, István. *A napfény íze* [Sunshine], scenario in Hungarian, dated May 25, 1998. Hungarian National Film Archive library, Budapest.

Szabó, István. "Hulljék mázsákban a popcorn" [Let popcorn flow by the ton], *Heti Student Express*, March 1, 2000: 1–2.

Szabó, István. "Personal Folders." Hungarian National Film Archive library, Budapest.

Szabó, István. "Szabó István beszélgetése Fábri Zoltánnal" [István Szabó's conversation with Zoltán Fábri]. *Filmkultura*, no. 3 (1965). Reprinted in part in *Beszélgetések Szabó István Filmrendezővel* [Conversations with Filmmaker István Szabó], edited by Zsuzsa Radnóti, 181–93. Budapest: Ferenczy Kiadó, 1995.

Szegő, András. "Ingerelnek a felfuvalkodott, gőgös emberek" [I can't stand swellheaded, arrogant people]. Interview with István Szabó (1987). Reprinted in *Beszélgetések Szabó István Filmrendezővel* [Conversations with Filmmaker István Szabó], edited by Zsuzsa Radnóti, 9–22. Budapest: Ferenczy Kiadó, 1995.

Szekfü, András. "Az álmodozásoktól a mesékig: Szabó István filmjeiről, a *Budapesti mesék* bemutatóalkalmából" [From Daydreaming to Tales: On the films of István Szabó, on the occasion of the premiere of *Budapest Tales*]. *Mozgó Világ*, April 1977: 78–86.

Szekfü, András. *Igy filmeztünk 2: Válogatás fél évszázad magyar filmtörténeti interjúibol* [How we filmed, 2: Selections from a half century of interviews about Hungarian film history]. Budapest: MMA Kiadó, 2019.

Varga, Balázs. "Hiányjel: Zsidó sorsok magyar filmben 1945 után" [Ellipsis: Jewish Fates in Hungarian film after 1945]. In *Minarik, Sonnenschein és a többiek*, edited by Vera Surányi, 24–35. Budapest: Magyar Zsidó Kulturális Egyesület and Szombat, 2015.

Vitányi, Iván. "Miröl szól *A Napfény ize?*" [What is the subject of *Sunshine?*]. *Élet és Irodalom*, February 25, 2000.

Walton, Chris. "Furtwängler the Apolitical?." *Musical Times* 145, no. 1889 (Winter 2004): 5–25. https://www.proquest.com/docview/210507175?parentSessionId=hLQXNkON8TY1MGKvwS9%2FtRrbV%2Bpua6tD6%2Bq8wu3r9PA%3D&pq-origsite=primo&accountid=11311 (accessed December 15, 2022).

Warchol, Tomasz. "Patterns of Central European Experience in István Szabó's Trilogy and *Sunshine*." *Social Identities* 7, no. 4 (2010): 659–75.

Weiss, Andrea. *In the Shadow of the Magic Mountain: The Klaus and Erika Mann Story.* Chicago: University of Chicago Press, 2008.

Zombory, Maté, András Lénárt, and Anna Lujza Szász. "Elfeledett Szembenézés: Holokauszt és Emlékezés Fábri Zoltán *Utószezon* C. Filmjében" [Evaded Self-Scrutiny: The Holocaust and Memory in Zoltán Fábri's film, *Utószezon*], *BUKSZ*, no. 3 (2013): 245–56.

Zsugán, István. "Mephisto: A Self-Absolving Character." *New Hungarian Quarterly* 23, no. 87 (1982): 85–9.

Figures

Films

Films directed by István Szabó, mentioned in this book:

Álmodozások kora [The Age of Daydreaming] (1964)
Álom a házrol [Dream about the House] (1971)
Apa [Father] (1966)
Az Ajtó [The Door] (2012)
Being Julia (2004)
Bizalom [Confidence] (1980)
Budapest, amiért szeretem [Budapest, Why I Love It] (1971)
Budapesti mesék [Budapest Tales] (1976)
Édes Emma, drága Böbe [Sweet Emma, Dear Böbe] (1992)
Hanussen (1988)
Koncert (1962)
Meeting Venus (1991)
Mephisto (1981)
Oberst Redl [Colonel Redl] (1985)
Rokonok [Relatives] (2006)
Sunshine (1999)
Szerelmesfilm [Lovefilm] (1970)
Taking Sides (2001)
Tűzoltó utca 25 [25 Firemen's Street] (1973)
Variációk egy témárol [Variations on a Theme] (1962)
Zárójelentés [Final Report] (2020)

Films by other filmmakers, mentioned in this book:

8 ½ (1963), dir. Federico Fellini
1945 (2017), dir. Ferenc Török
Bástyasétány 74 (1984), dir. Gyula Gazdag
Budapesti tavasz [Spring in Budapest] (1955), dir. Félix Máriássy
Casablanca (1942), dir. Michael Curtiz
Céline et Julie vont en bateau [Céline and Julie Go Boating] (1973), dir. Jacques Rivette
Doctor Zhivago (1965), dir. David Lean
Édes Anna [Sweet Anna] (1958), dir. Zoltán Fábri
Éjfélkor [At Midnight] (1957), dir. György Révész
Entr'acte (1924), dir. René Clair

Gentlemen's Agreement (1947), dir. Elia Kazan

Hideg napok [*Cold Days*] (1966), dir. András Kovács

Job Lázadása [*The Revolt of Job*] (1983), dir. Imre Gyöngyössy and Barna Kabay

Jules et Jim (1962), dir. François Truffaut

Két félidő a pokolban [*Two Half-Times in Hell*], dir. Zoltán Fábri

Körhinta [*Merry-go-round*] (1955), dir. Zoltán Fábri

Les 400 Coups [*The 400 Blows*] (1959), dir. François Truffaut

Nappali sötétség [*Darkness in Daytime*] (1963), dir. Zoltán Fábri

Nuit et Brouillard [*Night and Fog*] (1956), dir. Alain Resnais

Párbeszéd [*Dialogue*] (1963), dir. János Herskó

Saul fia [*Son of Saul*] (2015), dir. László Nemes

Shoah (1985), dir. Claude Lanzmann

Smiles of a Summer Night (1955), dir. Ingmar Bergman

Szegénylegények [*The Round-Up*] (1966), dir. Miklós Jancsó

Tár (2022), dir. Todd Field

Teströl és Lélekröl [*On Body and Soul*] (2017), dir. Ildikó Enyedi

The Jazz Singer (1927), dir. Alan Crosman

Utószezón [*Late Season*] (1967), dir. Zoltán Fábri

Valahol Europában [*Somewhere in Europe*] (1948), dir. Géza von Radványi

Index